THE BOOK OF
WENDLING, LONGHAM and
BEESTON with BITTERING

Over 700 years of Village Life

STEPHEN OLLEY

HALSGROVE

First published in Great Britain in 2005

British Library Cataloguing-in-Publication Data.
A CIP record for this title is available from the British Library.

ISBN 1 84114 417 7

HALSGROVE

Halsgrove House
Lower Moor Way
Tiverton, Devon EX16 6SS
Tel: 01884 243242
Fax: 01884 243325
E-mail: sales@halsgrove.com
Website: www.halsgrove.com

Printed and bound in Great Britain by CPI Bath

*Whilst every care has been taken to ensure the accuracy of the
information contained in this book, the publisher disclaims responsibility
for any mistakes which may have been inadvertently included.*

*I would like to dedicate this book to the memory
of the late Richard H. Butler-Stoney OBE.
Although I only knew Richard for a couple of years
before he sadly passed away, he and his family
have been a great inspiration to me.*

CONTENTS

Acknowledgements

I am deeply indebted to the staff and pupils of the schools in Beeston and Litcham for their hard work and dedication to this book.

I would also like to thank all those who have helped me with my research or contributed material, including Ron Shaw of the Litcham Historical & Amenity Society, Mrs Joy Hammond, Mrs D. Walthew, Mr Ralph Cross, Mr Ralph Pooley, Mrs Jolly, Mr John Rupp, Mrs Linda Winterbone, Mr and Mrs K. Evens, Mrs Short and the family of the late Richard Butler-Stoney OBE.

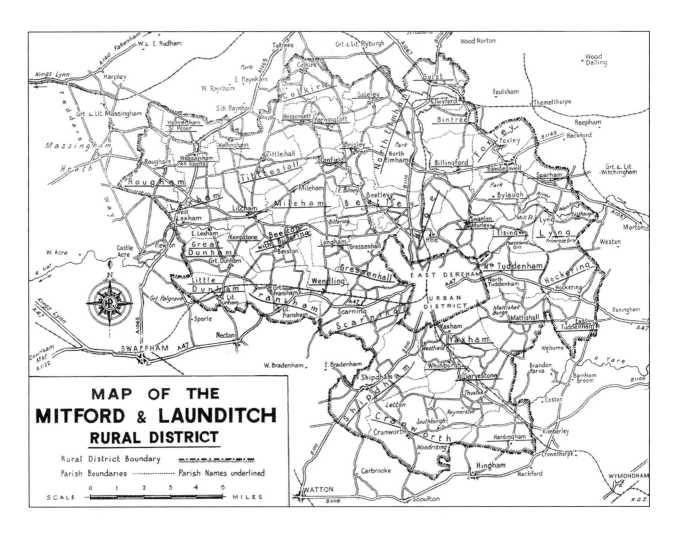

MAP OF THE
MITFORD & LAUNDITCH
RURAL DISTRICT

Rural District Boundary
Parish Boundaries .... Parish Names underlined

SCALE 0 1 2 3 4 5 MILES

INTRODUCTION

This book has been compiled to celebrate the history of these very individual villages which surround the Second World War American airbase. It has long been my ambition to see the history of this area in print and to hopefully answer many of the questions that have been asked in the past, such as: why is Station Road called Station Road and why is Wendling Airbase not that of Beeston or Longham? This was often the topic of much lively playground debate at Litcham High School; I don't have to say which villages the other lads lived in!

In this book you will find interesting facts along with photographs and images, many of which have not been published before. The book includes research on Wendling Abbey through to a section from Beeston Primary School's pupil admission book, which covers the period November 1945–47. This shows how a number of families came to Beeston to live in the old buildings on the airbase when the Americans went home. Some of the text has been reproduced in the same way it would have originally been written, to help preserve the full history of this text.

As many people across the area have requested information from census returns and registers from the nineteenth century, some extracts have been included at the end of this book. On a lighter note, there are also extracts from a book written by local man Dick Mason, who spent his childhood living near the base. Later in life he decided to commit many of his memories to paper but sadly Dick passed away before he could get his work published.

All information in this book is correct to the best of my knowledge but if any mistakes are present within these pages, I sincerely apologise. Researching, writing and producing this book on these wonderful villages has been a great experience.

Stephen W. Olley, 2005.

Seal of Wendling Abbey dated 1456.

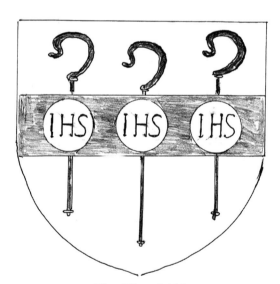

The Abbey shield.

PART I: WENDLING

Chapter 1

Early Wendling and the Abbey

The village of Wendling derives its name from a stream called 'Wandle' which runs through it. The 'ing' part of the name means meadow. It is thus claimed that Wendling means 'the winding stream by the meadows'. Before 1267 the village was known as Wendlyng.

In the time of Edward the Confessor (1042–1066) Wendlyng was in the manor of Bury. The survey conducted during the time of Richard I (1189–1199) revealed that the settlement consisted of a caracute of land (possibly larger than an acre), two villeins, six borderers, six acres of meadow, one caracute in demesne, and one and a half caracutes amongst the tenants. It also included paunage for 100 swine and one stockman who had a dozen acres.

Wendling Abbey

The abbey, founded in 1267 by William de Wendling, one of Henry III's judges, once stood on marshy ground near a rivulet (small stream) which runs to the south of the village. The abbey and outbuildings covered approximately two acres of ground, although they stood within ten acres of land. In 1218 William de Saham, clerk son of Robert de Saham held lands in the town and was a benefactor to Wendling Abbey.

The Abbey's Foundations

Sir William de Wendling, referred to in some records as 'clerk son of William', and in others, 'son of John de Wendling' was master of the hospital of St Cross near Winchester in 1295. A William de Wendling farmed the manor of Brandon Ferry in Suffolk, which belonged to Hugh Bishop of Ely in 1259. Sir William de Wendling, son of William de Wendling, gave the hospital the Church of St Clement of Conisford in Norwich with several houses near to it. In 1267 Sir William established himself on 10 acres of land in Wendling (on which the abbey was built) with 3s. rent in Baldeswell (sic) by a fine levied between himself and Nicholas, abbot there.

It does not appear that Sir William had any lordship in Wendling. The principal lord was Robert de Stotevile, son of William de Stotevile lord of the manor of Gressenhale, who granted the site of the

This bridge was one of the last pieces of Wendling Abbey to remain standing.

This small piece of abbey wall still remains next to the lane that leads to Abbey Farm.

new abbey church in 1273. He and his heirs gave their patronage to the new place of worship.

In 1267 Sir William de Wendling also settled on Nicholas, abbot of Wendling, and his successors 5 messuages, 87 acres of land, a mill and 10s. rent in Scarning. He granted this to the then church of Longham, which was appropriated to Wendling Abbey. Nicholas was rector of Nedham in Holt Hundred, and in 1257 William de Wendling was King Henry III's exchequer.

The donations of the abbey founder, along with those of Rayner de Gimmingham, Robert de Stotevile and Jordan Foliot Knights were confirmed in 1333.

William de Wendling gave to the canons the rents that he paid on Langham, Yaxham Reymerstone,

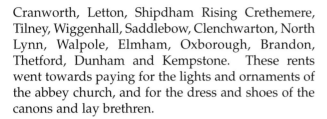

Cranworth, Letton, Shipdham Rising Crethemere, Tilney, Wiggenhall, Saddlebow, Clenchwarton, North Lynn, Walpole, Elmham, Oxborough, Brandon, Thetford, Dunham and Kempstone. These rents went towards paying for the lights and ornaments of the abbey church, and for the dress and shoes of the canons and lay brethren.

Abbots of Wendling

Nicholas	1265–73
Robert	1286
John (resigned)	1329
William de Saxlingham (elected)	1329
John de Norwich (died)	1339
John de Tytlesvalle (elected)	1339
Thomas	1352
John	1377–98
Ralph	1425
Edmond	1432
John Skerning	1432
Thomas Walsokes	1503
John York	1509
George	1529
Thomas Ellington	1535

In 1291 the abbey held possessions in 29 Norfolk parishes, of which the annual value was £39.19s.7½d. This value was slightly augmented over the years by occasional gifts of lands and rents, thus in 1306 the abbot and convent were licensed to accept gifts by Nicholas de Stokerley, of a messuage (a dwelling-house), a mill, 3 acres of land, 3 acres of meadow and 26.8d. rents in Yaxham.

The abbey obtained the royal license to appropriate the church of Langham in 1329 and that of Yaxham in 1363. Such additions meant that by 1535, when Thomas Ellington was abbot, the annual value of the abbey was declared as £55.18s.4½d.

In September 1327 the constable of Dover Castle was ordered to permit the abbot of Wendling to cross the Fens to attend the General Chapter (a type of church meeting) at Prémontré in France, home of the Premonstratensian order, and to supply him with 20 marks towards his expenses.

In 1411 Pope John XXXII granted an indulgence of 100 days to penitents who, on certain specified feasts visited the church and gave alms for the repair of the monastic church of Wendling.

On the death of abbot John de Norwich in 1339, the canons proceeded at once to the election of a successor, without waiting for the necessary formalities. The abbot of Langdon, who was acting as commissary for the abbot of Prémontré wrote to the abbot of Dereham stating that the late John de Norwich was an unworthy man who should not have been abbot. He also pointed out the errors of the canons who had procured to make another unworthy election. After quite some debate, the full

details of which are unknown, a John de Tytleshalle eventually succeeded as superior.

During his first visitation tour as commissary of the abbot of Prémontré in 1475, Bishop Redman stayed at Wendling between the 28 and 30 June. Three years later he was again in Wendling on 30 June. The abbot was ordered to regulate the hours of worship and rebuild the church, which had been destroyed by fire, as soon as possible.

In addition to John Skerning (abbot in 1432) and John Grey (sub-prior) there were only four canons. They had three churches in their charge which were served either by regular curates or by canons who could be directed at will.

When Bishop Redman reached Wendling on his visitation tour of 1482 he praised the general condition of the house. Considerable progress had been made with the buildings but he urged for greater speed with the church. He gave some attention to the smaller details of worship, such as directing that Antiphons of the Canticles should be sung only by the priests.

In addition to abbot and prior, there were four other canons at this time, two of whom were novices. The numbers were the same at the time of the next visitation made on the 27 June 1488 when two of the inmates were sentenced by the bishop. In one case there had been rebellion and disobedience but the offender promised future obedience and was ordered to be castigated before the provincial chapter. The other offender was brought before the visitor for defects in singing the collects (short prayers). The bishop recorded that everything else was in good order and that there had been much progress in the building of the church.

At the visitation of September 1491 Thomas Milthorn, the rebel of the last visitation, had not improved. Indeed, he was sentenced to 40 days of penance and to three years' absence at Sulby. During this visit the abbot was ordered to raise the number of canons to a minimum of eight. There was, however, no improvement in numbers when the bishop again visited in 1494; the canons, including the abbot, numbered six. On this occasion there were various ritual injunctions and as a result of bad behaviour, John Barlyng was condemned to 40 days' penance plus two years at some other house.

At the visitation of 1497 there were five canons and two novices. On this occasion the bishop found nothing worthy of correction, the house was not in debt and was abundantly supplied. The abbot was ordered to repair the dormitory.

The last recorded visitation of Bishop Redman was in 1500, when there were six canons and two novices. The visitor found that all was in order.

In 1536 a confidential report alleged poor behaviour by the abbot. Later in the same year the county commissioners reported that the abbot and convent had, on 1 November 1534, leased a large portion of land and possessions to Richard Southwell (one of the commissioners) and Robert Logan. There were also two hinds and ten servants at the abbey. The lead and bells were worth £100, but the house was in decay. The goods were worth £12.8s.9d. but the house owed £66.17s.11d. According to the same commissioners' certificate dated 27 January 1537 the staff of this house were sold to Robert Logan for £13.6s.8d. The plate valued at 41s.8d. was received by Richard Southwell on 6 February 1537, and former abbot Thomas Ellington was assigned a pension of 100s. in spite of the charge of 'incontenency' (poor behaviour).

A painting showing how Scarning Dale originally looked. Some of the remains of Wendling Abbey were taken to build the main house and outbuildings at Scarning Dale.

Below: *Although the house has been extended through the years old timbers taken from the abbey can still be seen inside the main house.*

This small abbey was one of those whose dissolution was permitted by Clement VII's bill of 1528, and whose possessions were granted to Cardinal Wolsey. However, Wolsey's fall prevented that dissolution being carried out. Eventually, in 1546, Henry VIII granted the abbey to the dean and chapter of Christ Church, Oxford at the latter's foundation.

In 1810 the last of the remains of the abbey that could be seen above ground were used for repairing roads in the locality.

Plan of Wendling Abbey
(Extract from *Norfolk Archaeology*, Vol. 5)
A plan of the abbey was prepared by Revd W.T. Spurden in 1810.

Travelling through the village I was just in time to take a ground plan of the ruins, none of which stood more than about a yard above the ground, and the whole were then being picked up by day labourers from their very foundations for repairing the roads.

The pillars of the nave had been erected upon a continuous bed of very hard concrete. The whole was in a condition to be very intelligible. The entire length of the church from west to the east, was about 184 feet within the walls. There remained not a fragment of an arch, pillar, string-course or moulding to indicate the character or date of the edifice or any of its parts. It is suggested by Mr Harrold that the passage between Nos. 7 and 9 led to the infirmary which in ancient times generally stood apart, traces perhaps might still be found east of the cemetery and he also observes that the room marked No. 9 was probably under the dormi-

tories, and used as the winter parlours by the monks, that Nos. 12 and 13 were the cellar or buttery and kitchen and that possibly the four strangers ran along the west side of the cloisters. Three stone coffins were found in the garden or cemetery.

Premonstratensian Canons

The founder of this order was a priest from Lorraine, named Northbertus, who formed the rule for his new order along similar lines to that of St Augustine. It was later approved and confirmed by Pope Calixtus II in 1120. Representatives of this order came to England in 1140 and it was not long before abbeys within this order were founded in Norfolk (West Dereham and Langley abbeys in 1188, and Wendling in 1267).

Premonstratensians, also called Norbertines, wore traditional dress that consisted of a habit, a linen surplice, a long white cloak and a white cap or hat when they went abroad. Underneath all this they wore doublets, breeches, linen shirts, shoes and white stockings.

In 2004 the order is strongest in Belgium.

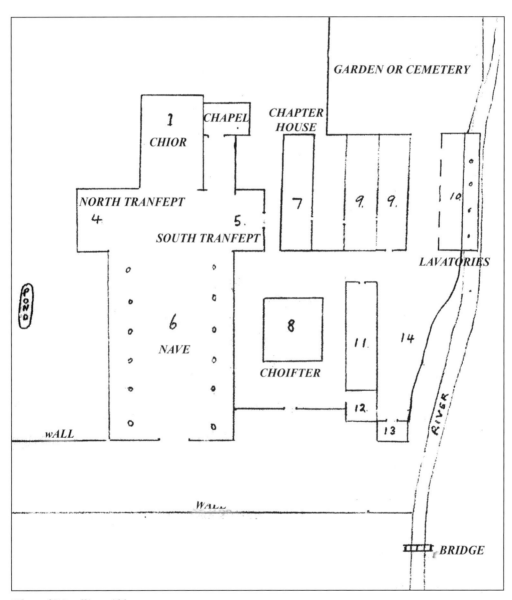

Plan of Wendling Abbey.

Chapter 2

Wendling Church and Chapel

Church of St Peter and St Paul

As Wendling church was under the spiritual charge of the abbey, and was served by one of the canons, there was no vicarage.

The church of St Peter and St Paul consists of a nave and chancel with a low square tower at the west end. There is also a small chapel on the south side of the nave (about 45 feet long) and a south porch made of flint rubble. The roofs are plain, of a low pitch and covered with lead, the east gables surmounted by crosses. The dimensions of the interior of the chancel are about 21 feet by 15 feet. It is lit by a Perpendicular (fifteenth century) east window of three cinquefoil headed lights, and on the south by two windows, one on each side of the priest's door. They consist of two trefoil ogex headed lights with a quatrefoil in the head. The arches as well as that of the priest's door appear equilateral.

The porch dates from the Perpendicular period. The doorway has a rolled mould with head stops typical of that time. Above the entrance is a fine carving of a Norman head with beard and moustache, wearing chain-mail head-dress.

Under the easternmost window is a stone seat in the angle of which is a holy-water drain. Near the centre of the north wall is a niche or cavity perhaps used for an early sepulchre. The arch opening to the nave is a flat four-centred arch of the Tudor era with late mouldings. Immediately projecting from this on the south side of the nave is a short transept or chapel under a low plain arch, the ends of which die in the wall. In this chapel is a large window of four lights and Perpendicular tracery.

In the north wall are two windows, each of three lights; the easternmost one is of Perpendicular style under a flattened Tudor arch. The other has the common drop arch and tracery of the early Perpendicular period.

Church of St Peter and St Paul.

Fourteenth-century priest's door.

This Norman head can be found in the church porch above the door.

Inside the church, looking west.

The church pulpit.

Left: *Inside the church, looking east.*

Perhaps the most outstanding feature of this church is the carved medieval font; it was made by a local craftsman which is unusual because most fonts were made at the quarry site to save the cost of transporting an unnecessary weight of stone. This one, sadly, has received the attention of vandals, who removed the heads of all the figures and the base. The sides of the font depict the seven sacraments as follows: east: matrimony; south-east: extreme unction; south: baptism of Christ; south-west: baptism; west: confirmation; north-west: penance; north: mass; north-east: ordination.

The church altar.

This font (below) *was made by a local craftsman.*

The Methodist Church

The Revd John Wesley often passed through Wendling on his journeys to Lynn from Norwich. On his visit to Norfolk in October 1790, the 87 year old Evangelist rose at 4a.m. on Monday 18 October and after prayers, left Norwich for Lynn at 7a.m. in a two-horse post-chaise with a companion. He stopped at Dereham and spoke to some Methodist members, but was unable to obtain fresh horses and had to set out for Swaffham with the same animals. At about 11a.m. that bitterly cold autumn morning, he passed within 4 yards of where a Primitive Methodist chapel was to be built, and some 30 yards from the present chapel. After a meal, and meeting members, he had to journey on to Lynn in a one-horse chaise. It was a miserable day and he said:

The wind blew, a drizzling rain fell in our faces and we had nothing to screen us from it so that I was thoroughly chilled from head to foot before I came to Lynn. But I soon forgot this little inconvenience, for which the earnestness of the congregation made me large amends.

This spirit of endurance and sacrifice also animated the Primitive Methodist missionaries who came from Lincolnshire to Norfolk, via Lynn, in 1821. A few years later the Gospel was being preached in Wendling by men such Mr Pilgrim and Mr James Fuller of Swaffham. On 17 December 1838, Wendling was shown as a preaching place on the Swaffham Circuit. For ten years services were held in local cottages, then in 1846, Mr Thomas Warner of Dereham gave a plot of land (now overgrown) close to the railway station, behind the Railway Tavern public house where a connexional chapel was built at a cost of £100. It was probably a wooden structure with a tiled roof and measured 24 feet by 17 feet. The *Primitive Methodist Magazine* for 1848 records, 'It was opened on June 11th, 1848'. A Sunday school was started and the opening sermon was preached by Mr C. Goodrich of Swaffham probably a relative of the Mr Goodrich mentioned by Wesley when he went to the town in 1790.

In 1877, a larger chapel was built by Mr W. Green, who was the society steward and Sunday school superintendent. (This good man carried the church offices for many years almost single-handedly). It stands next to the Post Office and, after being sold in 1920 for £90 was used for years as a store and as a centre for the local St John's Ambulance Brigade. It has since been converted into residential flats. The cause certainly flourished for at the Primitive Methodist centenary in 1907, the chapel had 69 members, a Christian Endeavour and a Junior Endeavour Society, a large Sunday school, and a Band of Hope with 130 members. At that time the need for a larger church was evident and in 1910 a site was bought for £40, on borrowed money, in Station Road. In 1914, Mr Albert Boddy of Tittleshall, built the present place of worship to seat 100, at a cost of £520 (£270 was raised and £250 borrowed). The chapel was opened on Easter Monday 1915, by Mrs C. Warmer with the opening sermon being preached by the Revd Joseph Mantripp. Mr W. Eagle and Mr A. Land were Society stewards (similar to church-wardens). There were eight local preachers.

The Band of Hope held a remarkable Temperance Demonstration each Whit Monday; the Dereham Salvation Army Band led the parade around the village and a public tea was held on premises that belonged to a Mr W.J. Balding, a local landowner and headmaster. On Whit Tuesday trains brought folk from a wide area to a sports day held on the Common. On one occasion 8,000 people were reported to be present. Teas were served from the chapel. It was one of the biggest holiday events in rural Norfolk.

In 1932 Wendling was transferred to the Dereham Circuit and in 1975, with the amalgamation of the Dereham and Swaffham Circuits, the cause returned to the Swaffham Section of the combined circuit.

In recent years an organ from Weybourne Methodist Church replaced the original instrument. The old heating system gave way to electric wall-mounted fires and foam cushions were provided for all pews. The old boiler-room and vestry was converted into a small schoolroom.

Wendling Methodist chapel.

The old chapel in Wendling, c.1900.

Chapter 3

Views of Wendling

Some of the local street names in existence today have very early origins. For example, Carr Lane derives its name from Wendling Carr, a lowland area covered with water, which lay on the north side of Abbey Farm towards Gressenhall. Also, there is a 1590 reference in 'The Hundred of Launditch' to Hulver Street.

This was once the heart of the village with the village bakery (behind Vine Cottage), the village shop, the Methodist chapel on the left-hand side of the road and the Rose Cottage public house. The Dame School was built onto the side of the house next to the pub.

Swaffham Road, c.1890. Note the Rose Cottage public house on the right.

Post Office and General Stores, c.1977.

Rose Cottage public house, c,1980.

Abroath

by Mrs Mollie Gooch

Arbroath, Hulver Street.

We bought our first house in 1961 for the princely sum of £1,400! It was an old cottage built at right angles to a country lane (as so many Norfolk cottages), right on the outskirts of the village. When we moved into the house in September I was expecting my third child. She was born at home six weeks later, delivered by my husband.

The house was still in a muddle and I remember the floorboards on the landing being up as electricity re-wiring was in progress.

The cottage had a very small kitchen, which we decided to enlarge straight away. This meant that I cooked Christmas dinner for my husband's family in a kitchen with no back wall, only a tarpaulin and brick dust everywhere! Not to mention a two-month-old baby plus a four-year-old and a two-year-old! I won't forget that Christmas in a hurry.

We had to pump up water from the well by a handpump, which we later changed to an electric one. The village wasn't put on mains water until 1965.

The garden, a quarter of an acre, was soon planted with all manner of vegetables and fruit, as my husband was a keen gardener. We also had a hive of bees situated on a small lawn. Every time I cut the grass I was stung on the head and had to go rushing next door to have the sting removed.

As the years passed we improved the property, buying more land on which we had a tennis-court built. This meant we had more grass to mow! By this time my husband was well into bee-keeping and had several hives, which were well away from the house. He made a summerhouse at woodwork classes, transporting it home in pieces to be erected in the garden. Most people just make coffee tables!

After several holidays in Norway he decided that pine panelling would be a good idea. Now every room has some pine panelling. The trouble came when he decided to do the same with the dining-room ceiling; being wattle and daub, a couple of bashes with a spade and the whole lot came down in a cloud of dust! We had to shovel the rubble out through the window.

My son had the smallest bedroom with a built-in bed. As he got older he grew too long for it so the room had to be extended by knocking out part of the wall on the landing. My husband has constructed built-in beds, wardrobes, dressing-tables and cupboards so that if we ever move we'll have hardly any furniture, as it's all part of the house! As we've lived here for almost 41 years that may never arise. To us it is, and always will be our very special home.

Station Road, 1903.

Mills

There was a water-mill at Wendling in the Middle Ages, probably in the abbey grounds, but its site is uncertain. Windmills were built at Mill Farm, the home of Miss K. Archer, on the A47, and are shown on following maps dated 1797, 1826, 1834, and 1838.

The first windmill was a post mill and the earliest known miller was John Beeston. In 1785 the mill was sold with the following advertisement in the *Norfolk Chronicle* of 25 June, 1785:

To be sold that well known WIND MILL with all its going gears situated in Wendling in Norfolk. Stands well for trade... also a good little Dwelling House near the said mill, with an acre of good land and a right of commonage. Immediate possession may be had. Further particulars from Mr John Beeston of Wendling aforesaid.

In the *Norfolk Chronicle* and *Norfolk Gazette*, 21 December 1850, the following advertisements appeared:

To be sold by auction by J.S.H. Greenacre at King's Arms Hotel, Dereham, on Monday 6th January, 1851 at 5 o'clock.

A very desirable Estate situated at Wendling comprising a convenient and substantial brick and tiled messuage recently erected with Baking Office and General Grocers and Drapers Shop, Stabling, Outbuildings and Warehouses, yards and garden. Also a capital POST WINDMILL driving two pairs of stones with roundhouse, patent sails, and all requisite machinery and going gears. Also four cottages. Apply to Messrs J.B. & N. Girling Solr. or the auctioneer.

The *Norfolk Chronicle* of 20 May 1871, carried this advertisement:

The late Mr John Mason's Freehold, Copyhold and Leasehold Estates at Wendling and Scarning with frontages to the railway near the station at Wendling which Messrs Butcher are instructed to Sell by

Auction at the King's Head Inn, East Dereham on Friday, 30th June 1871. Freehold and Copyhold. Farm House etc.. occupied by Mr Alfred Henry FOGG. Also a House, Bake Office, WINDMILL & PREMISES etc. occupied by Charles HORSLEY. Particulars of Messrs. Glazier & Mason, Solrs. King's Lynn, of Mr John Coleman, the Executor, at the place of sale, and of the Auctioneers, Norwich.'

In June that year, the same paper carried a similar advertisement but stated:

Lot 2 – A well situated Dwelling House, Bake Office and TOWER WINDMILL with the sails, going gears, etc. and the Warehouses, Counting Room, Stables and other buildings and a Pightle of Land abutting on the Turnpike Road, containing 1a 2r 8p in the occupation of Charles Horsley...

On 5 August 1871, Messrs Butcher were again offering the tower mill, 105 feet above sea level, with possession at Michaelmass next. The tower mill was demolished late in the nineteenth century, although one of the grinding stones is fixed into the floor of the farmhouse and the large baker's oven remains.

Wendling Station

Wendling was a crossing place on the single line from King's Lynn to Dereham, the signal-boxes on either side of it being Dereham West Junction and Dunham. Although Wendling Station was well situated relative to the village it served, the principal destinations for passengers were Swaffham and Dereham, which included schoolchildren to the Grammar Schools at these two locations. During the late 1940s and 1950s it was unusual for more than the odd wagon load of freight (mainly domestic coal for the village) to be dealt with daily. This all changed during the sugar beet season when the station would fill with wagons to be loaded up with beet from local farms ready to be transported to the factories.

In addition to the crossing loop and two goods yard sidings there was a refuge siding, situated at the east end of the station, which could accommo-

View of the station from the bridge.

date 46 wagons plus an engine and brake van. This facility proved to be very useful on Wednesday 5 October 1949, although not in the way it was intended. During shunting operations at Fransham, the rear portion of the 8.55a.m. freight, Dereham–Kings Lynn, ran back towards Wendling, arriving there at an estimated speed of 40mph, in thick fog. The Wendling signalman, Mr H. Bilverstone had already been warned of the train's movements by telephone from Fransham, so he diverted the runaway wagons into the, luckily clear, refuge siding. The wagons demolished the buffer stops, overshooting them by about 30 yards. Five of the wagons rolled down an embankment, taking telegraph wires with them.

On Monday 7 October 1912 the 6.00p.m., a goods train from Norwich to King's Lynn, was waiting at Wendling Station for the 5.43p.m. King's Lynn–Norwich passenger train to arrive. When the passenger train arrived the points were set wrong directing it into the freight train. A locomotive had to be sent from Dereham to tow the goods train clear and then take the rear coaches of the passenger train back to Dereham.

The last stationmaster was Mr Len Tuck. He held the position for about 15 years until it closed c.1968.

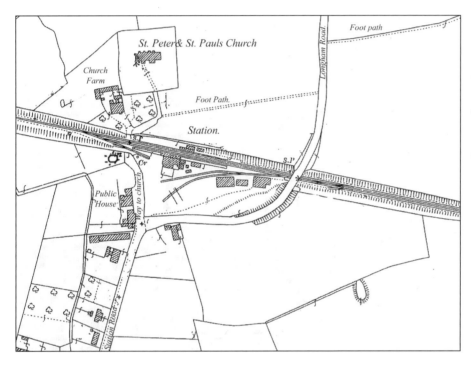

A plan of Station Road and the station before the bypass and flyover were constructed (c.1960). At this time people had to go to church by walking across the railway line beside the station.

Plan showing new roads, c.1975.

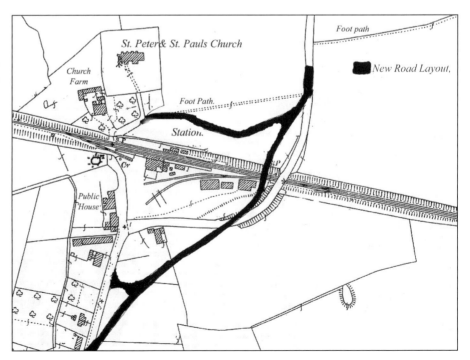

Ammunition being unloaded in a siding at Wendling Station ready to be taken by road to the American airbase.

Above: *Wendling Station looking towards Swaffham, c.1932*

Right: *The platform at Wending Station looking towards East Dereham, c.1940. Most of the line between East Dereham and Swaffham was single track but it divided into two at Wendling to allow trains to pass.*

Wendling Station with the crossing to Church Farm and the church in the foreground.

A photograph of Wendling Station, 4.11p.m., 19 July 1958.

The waiting-room and signal-box at the station, 1944.

The storage barn at the station.

This sign stood on the platform.

The bridge beside the station.

This bridge, pictured c.1978, stood behind the cottages in Carr Lane to allow the cattle belonging to Abbey Farm to pass beneath the railway line.

Chapter 4

A Vibrant Village: People and Events

Most community events in Wendling were once centred on the village school or the church. These events often included fireworks displays, carol services at the church with the schoolchildren putting on a play and a large village fête held on the school playing-field. The most prominent of these occasions was Wendling School's centenary fête held on 17 July 1976. It had a Victorian theme with the entire village dressing up in period costume. There were Victorian games as well as the pupils' annual country dance display. When the village school closed the local pub took over hosting such events for a short time, but at the time of writing, with the school and pub closed, it is left to a small army of locals to run a village fête in the village hall.

Village fête held at The Grange, mid-1970s.

Children from the village school entertain the public with a song accompanied by their headmaster Mr Bob Moore, 1970s.

Every one joins in with the country dancing on the front lawn of The Grange.

Revd Hugh Davis in for a ducking at a fête held at The Grange, mid-1970s.

Anyone for a ride? Local villagers take a wagon ride around the grounds of The Grange, mid-1970s.

Whitsuntide at Wendling

The Whitsuntide celebrations in Wendling used to last three days and were renowned throughout the county, although disappointingly no photographs were available of these events. Mrs Jolly unearthed the following text (possibly originally compiled by local man Mr Godfrey Windham using local dialect) which describes these events better just as well as photographs. The date of the piece is unknown:

My native village, Wendling, lies along the highway that winds its way from Yarmouth to King's Lynn. There is nothing to distinguish it from any other village and the traveller may well pass through it without being aware of its existence. Yet in my youth it was my world, and not a dormant world, particularly at Whitsuntide, when lilacs and laburnum were in full bloom and the lanes were perfumed by the smell of hemlock and sweetbriar. In the evenings, bells from a dozen churches rang out their joyous peals over meadows carpeted with buttercups which left a deposit of gold on the boots of the labourers returning home.

On Whit Sunday, the chapel held its school anniversary in a neighbouring barn. For weeks past the children had practised their songs and 'pieces', waiting impatiently for the day when they could put on their new suits and summer frocks and, standing in front of a platform made from sheep hurdles and wooden planks, display their knowledge of elocution.

Each year a favourite local preacher was invited to conduct the anniversary services. One year it was George Langdon, a huge, bearded man with beaming face and thunderous voice. He had walked some three or four miles from his little farmstead. On entering the barn, he removed his bowler hat. Wiping the sweat from his brow, he said how glad he was to be with his Wendling friends again and announced the first hymn. After the hymn, George knelt on the platform and prayed a long and ardent prayer and when he rose tears streamed down his face. For no good preacher could pray without emotion and the depth of his emotion was the standard by which he was judged. He wiped away his tears and his face transformed immediately into a beaming smile. He called Winnie Walker to say her 'piece'.

Winnie was four years old and in a lisping voice began, 'God who made the daisies and all the pretty flowers...' But at this juncture some of the boys at the back of the platform started to giggle and, in attempting to smother their merriment, over-balanced and sent the form on which they were sitting crashing to the floor. This commotion was too much for Winnie. With her little face sad and puckered she burst into tears and ran back to her place.

The next item George announced was the anthem by the choir. Now, for a small village, the choir was well trained and sang in perfect harmony. There was a hush over the congregation as the anthem swelled out:

'Send us Thy Light and Thy Truth:
Let them lead me,
0 let them lead me; 0 let them lead me to Thy holy hill.'

Loud and soft, soft and loud, the words were repeated with growing fervour until the whole place seemed inspired and infused with the very presence of the Eternal God. There is no one who, having experienced such moments as these, in which earth meets heaven and the spirit of man links up with the Heart of God, can return to the daily round and common task without being influenced thereby. Neither is the influence fleeting, for it lingers over the years and is a sure and certain anchor for a faith which may be torn and shaken by the winds of time and chance.

The afternoon service ended, George Langdon tramped home to milk his cows and back again to preach the evening sermon. This was a repetition of George's usual discourse, without reason or cohesion, but eloquent in its sincerity and moving in its direct appeal. When he had ended, he carefully wiped his eyes and said: 'Now, my friends, I expect you would like me to sing.'

It was characteristic of this tireless man that, after preaching, he must sing a song which he called 'Exalted High'. All the boys knew George's song and used to imitate his manner of singing it, to the amusement of their elders. With handkerchief in hand and head thrown back, he would close his eyes and begin, very softly:

'Exalted high, at God's right hand,
Nearer the Throne than angels stand
With glory crowned in white array
My wondering soul cries: Who are they?'

The first two lines were sung slowly and the second two equally fast and so on, over and over again, first repeating one line and then another until, mopping his beaming brow, he would work up into a crescendo of excitement which stopped suddenly at the last line. And then came the answer:

'These are the saints, beloved of God,
Washed are their robes in Jesus's blood.
With angels, clothed in spotless white
They shine in uncreated light.'

It was a storm at sea, with the winds lashed up into a fury and then dying down into perfect calm.

Such were those men whose hands were rough and hardened through wresting a living from the land, whose clothes were coarse and badly fitting, but whose faith burned within them like a living fire, a fire which consumed all petty jealousies, all desire to ride roughshod over the feelings of their fellow men in pursuit of their own ambitions, and brought into their lives a peace like the whispering of leaves in a summer breeze.

On Whit Monday the Band of Hope annual fête (or treat, as it was called) was held in a meadow adjoining the barn. Wendling boasted a vigorous Band of Hope and this treat was a highly-organised affair. To begin with, the Salvation Army band from Dereham headed a long procession of blue ribboners who marched and sang around the village. Hale and hearty fellows were those bandsmen, particularly the drummer who, in the pauses between playing, would take off his red cap and wipe his perspiring head. It so happened that he had a particularly shiny bald head and, much to the amusement of his pals, one of the small boys called out: 'Coo look! Ole Harry 'a bin usin' metal polish.'

After the procession had returned to the meadow, an ambitious sports programme began. This included tug-of-war, pole-jumping, pillow-fighting on a greasy pole, egg-and-spoon races for the children.

At one side of the field a cricket match was held between teetotallers and beer drinkers. The captain of the teetotallers was a tall and rather handsome young man called Fred Butcher. Bill Bradley was the beer drinkers' captain (both on and off the field). These two wore cream shirts and trousers but most of the players were in their black Sunday suits, starched collars and bowler hats.

The beer drinkers won the toss and batted first. Bill Bradley took the first ball, which went miles wide of the stumps, beat the wicket-keeper all endsup and produced two easy runs. The next ball was a full toss, which Bill swiped into the field with a resounding smack. It sped towards the fieldsmen head high, and smashed into the bowler hat of a short, fat youth of 20, named Charlie. A roar went up from the onlookers. 'Good ole Charlie. Keep yow yar hat on bor. You'll catch him out if he send yow another like that there!' And so the game went on; full of fun and everybody in a good humour.

At the end of their innings, the beer drinkers had managed to knock up 56 runs and by this time tea was ready in the barn. Everyone in the village who could walk came to this tea. They sat on long wooden forms on either side of trestle tables covered with plates of ham sandwiches and fruit cake. The tea was free for all, provided out of the Band of Hope funds and, for the older folk, was the event of the day. There they would sit and talk about their rheumatics to their hearts' content. The children competed with one another in the number of sandwiches each could consume, dodging under the tables to avoid the restraining influence and admonishments of their parents.

When the tea was over, they rushed back to the meadow, most of them stealthily darting behind the bushes to prevent themselves from bursting with tea and lemonade. Games were resumed and the teetotallers began their innings on the cricket pitch. Five

wickets fell for 14 runs and things looked bad. But at this stage Alfred Butcher and Maurice Carter made a stand, bringing the score to 38. Then the beer-drinking bowler took off his hat and coat, rolled up his sleeves and called out: 'Yow're bin in there long enough together. I'm agoin' ter git one on yer out or I'll eart my hat.'

So saying, he walked back about 20 yards behind the wicket and, turning round, loped back again, gathering speed all the time. His hairy arm went over and, an instant later, so did Alfred's middle stump. It was soon all over after that and the honour of the beer drinkers was upheld by 13 runs.

By this time the evening shadows were extending from the towering elm trees and, over the little stream which wound its way along the far side of the meadow, a film of mist was rising, forecasting a fine day on the morrow. As soon as the sun had set there was a sudden swish like the hissing of escaping steam and, high above the heads of the happy crowd, a cluster of multi-coloured lights spread out like a gigantic fan. The firework display had begun. Children clapped their hands and danced with glee and old men stared with mouths wide open.

When the display was over, there were cries of 'Come on Willie Harbut... Gordie, thas time we wurra goin' boom' and, one by one, the little family groups disappeared into the quietness of the night. For youths and maidens the fun was not yet over. Linking their hands together, they formed a circle and began the age-old game of kissing in the ring. Three boys and three girls started walking round the ring, the boys in one direction and the girls in the opposite. Each had a white handkerchief and dropped it on the shoulder of a willing victim. Then began the chase. Girls ran giggling and screaming in all directions, each followed by an eager male. The first chase was a long one for as yet there was no competition. Each had chosen his or her favourite and the boys made sure that the girls reached the extremities of the meadow before they were caught. Then, with arms enfolded around each other, they kissed and sauntered back to the ring. From now on there was competition for the prettier girls and more handsome boys but, as time wore on, none was left out of the game.

On Whit Tuesday, Wendling was the centre of attraction for a host of people from all parts of the county. Posters printed in red, white and blue advertised a grand sports meeting which included trotting matches, hurdle races and cycle handicaps. Large refreshment booths were provided and innumerable side shows. The meeting would be attended by the band of HM Norfolk Regiment which, by kind permission of Colonel Trollop, would play selected musical items. Special trains were run by arrangement with the GER.

The meeting was held on the village Common, by the side of the turnpike. In the morning the Common was the scene of feverish preparation. The competitors' ring was roped off and the racing tracks mown and rolled. Marquees and stalls sprang up more quickly than mushrooms ever did and an air of cheerful expectancy prevailed. The proceedings were timed to start at two o'clock and at half past one the first special train steamed into Wendling Station which, strangely enough, was in the centre of the village and quite close to the sports meadow. The Station Road joined the main road opposite the chapel and, although there was a strong puritanical disapproval of this meeting among the chapel elders, they saw no harm in diverting some of the devil's money to a better cause. So all day long the chapel was open, not for prayer, but for the provision of light refreshment at modest charges.

The chapel yard formed an excellent vantage point for watching the crowd of spectators on their way from the station to the meadow and there was much friendly banter between the local young folk and the visitors. Some 8,000 people came to Wendling sports every year. This was verified by William Green, whose house adjoined the chapel; all day long he sat at his window and counted them as they went by.

Great excitement arose when the trotting ponies were detrained and led to the meadow, followed by the little machines to which they would be harnessed. These were drawn by stable lads in jockey caps and racing colours. A corner of the field was reserved as a paddock and the race-meeting atmosphere was completed by the bookies, wearing loud check suits and brown bowlers. There was Jack Lees of Norwich, Tom Smith of Yarmouth and a host of others, each having an enormous Gladstone bag and his own little stall. These soon got started with their business. 'Who says a bob on Black Jack?' 'Two to one Happy Lass'. Fools and their money were soon parted.

The first race, a trotting match, started promptly at two o'clock and there were six runners. Spectators surged towards the ropes, jostling each other vigorously for the best positions. From every quarter there were shouts of 'Go it, Black Jack', 'Come on Merry Weather', 'Let him have it Davy bor', 'Look out Sam, George is arter ye'. It happened that one of the horses was observed to be breathing very loudly. He had a broken windpipe and was breathing through a tube protruding from the middle of his neck. An excited voice called out: 'Wur look at that, Charlie, that ain't a hoss, thas one of ol' Johnson's traction ingines.' The race went off without incident and sure enough the traction engine won!

The next event was a cycle race and this aroused more local enthusiasm, for Jim Barton, a member of the chapel choir, was the favourite competitor. For weeks past Jim had been racing along the local roads and his speed was the talk of the village. But now he had to compete with some of the best riders in the county. Round the course he raced, down the slope towards the railway and up the other side, riding for dear life. Soon it was over and the stately bell-ringer announced: 'Morton first, Chaney second, Wharton third'. Murmurs of sympathy for Jim were mixed with caustic comments from the locals. One boy called out: 'You'll hitter pull yar socks up afore yow ride agin, Jim.' Someone clipped the lad over the ear and the next race began.

The sonorous voice of the ringer rose above the chattering crowd. 'Heer ye, beer ye, heer ye. Two hundred yards obstickle race is now agoin to start.' There was a rush towards the rope to see the fun. The two chief obstacles were a stack-cover, under which the competitors had to crawl, and the usual suspended barrels. Big Bill Bradley was one of the runners, but Bill had spent most of the time before the race in the refreshment booth and was not in the best of condition. The pistol shot cracked out and the dozen runners lurched forward together. As they came to the tarpaulin there was a scuffle for the outside places and Bill was wedged into the middle. There were moving bulges corresponding to the individual bottoms of the competitors and that of Bill Bradley was gyrating round the middle of the sheet. The crowd roared and egged him on. 'Wur, whatter yow arter, Bill? Yow're goin' the wrong way. Git yow back agin, bor.' And so Bill struggled, first one way and then another, until he finally collapsed inside the sheet without seeing the light of day. They pulled the cover away and a dejected voice called out: 'Where's that there boy who told me to go t'other way? I'll what yer call lather him.'

Meanwhile, the older members of the crowd were regaling themselves with saucers of cockles or plates of shrimps, according to their taste. Here and there would be seen little groups, pouring out their beer from brown and white stone bottles covered with wicker basket work. These were the days when beer was beer and potent in its effect.

The sports ended at six o'clock and the chapelites hurrried to their observation post to watch the crowds go home. The greatest sport was taunting the drunks who spewed their way along the roadside. There would be outpourings against drunkenness at the next Band of Hope meeting and extra fervour put into 'Hold the fort, for I am coming.' But there was no questioning that beer drinkers and teetotallers alike had had a wonderful Whit Tuesday.

Harvest Supper Celebrations

Mollie Gooch performs Albert and the Lion, *1999.*

Soldier, Soldier *by Mollie Gooch and her daughter Gillian, c.1999.*

Supper time, 1999.

Jubilee Celebrations

Above and below: *Entertainment was laid on by kids of all ages to celebrate the golden jubilee, 2002. Below, left to right: Mollie Gooch, Danielle Hobbs, Bethany Howlett and Philip Hobbs.*

Local girls dress up to celebrate Her Majesty Queen Elizabeth II's silver jubilee on the 7 of June 1977. Lucy Futter is dressed as Elizabeth I while Ann Massey is Richard of York (front left) *and Louise Massey is Edward IV.*

Waistbands expand as the people of Wendling and their friends from surrounding villages tuck into a special meal in the village hall as part of the golden jubliee celebrations in 2002.

Village Fun

The founding members of Wendling's village hall committee, 1953. Left to right, back row: Ted Violin, Mr Tuck, Mr Hannant; middle row: Bertie Neave, Ann Claxton, Olive Horningold, Mrs Meen, Mrs Parker, Mrs Hannant, Stanley Claxton; front row: Mr Huggins, Miss Huggins, Mrs Tull, Revd Tull.

Local schoolchildren c.1948.

Dolly Willmot and Susan Canham, c.1974.

Village Fun

Easter bonnet parade in the village hall, 2002.

The 1st Wendling Brownie pack, c.1982. The pack at that times was comprised of the following members: Ann Massey, Carrianne Butcher, Catherine Jewers, Clara Wiseman, Clare Kiley, Donna Bush, Donna Moulding, Elaine Ray, Jeanette Bush, Julie Webster, Louise George, Louise Massey, Lorraine Cook, Lucy Futter, Melanie Simonds, Michelle Baxter, Nicola Butcher, Samantha Pates, Sharon Parling, Susan Kirk, Theresa George, Tina Forster, Virginia Coggles, Yvonne George. The pack was run by Mrs Massey, Mrs Walters and Mrs Brooks.

Carol singers at The Grange, 1998. The picture shows: Bert May, Mollie Gooch, Sir Ralph Howell, Ella Howell, Richard Dunsire, Sheena Bush, Edward Hill, Freddie Howell, Lucy Gould, Charmain Mulligan, Jessie Hill.

Village Fun

Clockwise, starting above left:
A very popular game at the 2002 fête: find the full wine bottle and empty it when you get home! Derek Buck is on the far right.

Local ladies Pam Yaxley, Lucy Row (née Futter) and Sally Futter, stop for a chat while looking around the stalls in the village hall's car park at the fête in 2002.

Jake, Tazmin and Matthew Olley have a go at water skittles at the fête, 2002.

Unveiling the village sign, 1994. Some of those pictured are: Richard Dunsire, Ella Howell, Olive Willis, Verity Howden, Michelle Dunsire, Emily Dunsire.

At Work

Workers at Grange Farm take a hard-earned lunch break, c.1924.

Clockwise, starting right:
Mrs Bennett in her greenhouse.

Mrs Hannant, Mrs Chaney, Mrs Woods, Mrs Claxton and Miss Eagle, members of the Wendling St John's Ambulance Brigade, late 1950s.

Local farm hand Ernie Pooley, who worked in the area.

At Work

Staff at the bakehouse in the 1940s: Ted Langley, Dennis Neil, Maurice Barber, Reggie Meen, Amos Parker.

Snipper, the bakehouse horse, standing outside some cottages in Hulver Street, c.1940s. These cottages were demolished a number of years ago and a bungalow now stands on this land.

At Work

Bruno Brown checks the tomatoes in Mr Hannant's greenhouse, which was located in front of the council-houses in Grange Road, c.1950.

Emily Canham (née Brown) and 'Girlie' Robinson potting up at Norfolk Herbs.

The Parker Family

Mr Parker delivering bread with the help of three local children, c.1940s.

Mr Amos (Martin) Parker with one of his two daughters, c.1946. He is proudly standing beside Wendling's first delivery van, which he drove around the local villages delivering bread.

The Parker Family

Mr Parker of Station Road, Wendling.

Mrs Edith Leah Parker (née Spurn) standing in front of her cottage in Station Road. Mrs Parker's parents came from the distant village of Scarning.

Two young members of the Parker family standing outside the bungalows near the entrance to Grange Farm.

Mr Parker with the baker's van, c.1950. As you can see this van was not only used for delivering bread.

Brown • Canham • Freeman Families

Above: *Mrs Brown with one of her grandchildren, Susan, 1963.*

Left: *A very young Emily Brown, August 1935.*

Below: *Susan Canham holding her little brother Philip, 1968.*

Brown • Canham • Freeman Families

Emily Canham arrives at chapel on the arm of her father Bruno Brown on her wedding day, 5 April 1958.

Left: *Ralph and Emily Canham cutting their wedding cake.*

Below: *Emily and Ralph's wedding guests outside Wendling chapel.*

Brown • Canham • Freeman Families

Keith and Susan Freeman (née Canham).

Newlyweds Susan and Keith Freeman departing from the chapel in style.

Susan and Keith Freeman at their daughter Amy's christening. Their other children are Esther and James.

The Gooch Family

Gillian, Simon and Jane Gooch playing in their garden, 1965.

The Gooch family taking a walk along Hulver Street, 1961.

Gillian Gooch on the day of her marriage to Chris Hobbs, 1984.

Jane Gooch with her new husband, Paul Tooby, departing from the church in Wendling, 1977.

The Lawes Family

Mary Lawes at her wedding to Alan Sadler, 10 June 1972. The bridesmaids were Olive Lawes, Norma Gilding and Hazel Parnel.

The Lawes family at Mary's wedding, 1972. To the left of the happy couple are: the groom's father Mr Sadler, Joyce Lawes and best man Michael Potter. Basil Lawes is standing to the right of the bride.

Wendling WI

WI Christmas Party, c.1952. The photograph includes: Mrs Claxton, Mrs E. Wright, Mrs Waters, Mrs Sayer, Barbara Wright, Mrs Rogerson, Mrs Meen, Mrs Parker, Miss Eagle, Mrs A. Wright (née Suggins), Mrs Butcher, Margaret Meen (now Parker), Emily Brown (née Canham), Mrs Palmer (née Mitchell), Mrs Ruby Cowles, Mrs Brown, Mrs Symonds.

Wendling WI gather for a Christmas party in East Dereham, c.1985. Left to right, back row: Val Keron, Lucy Massey, Girlie Robinson, Emily Canham, Sally Futter, Mary Olley, Jenny Thurston; front row: Edna Wright, Vera Offard, Mrs Smith, Olive Hornigold.

Wendling WI

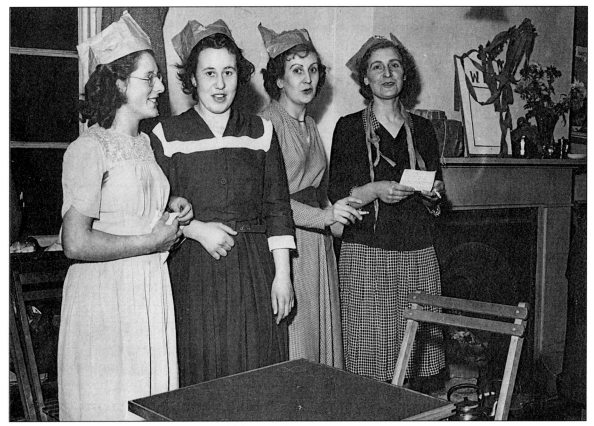

WI Christmas party held at the Rose Cottage club room. c.1951. Left to right: Margaret Meen (now Parker), Emily Brown (later Canham), Barbara ? (née Wright), Ruth Rogerson (née Wright). Barbara married an American and was on a visit home from the USA when this photograph was taken.

In 1973 a pair of silver birch trees were planted in the playing-field of Wendling Primary School by Mrs Mollie Gooch of Wendling WI to celebrate the WI's silver jubilee. This was done under the gaze of: Mrs Akehurst, Mrs Massey, Mrs Hornigold, Mrs Woods, Mrs Wright, Mrs Claxton, Mrs Fairhead, Mrs Parker, Mrs Keron, Mrs Sally Futter, Mrs Howell, Mrs Prior, Mrs Mary Olley, David Olley, Stephen Olley, Mr Moore, Darren Meen, Jane Futter, Garry White, Carol Simpson, Adele Meen, Andrew Woods, Sharon Simpson, Jocelyn Fenn, Jill Long and Angie Simpson.

Chapter 5

Wendling School

Before Forster's Education Act of 1870 was passed, which provided primary education for all, there was throughout the country, a network of Voluntary Schools which had been given and often also maintained, by private generosity and religious or sectarian zeal. This included numerous National Schools, so called because they were founded by the Anglican National Society.

White's *Directory of Norfolk* for 1846 shows Mrs Ann Atthow as schoolmistress, and for 1854 Robert Claxton is schoolmaster. In 1864 Dinah Badcock is shown as Schoolmistress.

Mrs Bennett's house, 'Clear View', has an annex bearing a stone tablet inscribed 'WENDLING SCHOOL – Erected AD1869 by Messrs BULLARD & SONS of NORWICH for the use of the Parishioners of Wendling.' This property at one time belonged to the Rose Cottage public house, and the brewers obviously provided this room for a school.

The Act of 1870, doubled the state grant to existing Church Schools and introduced publicly controlled schools to fill the gaps in the educational map of the country. These new schools were called Board Schools and were paid for by local rates and government grants. Between 1870 and 1890, the average school attendance throughout the county rose from 1¼ million to 4½ million, and the money spent on each child doubled.

In Wendling the School Board, with five members, was not established until 16 March 1875, nearly five years after the Act was passed. The school itself was probably built that year at a cost of about £500 and Kelly's *Directory of Norfolk* shows the Board School as vacant at that time. It was opened in 1876, but the school logbooks, unfortunately, do not begin until July 1878. Mrs Cecilia Lovett is the first mistress shown in the logbooks. The first book records the visits of the rector, Revd W.R. Easton, as well as admittances, average attendances and standards of proficiency. Over the years average attendance fell as low as 39, but also rose to well over 80. There was a large main classroom and a small one for infants, the children at the rear of the class sitting on a four-tier platform.

One Friday afternoon in March 1947, a pupil drew Mrs Rowell's attention to water seeping under the classroom door. Thinking a tap was left on, she hurried into the cloakroom only to find the floor, the playground and the surrounding meadows under water. The flood water rose to 2 feet in the school which was closed for several days. Some of the staff and scholars had difficulty getting home.

Wendling School celebrates its centenary, 1876–1976. It closed in 1982.

Robin, Sally, Jane and Lucy Futter dressed up in their Sunday best, ready to go into Wendling chapel for a service of as part of the celebrations to commemorate the village school's centenary, 1976.

Head Teachers at Wendling School*

1883	*Miss Anna H. Hill. She married Mr Robert Huggins, and after his death, Mr Boddy. She moved to Fransham, but some later years returned to Wendling.*
1888	*Miss Agnes Bowie.*
1890	*Mr Abraham Bartle of Honeypot Farm.*
1891	*Miss Clara Habblethwaitte.*
1894–1922	*Mrs A.H. Boddy She was also organist at Scarning Church for a record period. She died in 1952.*

1900 W.J. Balding was headmaster.

1902 Balfour's Education Act abolished the School Boards.

1907 The school was enlarged to accommodate 90 scholars and was closed for 15 weeks while alterations were completed. Average attendance was 78.

1909 Miss Laura Eagle became monitress and served as teacher with a few years break while at Beeston until 1957.

1922–26	*Miss Norah Layer.*
1926	*Miss H.F. Catton.*
1931	*Miss I. Hillier (later Mrs Gillett).*
1933–72	*Mrs F. Rowell. Average attendance at this time was 50.*
1973	*Mr R. Moore became head teacher. He is assisted by Mrs D. Howe.*

A number of head teachers followed Mr Moore until the school closed in 1982.

* Names and dates have been gleaned from a variety of directories.

Left: *Suzanne, Pam, Tony and Jennifer Yaxley dressed up for a chapel service.*

Below: *Mothers' race on the school playing-field, 1976. Left to right: Jackie Campen, Jackie Harnson, Janet Meen, Christine Warlidge, Sheila Forster, Margaret Parker.*

Wendling School, 1914.

Wendling School, 1919.

Wendling School, 1920.

Wendling School, 1922.

Wendling School, 1976. The teachers at the back are Mr Moore and Mrs Howe. Left to right, back row: Tracy Simpson, Darren Meen, Jocelyn Fenn, Suzanne Yaxley, Carol Simpson, Mark Hannant, Jane Futter, Mark Seekings, Garry Simpson; middle row: Carl Warlidge, Anita Pool, Paul Forster, Sean Webster, Rachel Woodrow, Melanie Simonds, Mandy Seekings, Tracy Campen, Jennifer Yaxley, Louise Massey; front row: Richard Stokes, Stephen Olley, Lucy Futter, Claire Harrison, Theresa Simpson, David Olley, Julie Webster, Rodger Harrison, Carrianne Butcher, Tina Forster.

Wendling School, c.1982. Left to right, back row: *Mrs Spooner, Samantha Pates, Lorraine Cook, Jason Warlidge, Karen Pates, Hugh Coggles, Mr Laycock;* middle row: *Tony Forster, ?, Nicola Butcher, ?, Sharon Parling, Tony Butcher;* front row: *Lucy Pates, Matthew Olley, Eleanor Laycock, Annie Massey, Tracy Parling.*

Wendling School.

Wendling School mid-1950s. Left to right, back row: *Tommy Brown, Tony Goodson, David Gilbert, Cecil Brown, Gregory Forster, Eric Howe;* third row: *Marlene Leggatt, June Eastham, Linda Fiddy, Betty Steere, Pat Goodson, Vilanda Cowles, ?, Diane Palmer, Kathy Gilbert;* second row: *Pam Meen, Nicola Chittock, John Fiddy, Steven Baker, Maurice Cowles, Brian Poole, Ivan Brown, ?, John Poole, Michael Wright, Doreen Meen, Linda Eastham, Christine Purple, ?;* front row: *Janet Meen, ?, Robert Tuck, Geoffrey Eastham, Valerie Eastham, Yvonne Leggatt, Gillian Butcher, Jenny Meen, Carol Rix, Linda Barber, Janet Claxton, ?, Clive Hannant, ? Brown.*

Miss Laura Eagle of Station Road, Wendling, had a teaching career spanning nearly 50 years. Miss Eagle was a pupil at the school for one term in 1909. Then. after Christmas, she was an apprentice teacher aged 14. Miss Eagle spent all but seven years of her teaching career at Wendling School teaching children from the ages of 4 to 8 in the same small classroom. Hundreds of pupils have been taught the Three Rs by Miss Eagle who would think looking around the class 'I taught most of their parents' (not many teachers could say this today). Each year Miss Eagle gave her class presents from the Christmas tree; this must have become easier as time when by as the number of pupils in the school dropped from 80 to below 40. Miss Eagle played a big part in village life as she was also a member of the Parish Council, the WRVS, St John's Ambulance Brigade and the Women's Institute. She also played the organ for the village Methodist church for over 40 years.

The Second World War and the Airbase

Dick Mason spent his childhood living and playing near the airbase and later committed his memories to paper. What appears below may not be 100 per cent accurate or entirely politically correct to today's reader, but it serves as the true thoughts of someone who lived in this area during the Second World War.

The Home Guard

By Dick Mason

The LDV, later the Home Guard, came into being and all more or less able-bodied males were expected to participate. Father's initiation took place one Sunday morning and was very brief – about 20 minutes. He was livid [and referred to the man in charge as an] 'Ignorant boy, wet behind the ears, never seen a shot fired in anger, jumped-up nobody'... When he eventually calmed down, it emerged that a local farmer's son who had mysteriously rocketed to the rank of sergeant, had addressed Father by surname only. 'Over there Mason'. That did it! Funny to reflect that in those days the aristocracy always addressed one another by surname, yet at our level it was considered an insult – especially if you were being addressed by an 'ignorant boy, wet behind the ears who had never seen a shot fired in anger'!

Delicate diplomacy eventually prevailed and Father returned, but only after a lengthy cooling-off period, and on the definite understanding that he would accept no orders from the offending sergeant even if the Jerries were at our very door. Fortunately, the corporal was a First World War veteran and as such, much more acceptable. Some time afterwards Father brought home an old but serviceable rifle which he cleaned and oiled with love and care. 'If that old Jerry Blenheim come this way agin he'll be on the wrong end o' this.' The fighting spirit of the Home Guard summed up in one short phrase. He couldn't resist one trial shot – in the air – which depleted his ammunition allocation by some 20 per cent at a stroke, so to speak. I do not doubt that the Home Guard would have acquitted themselves bravely in our hour of need had it come, but I also understand how the activities of Captain Mainwaring and his comrades in 'Dad's Army' strike a chord of authenticity in those who lived through those anxious days. This reminds me of a story I got second-hand, debatably true, but worth telling anyway.

*Some boys were in a wood one dark night when the local Home Guard patrol passed by, during the middle of one of many scares about enemy paratroops. The boys crashed around noisily and the patrol halted. 'There's somebody in that there wood, hold you hard' said the corporal. All quiet until the patrol started to move off, then more crashing around. 'I think you be'er load yar guns'. Rattling bolts, 'blast I're nipped my fingers'. (The rear bolt extension on those old rifles could be spiteful). Then 'b***** me I're dropped my cartridges'. Matches were being struck to find them as the boys stole away, with some difficulty, being literally doubled up with mirth.*

One may reflect on the thoughts of a toughened German paratrooper, had there been one, and his subsequent report to his superior officer. 'The cunning English have a new tactical ploy mein Sturmbannführer – they us make laugh so much we can't shoot'!

The Home Guard had a variety of weapons, some obsolete, some improvised, including what I believe were known as ball cartridges, to use in a sporting 12-bore gun... and as such would have done considerable damage to a person if moving fast enough – which by and large they failed to do (I would guess at an effective range of about 50 yards, at which distance the victim might well suffer a nasty bruise). You veterans out there, please correct me if I'm wrong. It goes without saying that the effect on a Tiger tank would have been negligible at any range! I'll come to the HG's anti-tank armoury later, first let me tell you how I had another experience of 'friendly fire'.

I was (rather reluctantly) helping Father on his field late one summer evening, while the Home Guard were practising with ball ammunition, firing in our direction but into a railway embankment between us and them. Quite a substantial embankment, about 25 feet high, which should, theoretically, have left us quite safe, especially as we were some distance away from the action. I heard 'buzzz', then shortly afterwards 'buzzz' again. I thought [the noise was coming from] flying black beetles which were often around at dusk and made a similar noise.

I realised my mistake when Dad grabbed me by the scruff of the neck, pushed me face down into a furrow and led me at a crawl to the safety of the nearest ditch.

Father knew from experience the sound of nearly-spent bullets, but I have never been able to figure out how they got over the embankment to us. The only possible explanation would seem to be a howitzer-like trajectory. Perhaps they hoped to apply plunging fire and drop one into a Tiger's open hatch!

At a later stage, the Home Guard received an issue of Sten guns. The Sten, as many will know, developed into a useful weapon, especially at close quarters, but the early marks represented a somewhat experimental project to make a weapon without too much precision engineering, embodying pressed metal, welded components, unskilled labour and generous manufacturing tolerances. This principal continues to this day with the famous and abundant Kalashnikov.

We had to start somewhere, hence the MK1, on which Father received instruction in spite of his utter contempt for it. He told of setting it for serial fire, whereupon it fired a single shot. They tinkered with it and attempted single shot fire whereupon it emptied the magazine. Tinkered again, loaded it, paused for tea, stood it down on it's butt set to 'safe', whereupon it emptied itself into the ceiling! Later marks were better, as I am sure many veterans will confirm and the Germans (amongst others), later paid the Sten the ultimate compliment of copying it.

The Home Guard had their own unique weapons, hastily improvised by various engineers and made of whatever was available to them, all of which interested me greatly as can be imagined. My problem was getting a close look. One, which I believe was called the Northover Projector was a length of what looked like drainpipe, on a tripod with a very rudimentary opening breech, firing grenades and bottles of phosphorus and perhaps other mildly lethal missiles – not very far – presumably using some kind of separate propellant charge. I never got close enough to find out.

Then there was a kind of spigot mortar where the fixed part which would normally be the barrel, was a length of solid rod, and the bomb, which seemed huge to me, included a tubular barrel which slid over this rod and presumably contained the propellant. I have been told that the stainless steel spigots which can still be seen around set in concrete were strategically placed mountings for these weapons.

There was also a rifle-based grenade launcher – an old rifle tightly bound with wire to discourage it from bursting, at the muzzle end of which was a metal cup to accept a standard hand-grenade. One loaded a blank cartridge, popped in the grenade having first pulled the pin ('don't drop it now!'), rested the butt against a sandbag, registered the required elevation and azimuth (by eye presumably), pulled the trigger and off she went, arming lever falling off on the way, to explode some seven seconds later. Tiger tanks watch out!

These brave lads would have undoubtedly fought well, but I cringe at the thought of these devices and their handlers meeting the might of the Wehrmacht, just as I do when I look at the remaining pillboxes still

around and wonder how few rounds of 88mm shot it would have taken to obliterate one. The Germans didn't come, so we shall, thankfully, never know.

The Home Guard organised an open day on a field not far away, and local people attended in considerable numbers. Father decided to boycott it, so I went by myself. There was marching, rifle drill and various weapons on display, including the notorious Sten, which needless to say I gave a wide berth. First in the weapons demonstration came the firing of a machine-gun into a local pond, which resulted in a delightful rainbow effect from the spray thrown up in the sunshine. This was, however, somewhat curtailed when it was realised that bullets can ricochet off water in certain circumstances.

Next came the spigot mortar and its mighty cylindrical missile which was fired at a low angle at a big pile of old square army petrol cans about 50 yards away. Before travelling far, it grounded and slid along the muddy surface like a terrestrial torpedo, leaving a deep grove in its wake. I was impressed, but thinking back I do not recall a hit on the target and I remember wondering if it was standard procedure to lay a bed of mud prior to engaging the enemy.

The most spectacular of all was the Northover Projector which rounded off the live-firing demonstration, the chosen missile being phosphorus in glass bottles. Phosphorus as many will know, bursts into flame on contact with air, which can be very uncomfortable for the enemy provided you deliver him a bottle which breaks on him when it arrives.

On this occasion, however, the bottle broke either in the barrel or just out of it, spraying phosphorous which ignited on the scores of bikes leaning against a nearby tree! Panic ensued as bikes were valuable and new tyres virtually unobtainable. I never knew the extent of the damage, which was probably not that bad, but I grabbed my trusty steed which was fortunately parked elsewhere, and hurried it home for safe keeping, whilst resolving to stick to carbide in the future on safety grounds!

Wendling Airbase

392nd Bombardment Group
Information from *The Liberators from Wendling* by Robert E. Vickers junr

This group was activated in January 1943 at Davis-Monthan airfield, Tucson, Arizona and was equipped with B24 Liberators. The group trained at Biggs Field, El Paso, Texas and Alamogordo Army Airbase, New Mexico. The advance party of the USAF 392nd Bombardment Group, 2nd Air Division, 14th Combat Wing and the first B24H Liberator Unit assigned to the Eighth Air Force, European Theatre of Operation arrived at Station 118 on 22 April 1943. More men followed in August 1943 and were assigned to the Eighth Air Force at Wendling Airbase in East Anglia.

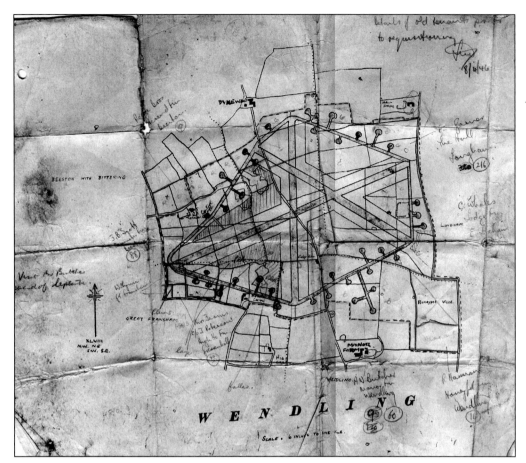

Old map of the airbase showing the field boundaries prior to the requisitioning of the land that took place late in 1941.

The group flew 285 combat missions, suffering 1,552 casualties, including 835 killed in the line of duty and 184 aircraft lost. In February 1944 the group was awarded the Distinguished Unit Citation for destroying an aircraft factory in Gotha, Germany. The group returned to the United States in June 1945 and was deactivated at Charleston AAF in South Carolina in September 1945.

The Missions

The first combat operation was a target at Abbeyville, France on 9 September 1943. Some 20 B24s were dispatched; two aborted but 18 reached the target and delivered 288–300lb general purpose bombs. All aircraft returned safely.

The Group carried out a total of 285 daylight missions with a total of 1,553 aircrew casualties suffered by the unit. A total of 170 men died while 1,202 were lost in action, presumed dead, and 181 were wounded in action.

Mission 8: 13 November 1943

For Mission 8, 24 B24s took off; 15 reached the target with eight having to abort due to mechanical difficulties and one because of poor weather. The bombs consisted of 500 general purpose weapons and bombing was accomplished even though the target was obscured by bad weather. Enemy defences were quite heavy and Group losses high. Some 50–75 single and twin-engine fighters pressed home attacks and anti-aircraft fire was some of heaviest seen on these early missions. The Group lost four aircraft; one due to enemy fighters and three to flak (anti-aircraft fire). An additional six B24s were damaged. Group gunners claimed seven enemy aircraft, but the unit suffered an additional 43 casualties – 40 crew members MIA and three injured. Total flight duration for this mission was seven hours. This was one of the costliest raids to the Group in men and aircraft during the early missions of the Second World War.

The Most Disastrous Mission

The deadliest mission carried out by the Group was a raid on Friedrichshafen on 18 March 1944, when a force of 28 aircraft started to take off at 10.00a.m. Four aborted due to mechanical difficulties, two collided over France (one chute was definitely seen and another was probable). A total of 15 aircraft were lost in action: one was last seen heading for Switzerland, one crash landed at Gravesend with two dead crew on board. Seven returned with extensive damage, the last aircraft landing at 6.45p.m. The total loss of life for this mission reached 154 men.

The Last Mission

The last mission carried out by the Group was on 25 April 1945. It was also the last mission to be carried out by the Eighth Air Force. One aircraft was lost, although the crew survived.

Wendling Airbase

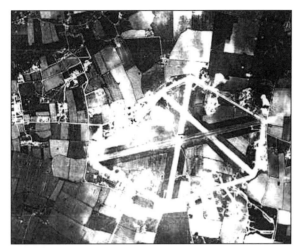

Aerial photograph of the base and surrounding area.

Standard living accommodation.

Sleeping quarters.

Base hospital.

Medics with the equipment they carried in their ambulance to transport the injured to the base hospital, c.1944.

Wendling Airbase

A typical office on the base.

Washing facilities on the base.

Parachutes stored in a protected storage area.

Bombs stored in Honey Pot Woods.

Base library.

Building a line shack, c.1944. These were made from discarded wooden bomb boxes.

Wendling Airbase

A dining-room on the base set out for Thanksgiving.

Escape Corner was an area of the base library where the contents of the escape packs were displayed. These packs were carried by airmen in case they were shot down behind enemy lines. They contained a silk map and a selection of false documents to help them find their way back to safety.

All the Americans were given bicycles to travel around the local area. At the end of the war all the bicycles were lined up along the main runway and a gun carrier was driven over them. But some were saved by the local 'enterprising' youngsters who managed to make off with them before they could be collected up.

Local bobbies visit the base, c.1944.

An armament mechanic cleaning the Plexiglas on the gun turrets, c.1944.

Wendling Airbase

The precision engineering tools used in the workshop.

Electrical testing equipment.

Tyre and wheel workshop.

Fabric-covered aircraft flaps waiting to be repaired.

Equipment in the engineering department ready to remove damaged aircraft.

The Weather Station

The weather station on the base, seen here in the middle of the picture, c.1944.

The weather station workroom, c.1944.

Weather officer John R. Borchert checking the readings, c.1944.

An aircraft being cleared of snow, ready to go out on a mission, c.1944.

Possibly Station Weather Officer John R. Borchert setting up the weather station equipment on the base, c.1944.

John R. Borchert, Third Assignment: Wendling

On September 4th I joined 392nd Bomb Group as Station Weather Officer at their base near Wendling. The place was terribly raw, unfinished and unready except for the runways and 'hardstands' for parking the bombers. There was construction and military equipment milling around in a sea of cold mud. I was Station Weather Officer and acting Group Weather Officer (i.e. Staff to the Group Commander). This was the first time I'd had responsibility for setting up and running a station. Here are a few vivid memories:

Pre-dawn briefings: dead-serious business as the group navigator and intelligence went over the route and target material with the flying officers and crews, and I laid out the weather forecast. Group weathermen like me were not allowed to deviate from the division/bomber command forecasts for the mission route and target. However, we were allowed to present our own forecasts for our local base weather at take-off and return.

On a few occasions my synoptic analysis, and resulting forecast, were not consistent with those at higher headquarters. There were always good reasons why the forecasters disagreed, and it gave the crews more confidence to get some insight into the complexity of the situation. A couple of times our commander called the division commander and asked him what was wrong: 'My weatherman knew damn well this mission was going to have to be scrubbed.'

The debriefings when missions returned were memorable. The guys were always exhausted; sometimes effusive, sometimes sombre, depending on the success of the mission. Sometimes they knew they had demolished the target; other times they knew they had missed, or were even uncertain that they had bombed the right location; sometimes they

were just uncertain of any results, pending the post-mission reconnaissance photos. They were always interested in the weather and anxious to talk about it, tell me what had been right and what had been wrong and we'd interpret it together. It was a priceless teaching experience.

This was the first time since commissioning that I had been responsible for a detachment of enlisted men. I recall many of them vividly. But the clearest memories are of Private Pollock. He was a very bright, direct, driven Brooklyn kid for whom the normal tasks of an enlisted weather observer just weren't enough to keep him busy. Within clear limits, I gave him a pretty free hand to go out and procure scarce supplies for the station – things like graph paper, purple pencils (believe it or not) for identifying occluded fronts on the weather maps, adequate teletype paper, barometer paper, and so on. Pollock was a genius. He would be able to get a jeep and go to other bases; he bamboozled supply sergeants; he'd come back with cartons of paper and purple pencils, spare instruments and parts.

Shtogren (now Major) had warned me that he was putting Pollock in my detachment out of desperation and because I was lowest base weather officer in the pecking order. The others found him disruptive but I found him very productive. Shtogren was astonished when, instead of asking to have him transferred, I recommended him for promotion to corporal.

Then there was Major Stonesifer, an old (age 50?) curmudgeon from Texas. He was a First World War reserve veteran who had volunteered for Second World War duty. He was the base station complement commander (i.e. cooks, janitors, guards, etc.). He fumed because the enlisted men in my weather station were on detached service from 18th Weather Squadron headquarters at European Theatre Command, hence completely free of his authority. He exploded at me once because he found my bed unmade mid-morning. With a smile, I told him I had been up since 4.00a.m. preparing the forecast and briefing the mission, had just gotten a bite of breakfast, and was now going to get a little sleep as soon he got out of my quarters. What made it worse for him: I was a mere 2nd lieutenant.

One morning about 2.00a.m. I had finished the forecast and crawled into my cold bed to get a couple of hours' sleep before briefing time. I awoke with a start as dirt and bits of plaster were falling on me from the ceiling (my quarters were on the ground floor in one corner of the control tower, next to the runway). I noticed the room was brightened by a flickering red glow through the window. An instant later there was a tremendous explosion out on the airfield, the red glow brightened, and more concrete crumbs fell on my bed.

German raid? Explosions in a bomb bay? It turned out that a gasoline-powered compressor had exploded on one of the 'hardstands' – the aircraft parking places dispersed around the perimeter of the field – while the ground crews were fuelling the planes and loading the bombs and ammunition. It had ignited a hose from a fuel tank truck. There were a couple of dozen B24 bombers parked on those dispersed hardstands, being fuelled and armed for the morning's mission. The service crew had pulled the hose away from the ship, but the flames ran to the 2,700-gallon tank truck and blew it up. Before the fire was brought under control, two more tankers went up. That's what the explosions were. Miraculously, no planes were damaged. Nor were any bombs or machine-gun ammunition ignited. The briefing and mission went off on schedule, but all of us missed part of the night's sleep.

392nd Bombardment Mission Logs

Date	Mission No.	Target	Planes Out	Planes Bombing	Result
9-9-43	1	Abbeyville, France	21	18	Good
2-10-43	2	Woensdrecht, Holland	21	0	No bombing
4-10-43	3	Enemy Convoy, North Sea	33	0	Air diversion
8-10-43	4	Vegesack, Germany	13	11	No results
9-10-43	5	Gdynia-Danzig, Poland	13	10	Longest miss
3-11-43	6	Wilhelmshaven, Germany	29	27	Good
5-11-43	7	Münster, Germany	27	24	Good
13-11-43	8	Bremen, Germany	26	12	Good
16-11-43	9	Rjuken, Norway	20	20	Excellent
18-11-43	10	Kjeller, Norway	21	21	Excellent
26-11-43	11	Bremen, Germany	24	14	Good
1-12-43	12	Solingen, Germany	21	12	Good
5-12-43	13	Cognac, France	21	0	Unsuccessful
11-12-43	14	Emden, Germany	21	20	Fair
13-12-43	15	Kiel, Germany	27	24	Good
16-12-43	16	Bremen, Germany	21	16	Good
20-12-43	17	Bremen, Germany	24	20	Good
21-12-43	18	Münster, Germany	23	11	Good
29-12-43	19	Tactical target	28	27	Excellent
30-12-43	20	Ludwigshafen, Germany	27	23	Good
31-12-43	21	St Jean-d'Angély, France	27	22	Excellent
4-1-44	22	Kiel, Germany	27	24	Good
5-1-44	23	Kiel, Germany	14	10	Good
7-1-44	24	Ludwigshafen, Germany	18	14	Good
11-1-44	25	Meppen, Germany	18	11	Good
14-1-44	26	Tactical target	28	27	Good
21-1-44	27	Tactical target	29	21	Fair
29-1-44	28	Frankfurt, Germany	28	26	Good
30-1-44	29	Brunswick, Germany	22	18	Good
31-1-44	30	Siracourt, France	22	22	Fair
2-2-44	31	Watten, France	27	27	Fair
5-2-44	32	Tours-A/F, France	13	13	Excellent
6-2-44	33	Siracourt, France	25	0	No bombing
8-2-44	34	Watten, France	28	27	Poor
11-2-44	35	Siracourt, France	25	23	Good
12-2-44	36	Siracourt, France	26	26	Good
13-2-44	37	Raye-Sur-Authie, France	24	22	Excellent
20-2-44	38	Helmstadt, Germany	36	34	Wrong target
21-2-44	39	Vörden, Germany	36	34	Excellent
22-2-44	40	Gotha, Germany	34	0	Recalled
24-2-44	41	Gotha, Germany	31	29	Excellent
25-2-44	42	Fürth, Germany	25	22	Excellent
29-2-44	43	Lottingham, France	27	25	Good
2-3-44	44	Dermbach, Germany	26	22	Very Poor
3-3-44	45	Oranienburg, Germany	28	0	Recalled
5-3-44	46	Cognac, France	28	28	Fair
6-3-44	47	Genshagen, Germany	21	21	Poor
8-3-44	48	Erkner, Germany	24	24	Excellent
9-3-44	49	Brandenburg, Germany	25	25	Unobserved
11-3-44	50	Siracourt, France	24	24	Unobserved
15-3-44	51	Brunswick, Germany	25	22	Fair
16-3-44	52	Friedrichshafen, Germany	29	29	Fair
18-3-44	53	Friedrichshafen, Germany	28	22	Fair
21-3-44	54	Watten, France	13	13	Good
23-3-44	55	Osnabrück, Germany	24	22	Hit rail yard
24-3-44	56	St Dizier, France	26	26	Excellent
26-3-44	57	Febvin-Palfart, France	24	22	Excellent

Date	Mission No.	Target	Planes Out	Planes Bombing	Result
27-3-44	58	Mont-de-Marsan, France	16	16	Excellent
1-4-44	59	Ludwigshafen, Germany	24	22	Unknown
6-4-44	60	Watten, France	2	2	Unknown
8-4-44	61	Brunswick, Germany	39	30	Fair
9-4-44	62	Tutow, Germany	34	12	Poor
10-4-44	63	Marquise, France	9	5	Unknown
11-4-44	64	Bernburg, Germany	26	25	Fair
12-4-44	65	Zwickau, Germany	26	0	No Bombing
13-4-44	66	Lechfeld, Germany	17	16	Excellent
18-4-44	67	Brandenburg, Germany	24	24	Poor
19-4-44	68	Gütersloh, Germany	23	21	Excellent
20-4-44	69	Marquise, France	27	7	Bombs In Area
22-4-44	70	Hamm, Germany	27	24	Good
24-4-44	71	Leiphien, Germany	28	25	Excellent
25-4-44	72	Wizermes, France	25	22	Good
26-4-44	73	Gütersloh, Germany	26	0	No Bombing
27-4-44	74	Moyennville, France	18	8	Excellent
27-4-44	75	Châlons-sur-Marne, France	26	25	Excellent
29-4-44	76	Berlin, Germany	18	11	Good (h/losses)
1-5-44	77	Liege, Belgium	24	0	No Bombing
3-5-44	78	Wizernes, France	23	21	Target obscured
4-5-44	79	Brunswick, Germany	25	0	Recalled
7-5-44	80	Münster, Germany	28	28	Bombs In Area
8-5-44	81	Brunswick, Germany	28	25	Unknown
9-5-44	82	St Trond, Belgium	28	27	Excellent
11-5-44	83	Mulhouse, France	24	10	Poor
12-5-44	84	Zeitz, Germany	18	15	Fair
13-5-44	85	Tutow, Germany	19	19	Bombs In Area
15-5-44	86	Siracourt, France	16	4	Bombs In Area
19-5-44	87	Brunswick, Germany	28	23	Good
21-5-44	88	Siracourt, France	17	16	Bombs In Area
23-5-44	89	Avord, France	30	30	Excellent
24-5-44	90	Melun, France	32	31	Excellent
25-4-44	91	Belfort, France	6	6	Good
25-5-44	92	Fécamp, France	28	26	Good
27-5-44	93	Saarbrücken	25	23	Excellent
28-5-44	94	Zeitz, Germany	26	26	Excellent
29-5-44	95	Pölitz, Germany	27	24	Poor
30-5-44	96	Rotenburg, Germany	26	25	Excellent
31-5-44	97	Brussels, Belgium	26	0	No Bombing
2-6-44	98	Berck-sur-Mer, France	23	21	Bombs In Area
4-6-44	99	Avord, France	36	26	Excellent
6-6-44	100	St Laurent-sur-Mer, France	36	22	Bombs In Area
6-6-44	101	Cerisy-la-Forêt, France	12	0	No Bombing
6-6-44	102	Vire, France	22	20	Bombs In Area
7-6-44	103	Lisieux, France	23	23	Good
8-6-44	104	Le Mans, France	35	26	Excellent
10-6-44	105	Orleans-Bricy, France	34	29	Bombs In Area
11-6-44	106	La Possoniere, France	23	23	Good
11-6-44	107	Monfort-Sur-Mer, France	6	6	Bombs In Area
12-6-44	108	Dreux, France	36	35	Excellent
14-6-44	109	Emmerich, Germany	36	36	Excellent
15-6-44	110	La Frillerie, France	24	23	Excellent
17-6- 44	111	Melun, France	11	0	No Bombing
17-6-44	112	Tours, France	12	11	Poor
18-6-44	113	Lüneberg, Germany	34	2.9	Good
19-6-44	114	Mont-Louis-Fernes, France	11	11	Bombs In Area

Date	Mission No.	Target	Planes Out	Planes Bombing	Result
19-6-44	115	Mont-Louis-Fernes, France	22	21	Bombs In Area
20-6-44	116	Pölitz, Germany	33	31	Excellent
20-6-44	117	Crépy	16	13	Poor
21-6-44	118	Genshagen/Berlin, Germany	33	27	Bombs In Area
22-6-44	119	Domléger, France	23	23	Poor
22-6-44	120	St Cyr, France	18	15	Poor
23-6-44	121	Léon/Athies, France	24	23	Good
26-6-44	122	Buc, France	24	0	No Bombing
28-6-44	123	Saarbrucken, Germany	22	21	Bombs In Area
29-6-44	124	Magdeburg, Germany	34	30	Poor
4-7-44	125	Conches, France	33	29	Bombs In Area
6-7-44	126	Kiel, Germany	34	31	On Target
7-7-44	127	Bernburg, Germany	42	37	Fair
8-7-44	128	Esternay, France	11	3	Unobserved
11-7-44	129	Munich, Germany	24	20	Excellent
12-7-44	130	Munich, Germany	34	31	Unobserved
13-7-44	131	Saarbrucken, Germany	28	23	Unobserved
16-7-44	132	Saarbrucken, Germany	36	35	Unobserved
18-7-44	133	Troarn/Troop Concentration	45	15	Poor
19-7-44	134	Koblenz, Germany	34	23	Very Good
20-7-44	135	Erfurt, Germany	24	23	Fair
21-7-44	136	Oberpfaffenhofen, Germany	24	23	Fair
24-7-44	137	St-Lo area	48	0	No Bombing
25-7-44	138	St-Lo area	48	48	Excellent
29-7-44	139	Bremen, Germany	34	45	Excellent
31-7-44	140	Ludwigshafen, Germany	36	30	Unobserved
1-8-44	141	Bolbec, France	36	21	Excellent
2-8-44	142	Corbie, France	34	22	Poor
3-8-44	143	Beveland, France	30	21	Excellent
4-8-44	144	Kiel, Germany	3	28	Poor
4-8-44	145	Villers 'L' Hopital	27	3	Good
5-8-44	146	Brunswick, Germany	28	25	Poor
6-8-44	147	Hamburg, Germany	24	25	Excellent
8-8-44	148	La Perthe, France	36	24	Excellent
9-8-44	149	Sindelfingen, Germany	36	27	Excellent
11-8-44	150	Pacy-Sur-Armançon, France	35	36	Excellent
12-8-44	151	Juvincourt, France	36	28	Excellent
13-8-44	152	Pont-Audemer	36	36	Poorly Planned
14-8-44	153	Lyon-Bron, France	36	36	Excellent
15-8-44	154	Whittmundhafen, Germany	36	27	Unobserved
16-8-44	155	Kothen, Germany	24	36	Excellent
18-8-44	156	Nancy-Essey, Germany	36	24	Very Good
24-8-44	157	Hannover, Germany	36	30	Very Good
25-8-44	158	Schwerin, Germany	23	35	Excellent
26-8-44	159	Salzbergen, Germany	36	22	Excellent
27-8-44	160	Heligoland (Diversion), Germany	11	24	Unobserved
30-8-44	161	Haut-Maisnil, France	24	0	No bombing
9-5-44	162	Karlsruhe, Germany	36	20	Good
9-8-44	163	Karlsruhe, Germany	36	31	Unobserved
9-9-44	164	Mainz, Germany	35	34	Near Target
9-10-44	165	Ulm, Germany	24	34	Unobserved
9-11-44	166	Hanover, Germany	28	19	Excellent
9-12-44	167	Hannover-Misburg, Germany	33	25	Poor
9-13-44	168	Schwäbisch Hall, Germany	40	12	Poor
9-18-44	169	DZ-Holland Supply	23	40	Excellent
9-21-44	170	Koblenz, Germany	24	12	Poor
9-22-44	171	Kassel, Germany	24	23	Good

Date	Mission No.	Target	Planes Out	Planes Bombing	Result
25-9-44	172	Koblenz, Germany	30	30	Unobserved
26-9-44	173	Hamm, Germany	30	29	Fair
27-9-44	174	Kassel, Germany	30	25	Unobserved
28-9-44	175	Kassel, Germany	30	27	Unobserved
30-9-44	176	Hamm, Germany	30	28	Excellent
2-10-44	175	Hamm, Germany	32	32	Fair
3-10-44	178	Gaggenau, Germany	39	37	Fair
5-10-44	179	Lippstadt, Germany	30	28	Excellent
6-10-44	180	Hamburg, Germany	36	34	Excellent
7-10-44	181	Kassel, Germany	36	34	Fair
9-10-44	182	Koblenz, Germany	22	21	Unobserved
12-10-44	183	Osnabrück, Germany	21	21	Excellent
14-10-44	184	Cologne, Germany	34	30	Poor
15-10-44	185	Cologne, Germany	28	23	Poor
17-10-44	186	Cologne, Germany	26	25	Unobserved
19-10-44	187	Mainz, Germany	30	30	Unobserved
22-10-44	188	Hamm, Germany	32	31	Unobserved
25-10-44	189	Neumünster, Germany	31	31	Unobserved
26-10-44	190	Minden, Germany	32	32	Unobserved
30-10-44	191	Hamburg, Germany	30	21	Unobserved
1-11-44	192	Gelsenkirchen, Germany	10	10	Unobserved
2-11-44	193	Castrop- Rauxel, Germany	19	19	Unobserved
4-11-44	194	Misberg, Germany	32	32	Poor
5-11-44	195	Karlsruhe, Germany	31	29	Unobserved
6-11-44	196	Minden, Germany	30	30	Unobserved
8-11-44	197	Rheine, Germany	10	8	Poor
9-11-44	198	Metze, Germany	29	28	Fair
10-11-44	199	Hanau, Germany	19	18	Unobserved
11-11-44	200	Bottrop, Germany	18	18	Unobserved
16-11-44	201	Eschweiler, Germany	37	37	Fair
21-11-44	202	Harburg, Germany	30	30	Unobserved
25-11-44	203	Bingen, Germany	18	16	Unobserved
26-11-44	204	Bielefeld, Germany	29	28	Fair
29-11-44	205	Altenbeken, Germany	19	18	Unobserved
30-11-44	206	Neunkirchen, Germany	19	19	Unobserved
2-12-44	207	Bingen, Germany	18	18	Unobserved
4-12-44	208	Bebra, Germany	19	18	Unobserved
5-12-44	209	Münster, Germany	9	9	Unobserved
6-12-44	210	Bielefeld, Germany	20	20	Poor
12-11-44	211	Hanau, Germany	40	32	Unobserved
12-12-44	212	Hanau, Germany	30	30	Fair
23-12-44	213	Ahrweiler, Germany	18	18	Excellent
24-12-44	214	Ruwer, Pfalzel, Germany	47	44	Good
27-12-44	215	Hamburg, Germany	18	17	Good
20-12-44	216	Kaiserslautern, Germany	29	29	Poor
29-12-44	217	Neuweid, Germany	29	25	Excellent
30-12-44	218	Remagen Bridge, Germany	29	27	Unobserved
31-12-44	219	Euskirchen, Germany	29	29	Unobserved
1-1-45	220	Engers, Germany	27	9	Unobserved
2-1-45	221	Engers, Germany	18	15	Unobserved
3-1-45	222	Landau, Germany	19	17	Unobserved
5-1-45	223	Neunkirchen, Germany	19	17	Poor
7-1-45	224	Landau, Germany	29	25	Unobserved
8-1-45	225	Dasburg, Germany	20	20	Unobserved
10-1-45	226	Dasburg, Germany	19	14	Unobserved
13-1-45	227	Kaiserslautern, Germany	18	17	Unobserved
14-1-45	228	Hemmingstedt, Germany	28	24	Excellent

Date	Mission No.	Target	Planes Out	Planes Bombing	Result
16-1-45	229	Lauta/Ruhland, Germany	28	26	Unobserved
21-1-45	230	Heilbronn, Germany	20	15	Unobserved
28-1-45	231	Dortmund, Germany	21	17	Excellent
29-1-45	232	Hamm, Germany	28	28	Unobserved
3-2-45	233	Magdeburg, Germany	30	28	Unobserved
6-2-45	234	Magdeburg, Germany	30	29	Unobserved
9-2-45	235	Magdeburg, Germany	30	29	Poor
11-2-45	236	Dülmen, Germany	30	30	Unobserved
14-2-45	237	Magdeburg, Germany	30	21	Unobserved
15-2-45	238	Magdeburg, Germany	29	24	Unobserved
16-2-45	239	Salzbergen, Germany	28	28	Unobserved
21-2-45	240	Nürnburg, Czechoslovakia	29	28	Unobserved
22-2-45	241	Northeim (Low Altitude), Germany	31	30	Fair
23-2-45	242	Weimar, Germany	31	27	Unobserved
24-2-45	243	Misberg, Germany	21	20	Unobserved
25-2-45	244	Aschaffenburg, Germany	28	27	Excellent
26-245	245	Berlin, Germany	31	29	Unobserved
27-2-45	246	Halle, Germany	31	30	Unobserved
28-2-45	247	Siegen, Germany	28	27	Unobserved
1-3-45	248	Ingolstadt, Germany	30	30	Unobserved
2-3-45	249	Magdeburg, Germany	21	21	Unobserved
3-3-45	250	Magdeburg, Germany	21	21	Excellent
4-3-45	251	Pforzheim, Germany	21	17	Unobserved
5-3-45	252	Harburg, Germany	11	11	Unobserved
7-3-45	253	Bielefeld, Germany	20	20	Unobserved
8-3-45	254	Siegen, Germany	28	18	Unobserved
10-3-45	255	Bielefeld, Germany	28	28	Unobserved
11-3-45	256	Kiel, Germany	30	30	Unobserved
12-3-45	257	Swinemünde, Germany	31	28	Unobserved
14-3-45	258	Gütersloh, Germany	31	30	Excellent
15-3-45	259	Zossen, Germany	31	29	Poor
17-3-45	260	Münster , Germany	31	30	Unobserved
3-18-45	261	Berlin, Germany	31	31	Fair
19-3-45	262	Neuberg, Germany	21	21	Very Good
20-3-45	263	Hemmingstedt, Germany	11	11	Excellent
21-3-45	264	Hesepe, Germany	29	28	Excellent
21-3-45	265	Essen, Germany	11	11	Excellent
22-3-45	266	Schabisch-Hall, Germany	30	30	Excellent
23-3-45	267	Rheine, Germany	21	21	Excellent
24-3-45	268	DZ-Wesel Supply, Germany	26	26	Excellent
24-3-45	269	Störmede, Germany	10	10	Excellent
25-3-45	270	Hitzacker, Germany	20	16	Excellent
30-3-45	271	Wilhelmshaven, Germany	31	31	Excellent
31-3-45	272	Brunswick, Germany	31	31	Unobserved
4-4-45	273	Kaltenkirchen, Germany	31	0	No bombing
5-4-45	274	Plauen, Germany	10	7	Unobserved
6-4-45	275	Halle, Germany	10	10	Unobserved
7-4-45	276	Krümmel, Germany	30	30	Very Good
8-4-45	277	Bayreuth, Germany	21	21	Very Good
9-4-45	278	Leipheim, Germany	31	31	Excellent
11-4-45	279	Regensburg, Germany	31	31	Very Good
14-4-45	280	Bordeaux-Pt. De Lusac, France	31	30	Excellent
15-4-45	281	Royan, France	33	30	Excellent
16-4-45	282	Landshut, Germany	31	31	Excellent
17-4-45	283	Beroun, Czechoslovakia	31	30	Excellent
20-4-45	284	Schwandorf, Germany	27	26	Excellent
25-4-45	285	Hallein (Obersalzberg), Germany	28	27	Excellent

Above: *A B24 on its way to Germany, c.1940.*

Right: *Aircrew double-checking the map before embarking on a mission, c.1940.*

Aircraft and Crews

Above, left: *'Short Snorter II'. This aircraft flew 118 sorties and then returned to the USA in June 1945.*

Above, middle: *'We'll Get By' flew 70 sorties and was then transferred to the 467 bomb group in May 1945.*

Above, right: *'The Wild Hair'. This aircraft only flew six sorties before returning to the USA in June 1945.*

Below, left: *'Star Swinger'. This aircraft flew 35 sorties and was then returned to the USA in June 1945.*

Below, middle: *'Rebel Gal'. This aircraft flew 89 sorties and then returned to the USA in June 1945.*

Below, right: *'The YMCA Flying Service'. This aircraft flew eight sorties and was then transferred to a different bomb group.*

Lt Paul Henderson (front row, second from left) *with the crew of 'Miss Minnie II', c.1944.*

Lt James E. Muldoon's aircrew, c.1944. This crew flew the majority of their missions in an aircraft called 'Jaw-Ja Boy'.

B24H 'Alfred' and its crew were well-known to the local children as the aircraft would stand close to the road on the Longham side of the base. The local children would sneak across to see the crew when they returned from their missions to see if there were any sweets or supplies left over. Although this was treated with great delight by the airmen, the military police were not so amused with these lapses in the base security. This memorial stands in the churchyard at Sheringham. It reads:

Remember before God with thanksgiving the gallant crew of B24H 'Alfred' of the 392nd BG USAAF which crashed near this spot on 4th January 1944 whilst returning badly damaged from a mission to Kiel.

In gratitude also to those who aided the survivors in the common cause of freedom.
2/Lt Colby A. Waugh, Pilot, KIA
2/Lt Arthur L. Cound, Navigator, KIA
2/Lt Virgil E. Thomson, Bombardier, KIA
S/Sgt Don C. Belden, Gunner, KIA
2/Lt James W. Barton, Co-Pilot
T/Sgt Lester L. Wagner, Engineer
T/Sgt Parke V. Kent, Radio Operator
S/Sgt Earl I. Johnson, Gunner
S/Sgt Henry Wilk, Gunner

'The Silver Queen', c.1944. Left to right, back row: Oscar Cushing (ball turret gunner), Walter Bohnenstiehl (radio operator), Louis Marcarelli (engineer), Herb Vaughn (top turret gunner), Don Good (armourer/waist gunner), Ben Bertalot (tail gunner); front row: Wilson Rapp (navigator), Ray Smith (co-pilot), Jack Stevens (pilot), Bill Voss (bombardier).

Volunteers taking part in an experimental flight. It was named the 'Black Widow' test and flew on 5 April 1945 in preparation for the journey home to America.

American Red Cross worker Miss Birdie Schmidt with the crew of the aircraft named in her honour, c.1944.

Christmas at Wendling
By Birdie Schmidt

On 2nd and 8th of December 1944, the 392nd celebrated their 200th mission which occurred on 11 November when the target was the oil refinery at Bottrop. According to Bob Vickers's book The Liberators from Wendling, *on the 2nd December, the 207th mission, target Bingen:*

'... would go down in the 392nd history as one of the roughest missions ever flown in terms of aircraft and aircrew casualties... It was ironic that the evening of this date, the 200th mission party celebration for enlisted men of the 392nd was planned.'

Before we knew about the losses suffered in the returning mission the celebrations had begun. The Aeroclub had thrown open its doors early for an afternoon tea dance, followed by an evening formal dance. The club was decorated with banners, greenery and flowers as well as an inverted parachute in the snack bar. The card room was a popular eating place lit by candles on each table. The food was free. Our kitchen staff had baked a large cake with the words 'Here's to The 200th Mission' decorating it. It disappeared as soon as it was put out. The officers served the men on this occasion. Working like beavers, they dished out ice-cream, opened cokes, checked coats, etc.

We helped host lady guests for the enlisted men's party on the 2nd and the officers' party on the 8th [December]. Guests were housed in a wing of the hospital.

We also celebrated with a Victory Dinner for the crew of the 'Birdie Schmidt'. They [the crew] had all finished their missions in one piece, although they were really shot up, with 'Eyes' (John Kamacho) wounded on the first mission.

The Aeroclub was thrilled to receive a citation commending our service to the 392nd from its CO Col Lorin L. Johnson, upon the occasion of our first anniversary on the base. It was read at the close of our anniversary program on the 23rd of December by a member of the Aeroclub Committee, Sgt George Bremer.

As there were to be three days of celebration our anniversary (the 23rd), Christmas Eve (the 24th), and Christmas (the 25th), we thought we should keep our anniversary celebration simple. Mrs Bone, our first cook, baked and decorated two huge cakes with congratulatory messages.

On Christmas Eve a candlelit singsong was featured in the club. The Base Glee Club presented a spirit-lifting program of songs concluding with carols – everyone joined in.

We woke up to a white Christmas day and a heavy hoarfrost covered the ground. The fog that went with it caused the mission scheduled to be cancelled. A party had been

planned for 130 orphans and refugees from Dr Barnado's Home for Boys in Lexham and the Home Hale Village School children as well as those of our staff. The men on the base acted as hosts. The party was under Jane Mallory's supervision and she related how it went:

'The children were taken to the perimeter where they had the opportunity to see inside a Liberator. This was quite a thrill for most of them as it was their first close-up view of an aeroplane. The GIs had their hands full in keeping order among the kids. The children were piled back into the trucks and brought to the theatre, which is next door to the Aeroclub. They were greeted by the base orchestra which rendered several numbers. The children put on a program of their own consisting of country dances, songs, and recitations, and this really brought the house down. They did an excellent job and to see some of the smaller children breaking forth in song and dance, was a sight to behold. The children were shown several movie cartoons, which they just loved.

Throughout all this the children were climbing all over the laps of the GIs, and it tugged at my heart to see the expressions on the faces of the GIs. Perhaps it being my first Christmas with the GIs I didn't know what to expect, but it certainly did move me greatly to see their reactions to these underprivileged children.

After the movies, the children were brought to the Aeroclub and seated at long tables in the snack bar, which was decorated with packages of candy wrapped in red paper and holly and Christmas greens placed along the tables. We served tea, cakes, and fruit jelly. We had planned to have ice-cream but at the last moment the freezing unit broke down. It was late afternoon so we drew the blackout curtains and lit the candles, and Santa Claus came bursting into the room, much to the glee and shouts of the youngsters. One of the GIs acted as Father Christmas and did an excellent job. He went up onto the stage where the Christmas tree stood with piles of presents stacked around it. These presents were bought with money donated by the GIs. There were 130 presents – one for each child. When we counted noses, however, we had 160 children, so we scurried around and made up 30 extra presents. Santa Claus read out each name and the GIs distributed the presents. With full stomachs and full of Christmas spirit the children got back into the trucks and were taken home.

On Christmas night we played the recording of Dickens's 'A Christmas Carol' by Ronald Coleman. There was free food in the snack bar: plum pudding with sauce, fudge, nuts, and apples. Lots of GIs told me it was the best Christmas they had ever spent away from home.'

Christmas tree and presents awaiting the arrival of local children, December 1944.

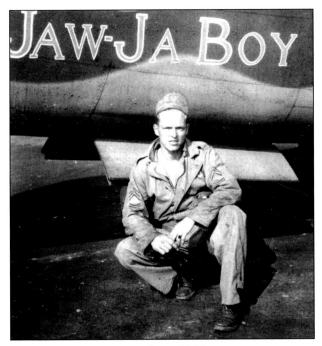

Master Sgt Ernest H. Barber, c.1944.

'The Yanks'

By Dick Mason

I shall never forget my first sight of our American allies, later to become universally known as 'the Yanks'. I hasten to explain that this title was in no way meant to be derogatory, more like a collective version of the affectionate family nickname which was more common then than now. When I first set eyes on them, they seemed to have the same number of arms legs, eyes, etc., as the people I had known before (although some of them seemed decidedly suntanned) and they later demonstrated that they were indeed fully equipped in a physical sense, at least to our level, sometimes perhaps beyond it.

But they were so different! Noisy, gregarious, boisterous, talkative, quite unlike our low-key culture. It was a wet day, and they were all wearing military style raincoats, which seemed to add to the impression of men from another planet as I stared open-mouthed at these intriguingly vigorous strangers in our midst. But they soon made an impression on our way of life, which remained long after they had left and they were soon welcomed into local homes – and not infrequently, also into local beds!

Our new visitors were members of the 392nd Bombardment Group, Second Air Division, Eighth Army Air Force, USAAF to give them their full title (The Mighty Eighth as they would come to be known) and they had come to operate from a local airbase recently built in some haste. They very soon made their mark and not only upon the enemy! The local girls soon found themselves treated like they had never been treated before and never would have been if it had been left to the locals. 'Are yer comin' out ternight gal' was superseded by 'come on babe let's roll' etc.

They dressed and talked like film stars and treated women like women like to be treated. No wonder they made the girls feel good, although like most young and fit men far from home, it wasn't just good girls they were really looking for!

They were truly marvellous people, kind, considerate and generous to us kids in spite of having to live from mission to mission where death and injury was an everyday event. They left an indelible impression on our society which endures to this day and an impression on me, which was confirmed in full measure when I eventually visited the USA many years later.

I have some good friends in Europe, which can be likened to favourite cousin relationships, but visiting Yanks on their home ground was to me, more like finding a long-lost family. Some of their ways did however, seem strange to us in the 1940s, in particular racial prejudices which were pronounced at that

A member of the ordnance personnel predicting the outcome of the war, January 1945.

Captain Wilbur H. Metz arming the bombs in the bomb bay, c.1945.

time. Black and white soldiers eating in the same mess hall, drinking at the same pub, or even sitting at the same table was absolutely taboo.

Blacks did the dirty work and the truck driving, the latter with considerable verve and gusto, occasionally with quite scary results. (An example of this is the occasion when several 500lb bombs came adrift in Swaffham and went clattering and bouncing down the Norwich Road. They were not fused of course and didn't explode, but the incident did, nevertheless cause a surge of adrenaline in a number of normally phlegmatic bystanders! Like much of our locality, Swaffham hasn't changed that much over the years – but it could well have done then!)

One facility missing from an otherwise generously-supplied US community was laundry facilities, the reason for which has never been clear to me, but this presented an opportunity not to be missed. It proved to be a ready market ripe for exploitation, to momentarily revert to modern jargon. Such a phrase would have meant nothing to us at the time of course.

So it was that enterprising youngsters reworked their pushcarts to be pull carts, made them bicycle-mobile (to coin a phrase), hooked them on to the back of their bikes and became laundry agents. In other words, they conveyed dirty laundry to the village ladies with their coal-fired coppers and fire-heated irons and back to the owner clean, accompanied by a modest bill. I don't remember any agreed commission scale for us, suffice to say we did alright – in both cash and kind. We 'made a few bucks', in the words of our newly-enhanced vocabulary.

Getting on to the base was a hit-and-miss process involving getting past the sentry, who lived in a little wooden hut equipped with a crank-up telephone and very big Colt .45 automatic pistol. There appeared to be no organised process for our admission in spite of what we considered legitimate official business and our reception would vary according to unknown influences and perhaps mood swings. Thus the two extremes of our reception would be 'roll on kid', or 1940s American-speak for 'push off'. The latter was happily rare and the former most common. Sometimes a guard would consult higher authority on his telephone, the results of which were often 'sorry kid no can do'. At this stage plan 'B' would be implemented. Over a field gate or two, through a gap or two in a few hedges, trailer and all, and we would arrive at our destination. Surprisingly we were never challenged actually on the base, where we roamed at will, nor on exit which would nearly always be past the aforementioned sentry who would often grin and wave as we passed by.

Our American friends were accommodated in what we call Nissen huts (I believe they were known to them as Quanset huts or some similar name). These were more or less half circles of corrugated metal with some form of token insulation and brickwork at each end containing the doors. Heating was by means of a

single 'tortoise' stove near the middle and one can imagine the manoeuvring to get a bed near to it because elsewhere arctic conditions prevailed for much of the year. These stoves had 'slow but sure combustion' cast into the top and combustion (not only in the stove), certainly did threaten, since they would often be stoked up to red heat in an effort to keep warm.

It was in such accommodation that I first heard of the Mason-Dixon line (finding it gratifying to lend my name to a line as well as a corner) and also of the ambitions of the inhabitants over and above that of getting the job done and getting back 'Stateside'. Suffice it to say, listening to these men talk provided significant enhancements to my education!

Another individual aspiration was to march down Unter Den Linden *[a street in Berlin that translates as 'under the lime trees'].*

Our accent intrigued some of our newly-found friends and vice versa. One always called me 'Maayson', as we would pronounce it. Another got me to say 'uniform' over and over, which produced a degree of hilarity when he tried to say it Norfolk-wise. We fought back; the dairy product spread on bread was definitely bu'er, not budderr – so there! In this way, really good friendships developed and it says a lot for the American character that these people who daily risked their lives, found time for us rustic kids.

Theirs was a land of plenty compared with what we could get. Cookies, candy, cigarettes (Camel, Philip Morris, Chesterfield, etc.) as well as many things we either never knew existed or had forgotten about, even flavoured chewing tobacco. We tried them all, sometimes shall we say 'blind', because our terminology was different and we didn't always know what was on offer. On the other hand, we never said 'no thanks' because this, whatever it might be, could be edible, drinkable, smokeable or sellable.

Thus it was that I said a blind 'yes please' to the question 'want chow kid?' I was lead to a huge mess hall, given a metal mess tin with a wire handle and lined up in the ranks for serving. As I approached the serving area, apprehension took hold, but my tin was filled without the slightest hesitation or comment and I sat down with the others to enjoy a real feast including I recall, raisin pie. Quite a jolly gathering, marred, but only momentarily, by me asking where the black ones were. Bong!

There were many examples of misunderstandings resulting from differing vocabularies. For example, the well-known word 'bum' was explained in a handbook issued to GIs, which stated, 'If you say bum in England, you will be referring to your own backside'. This was an easy one, others were less so, and reactions on both sides could be unexpected.

A village lady, married with two children, asked if she might accompany me on one of my collection/ delivery journeys, to which I agreed without asking why (tact or ignorance?) and we duly arrived at the relevant hut. Whilst I delivered the laundry, re-loaded another consignment and scrounged anything that was going, she chatted to the inhabitants and I overheard her say 'I recon yer think I'm a posh little piece don't yer?'. I think she must have got her message across in the end though as she didn't leave with me and she was afterwards seen wearing nylon stockings which were otherwise unavailable in England, whilst also affecting a passable rendering of a mid-western drawl from time to time!

Not far from the base was a dry pond which was used as a tip for the base's rubbish, or 'garbage' as the Yanks would have called it. Items to be found there could include flares, belts of live ammunition, pyrotechnic material and other debris of war in addition to what might be called domestic rubbish.

The base fire department extinguishing a practise fire.

Amazingly, the heap grew hardly at all, in spite of a constant stream of transport adding to it. This was because a veritable army of locals from miles around would be in constant attendance, raking around for anything useful and making off with it – on bikes, wheelbarrows, handcarts – or staggering under the load, on foot. Equally amazing is that nobody got blown up or burnt, not even me, as I made trails of cordite from dismantled live cartridges, ignited it and admired the flaring, smoking trail as it made patterns on the ground. This was better than carbide!

My friend Willy was not so fortunate. He tried to light a partially burned flare, utilising the time-honoured bonfire-lighting method of blowing on it to urge it on. He had a very high colour, very little by way of eyebrows and a natty crew-cut hairstyle for quite some time afterwards.

The 392nd were equipped with B24 Liberators. Big, four-engined bombers with big slab-sided twin vertical tail surfaces and four mighty and dependable Pratt & Witney radial engines, of which more later. Never attracting the glamour image of the B17 Flying Fortress nor it's successor the B29 Super Fortress, nor carrying the bomb load of the famous Lancaster, they were, nevertheless, a very effective workhorse, and made, I believe, in larger numbers than any other allied aircraft, by a number of manufacturers in the USA. This aircraft, originally designed and built by Consolidated Aircraft, developed over time as all do.

A Liberator bomber.

'Ours' were the 'H' model, the 392nd being the first unit in Europe to receive this up-gunned model with its electrically-powered gun turrets mounting .50 calibre Browning heavy machine-guns, which could shoot further and hit harder than the .303 calibre used by the RAF.

Any comparisons however, on subjects such as bomb load or defensive armament should take into account that the USAAF went by day, while the RAF went by night. Us kids of course, scrambled all over, and inside these massive machines. I remember being intrigued by the bomb doors, which slid upwards on the outside of the fuselage like a roller shutter garage door, worked by what I considered to be a kind of bicycle-chain mechanism.

'Our' B24s were made by Ford Motor Company at Willow Run Michigan, who proudly adorned the control wheel centres with a little blue and white oval badge just as you will find on any Ford product to this day – and, I suspect, on many a veteran's mantelpiece – they make excellent souvenirs. Virtually all maintenance was done outdoors, regardless of weather, thus did I become acquainted with the mighty Pratt & Witney at close quarters, which was quite an experience given my mechanical bent, enabling comparison with the nineteenth-century technology of the threshing machine, and helping to generate a lifelong love affair with the internal combustion engine.

The main runway ran approximately east–west, so take-off, which was mostly westward, meant flying straight over our house and surprisingly, landing would often be eastward, so we saw [the planes] all over again on their return. We spent hours noting aircraft serial numbers in each direction and we might typically say 'D hen't come back yet accord'n to my list' etc., quite oblivious to the risk to security. Just as well the enemy didn't nab us and pull our fingernails out to make us talk. Come to think of it, they probably wouldn't have understood our version of English anyway!

Left: *Ground crewmen. Left to right: Sgt George Kent, Sgt Delmer McCulley, Pvt Mauro Gentile, Sgt Robert Arpe, Sgt John Kallas.*

Below: *Fuel tanker used to refuel the bombers.*

A visiting British Halifax bomber. A number of Halifax bombers were sometimes seen towing large gliders to the base at Wendling during daylight hours. The air crew and the troops in the gliders would then wait at the base until nightfall before they departed on their missions.

A B24 entering a hanger for repairs, c.1944.

Equipment used to move ammunition around the base, February 1945.

Unlike the RAF, who departed in a stream more or less in line as they took off, the USAAF went in formation – necessary for daylight operations in order to present concentrated defensive fire to attacking fighters. Assembly prior to departure took what seemed like hours of droning around the sky and eventually assembling behind a 'lead ship', which would be a nearly time-expired ship (always 'ship', never 'aircraft' or 'aeroplane'), brightly painted in various colourful patterns, large spots, or a chequerboard pattern, for identification with its relevant Group, which it would eventually lead off in the correct direction, later peeling off while the rest continued on to the target.

In spite of all this activity, there were very few accidents during take-off and landing, but some seemed to literally scrape over two big elm trees near our house and you could literally count the rivets – if you were bold enough to keep your eyes open! One held one's breath on more than one occasion, especially after one tragic take-off accident when, as I understand it, both engines on the same side failed. Probably due to a fuel supply problem, just after take-off. The aircraft caught fire, bombs exploded one after the other, and all but one of the crew perished. The survivor was miraculously thrown clear on impact.

We might also claim a miraculous escape, because [our house was] right on the flight path about ¾ mile further on. Such are the fortunes of war. This event probably contributed to the eventual demise of our habitation – the end wall next door fell out some years later. It would have certainly been more than the end wall and somewhat sooner if those engines had run for a few seconds longer.

Bombers lining up ready for take-off. What a sight!

I have a mental close-up picture of the underside of a B24 clearly in my mind to this day, as well as the sound of those mighty motors giving all they'd got to get airborne with several tons of bombs and many other explosives and combustibles on board. I was not alone in my apprehension as they passed overhead. Mr G. from down the road said to me one morning. 'who deryersay meard them ingins boy?' 'Pratt & Whitney' I replied, with pride in my knowledge of the subject. Mr G. responded, 'Well I only hope Whitney meard them ones.'

To the best of my knowledge the base (always 'base', never 'station' as per RAF), had no ground defences but I have very good cause to remember one enemy night attack during which, according to my friends on the base, aircraft turret guns were manned in order to shoot back. I very clearly recall the pretty little red balls moving in what seemed a rather leisurely way across the sky (I later discovered this was tracer ammunition), but I am not sure which way it was headed – upwards or downwards.

What I did witness with ever-widening eyes was the antics of some Yanks who stopped by for a look on the way back from the pub, using a large straw stack within yards of our house as a vantage point, pausing at intervals to light cigarettes – and no doubt, cigars, with the attendant risk of firing the stack and in the process, drawing unwanted attention to themselves – and us! Mother suggested asking them in for a cup of tea, Father threatened to shoot them. They eventually went on their way, an inter-allied incident avoided and relative peace restored.

The 392nd contributed nearly 7,500 individual sorties in 285 combat missions, delivering some 17,500 tons of bombs and shooting down 283 enemy aircraft at the loss of 184 Liberators and at a human cost of 1,553 casualties, dead and wounded. They had undertaken many tough assignments including costly long-distance missions over Germany in daylight. They won a Distinguished Unit Citation for a mission to the Gotha Aircraft Works, which was Germany's largest producer of the Messerschmitt 110 fighter-bomber, where on 24 February 1944 they honoured it with 90 tons of bombs from an altitude of 19,500 feet, with 97 per cent impacting within 2,000ft and 70 per cent within 1,000 feet of the aiming point – an outstanding example of precision daylight bombing.

Losses on that day were heavy, with seven aircraft lost and 73 casualties, but the job in hand was, as usual, well done. There may have been a downside – there was a rumour that they bombed Switzerland twice, but this may have arisen from jealousy and sour grapes, which regrettably, did exist in a few quarters.

VE Day came and our Yanks prepared to leave, but they had no intention of doing so quietly – it would have been against their very natures! So they invited the locals to see what Saddam Hussein might

have called The Mother of all Firework Displays – mainly composed of parachute flares. These were spectacular, but of even greater interest were the neat little parachutes on which they were suspended. I decided that I must have one! Every time I tried to intercept my prize, I was shoved aside by a bigger boy or a grown man. Frustration reached a crescendo until at last I found myself positioned just right. Only a couple of little girls and their mother within striking distance. I made my move, only to be halted in my tracks in a vice-like grip on both arms and held rigidly to the spot by the substantially-built mother of the girls. I kicked, and no doubt swore, but to no avail, while the girls carried out a leisurely retrieval 'my' parachute, displaying self-satisfied smirks to add to my chagrin.

I vowed to be a lifetime misogynist there and then. This was one of my broken resolutions, which only remained intact until I met a very pretty girl from a neighbouring next village about a week later.

And so our American friends and allies went 'Stateside'. But they left us a legacy which I believe endures to the present time – and I don't just mean in the form of descendants – although this contribution was far from insignificant. I mean their influence on our attitude to life and to people. Gone was the shrinking, subservient demeanour, the gruff monosyllabic mode of communication. We held our heads high as they had done and we had become true believers in equality at all levels of society. Well, white society to be rather more precise, although obviously much change has since taken place.

Energy, resourcefulness, enterprise and independence of thought and spirit were now seen as assets, not a handicap and we would never again even think of touching our caps to anybody. Achievement became the criteria, not family background, and we made the vital link between personal endeavour and success, which to me at least, has proved invaluable. I suppose it is fair to say that other factors contributed to this process of enlightenment, but I give the Yanks due credit for influencing my life in this respect, although obviously I cannot speak for others.

Inside the cockpit of a Liberator bomber.

Clyde Whitt, c.1943.

In Memory of Clyde Whitt

Printed with the permission of Clyde's nephew Landon

When US gunner Clyde Whitt first arrived in the UK he was part of the following crew: Neil Larsen (pilot), Charles Stratton (copilot), Tom O'Neill (navigator), Tommy Hiller (bombardier), Clyde Whitt (right waist gunner), Henry Fox (radio operator), *Robert Wilcox (tail gunner), William Robinson (engineer), **Donald Barker (ball gunner), Gus Cristofaro (left waist gunner) & 'Gertie'.

* Wilcox was MIA 29 April 1944 while flying with Lt Shea's crew. He spent the rest of the war as a POW. His replacement was Stanley Prazak.

** Barker was transferred to the 578th Squadron before 4 June 1944. His replacement was Edward Davis.

Combat Diary of Clyde Gregory Whitt, 577th Squadron, 392nd Bombardment Group, 2nd Air Division, 8th Air Force

Monday – April 24, 1944: Flew with an old crew as right waist gunner. Had no fighter attacks and was I glad. Little flak although we got hit in right wing with 88mm. 18 degrees below although it seemed colder. My heated shoes and gloves went out but made it OK. Made a good hit on the target. Altitude 18,000ft. On oxygen 7 hours. 8 hours 35 minutes flying time. Airdrome in Germany (Leipheim) was target.

Thursday – April 27, 1944: Flew with own crew as right wing gunner. No fighter attacks. Lot of flak and it was real accurate. Altitude 20,000ft. 20 degrees below. Target was Châlons-sur-Marne, France (railway yards). 5 hours 5 minutes flying

time. No trouble with heated clothing. Did not drop bombs due to trouble with bomb bay doors.

Saturday – April 29, 1944: Flew with Lt Reed's crew as nose gunner. I checked my turret in the air and it would not work in elevation. Soon afterward I fixed it. The target was Berlin. We were about 15 minutes from the initial point when about 5 fighters attacked us from 12 o'clock. I put my sight on one and followed him through until he went under our right wing. We, then knowing we were hit, made a sharp turn to the left and got out of formation. We were at about 24,000ft when hit and, after turning, started down towards the clouds. Lt Reed then checked the crew to see if anyone had been hit. Everyone was OK. Lt Reed brought the ship to England. As soon as we got inland a few miles we bailed out. The ship was hit in #2 and #4 engines, Bombay, cockpit, and radio compartment. Shot out hydraulic lines and gas lines. We were hit by ME-109s. Bail out at 1:20pm. We all landed near Beckenville except the copilot. Lt Reed was unable to get out and went down with the ship. (Was my first parachute jump. When I made my jump I made a delayed one. I remember everything going down and did not have the feeling of fear as expected. Made a good landing.) I landed in an open field unhurt. Was picked up by local farmer and carried to nearest airbase. 5 hours 40 minutes flying time. Ship = 'Alfred II'. (Biggest air battle in history of war). The Lord was with us. (Sergeant Robert Wilcox, tail gunner and asst. engineer on my crew flew as a nose gunner on this Berlin raid with another crew. He is now missing in action as of this date.)

Tuesday – May 9, 1944: Flew with own crew as right waist gunner. No fighters and little flak. No damage. Altitude: 18,000ft. On oxygen for 3 hrs and 30 minutes. Ship #040. Good hit on target – Airfield at St Trond, Belgium (target near this town). Flying time: 5 hrs and 30 min.

Wednesday – May 10, 1944: Aborted or recalled due to weather.

Friday – May 19, 1944: Flew as right waist gunner with own crew. Lot of flak but we were lucky and didn't get any or very little. Lot of fighters – ME-109s. They didn't make a pass at us although they hit the element in front and behind us. I saw 3 B24s go down. Two chutes opened from the first ship and three from the second. Didn't see any chutes from the third. Many other B24s were seen going down. Target: Brunswick. Altitude: 25,000ft. On oxygen for 5 hours. Flying time was 7 hours 15 minutes. Temperature: -31 degrees. Ship #287.

Tuesday – May 23, 1944: Flew as right waist with own crew. Lot of flak but was real low. No fighters. Target was an airfield at St Avord, France. Made a good hit on target. Flying time: 7 hrs 30 min. On oxygen 5 hrs 30 min. Altitude: 18,000ft. Temperature: -20 degrees. Carried 12GP 300lb bombs. Ship #287. Smoke came up from target to about 2,000 feet.

Wednesday – May 24, 1944: Flew as right waist with own crew. Lot of flak. Continuous fire and very accurate. No fighters. Escort not so good. Target: an airfield at Melun, France. Made a good hit on target. Altitude: 21,000ft. Temperature: -20. Flying time: 6 hrs 15 min. Flak hole in nose turret. No injuries. Bomb load: 24GP 300lb. Briefing at 1:15. Take-off at 5:30. Ship #287. Got a view of Paris.

Thursday – May 25, 1944: Flew with own crew as right waist gunner. No flak over target but some on way back – very accurate. No fighters attacked. Good support = P-38, 47, 51. Target: railway yards at Belfort, France. Flying time: 7 hrs 30 min. Altitude: 20,000ft. On oxygen 6 hrs. Temperature: -20. Bomb load: 12 500lb GP. Good hit on target. No injuries. No damage. Briefing at 1:30. Take off at 5:30. Ship #287.

Sunday – May 28, 1944: Right waist gunner with own crew. Briefing at 6:15. Take-off at 10:45. Plenty of flak and accurate. No fighters. Good support. Flying time: 7 hrs 15 min. On oxygen: 5 hrs 30 min. Temperature -20. Bomb load: 52 100lb GP. Target: oil refinery at Zeitz, Germany. Made a good hit on target. Lot of smoke. Small hole in right wing from flak. Ship #040.

Monday – May 29, 1944: Was right waist gunner on own crew. Briefing at 4:30. Take-off at 8 o'clock. Lot of flak on way to target and a lot over target. Hit about 30 JU-88s and ME-109s just before and after the IP. Lucky they didn't hit our ship. Chris (left waist gunner) and Stanley (tail gunner) put in a claim for a fighter each. The fight was plenty hot. We made a good hit on target. The target was an oil refinery at Stettin, Germany. Flying time: 8 hrs 15 min. On Oxygen 5 hrs 30 min. Temperature -20. Ship #287. Bomb load 10 500lb GP. Squadron lost 4 ships. A B24 was on top of us on the bombing run and we thought his bombs were going to hit us. They missed us by a hair. Target: Pölitz, Germany, near Stettin.

Tuesday – May 30, 1944: Aborted due to problems with superchargers on engines 1 and 3.

Wednesday – May 31, 1944: Was right waist gunner on own crew. Briefing at 4:30a.m. Take off at 7:45. We were about 15 or 20 min in enemy territory when the formation turns back due to weather. We saw 8 bursts of flak on way back at 7 o'clock. Ship #432. Oxygen 3 hrs. Temperature -20. Flying time: 4 hrs 15 min. Clouds were as high as 20,000 and it was a very pretty sight to see. Target was to be Brussels, Belgium.

Sunday – June 4, 1944: Right waist gunner on own crew. Briefing at 1:30p.m. Take off at 3:45. We hit flak at the coast and over target. It was very accurate. We only got 3 holes in ship. No injuries. Coming back we did low flying and it was very foggy and getting dark. Landing at 10:00p,m. Bomb load: 8 500lb GP. Altitude: 18,000. On oxygen 6 hrs. Temperature: -19. Target: airfield at St Avord,

France. We hit this target on May 23, 1944. No fighters. Good support. We had no ball turret and flew a 9 man crew. Barker now with 578 Squadron. Ship #287.

Tuesday – June 6, 1944: D-MISSION. Flew with own crew as right waist gunner. Briefing at 1p.m. Take off at 6:30. Target was crossroads near St Lo, 14 miles inland in the invasion area. There was a heavy overcast and we didn't drop our bombs. Saw no flak and no fighters. This was the second mission on the invasion and the 100th mission for the 392nd Bomb Group. Flying time: 5 hrs 40 min. Bombs: 12 500lb GP. Ship #287.

Thursday – June 8, 1944: Flew as right waist gunner with own crew. Briefing at 1:45a.m. Take off: 5:30a.m. It was raining like H--- and a heavy overcast. We climbed to 25,000ft to form and it was cold as everything, -30. It was overcast up to 25,000 ft. We bombed from 17,000 carrying 52 100lb GP. Target was an airfield near Le Mans, France which was about 100 miles in front of our troops. No flak and no fighters were seen. Flying time: 6 hrs 20 min. Ship #287. This mission did not count on my finishing up combat.

Saturday – June 10, 1944: Flew as right waist gunner on own crew. Briefing was at 1a.m. and take-off was supposed to be 4:30a.m. The target was changed at take-off time and we didn't leave the ground until 10:20a.m. Altitude: 20,000 with temp at -21. Saw very little flak with no fighters. Bomb with PFF carried 24 250lb GP. Target was an airfield about 100 miles in front of our invasion troops.

Monday – June 12, 1944: Flew as right waist gunner with own crew. Briefing at 1:15a.m. Take-off at 5:45. Target was an airfield at Dreux, France. Flak was very accurate over target and plenty of it. Altitude: 20,000. Temp. -23. Flying time: 6 hrs. We carried a bomb load of 312 20lb fragmentation. Got a laugh from Fox (radioman) saying 'Gosh, I never saw so many bombs in my life'.

Sunday – June 18, 1944: Flew as right waist gunner on own crew. Briefing at 1a.m. Take-off at 5:30a.m. Flew across North Sea and very cold. We hit fighters just before we got to the coast – 109s. They were fixing to make a pass at us when some P-38 came out of nowhere, lucky for us. It seems like we went everywhere trying to find the target. We bombed the second target with 12 500lb GP. Altitude: 20,000. Temp: -25. Lot of flak but far out except over target. Flying time: 6 hrs. Target: Bremerhaven, Germany. [The crew could not find Lüneberg so they bombed Bremerhaven.]

Monday – June 19, 1944: Flew as right waist gunner with own crew. Briefing was at 4a.m. although we didn't take-off until 3:05p.m. Lot of flak over target. This was a No Ball (our first) Bomb load 52 100lb GP. Altitude: 21,000. Temp: -21. PFF job. Target was at Mont-Louis-Fernes, France. Trying to knock out the pilotless planes. Flying time: 4 hrs 5 min.

USAAF Missing Aircrew Report #06523

Aircraft: #42-50287 (NO NICKNAME), Mission 121 to bomb Léon in France, 23 June 1944.
Aircrew: 577th Squadron.

Pilot	1/Lt	Larsen, Neil R.	KIA
Co-pilot	2/Lt	Stratton, Charles R. Junr	KIA
Navigator	2/Lt	O'Neill, Thomas J.	POW
Bombardier	2/Lt	Hiller, Thomas B.	POW
Nose gunner	PVT	Davis, Edward T.	POW
Radio operator	T/Sgt	Fox, Henry H.	POW
Engineer	T/Sgt	Robinson, William F.	KIA
Waist gunner	S/Sgt	Whitt, Clyde G.	KIA
Waist gunner	S/Sgt	Cristofaro, Gus J.	KIA
Tail gunner	S/Sgt	Prazak, Stanley J.	KIA

Mission Loss Circumstances

An eyewitness (Lt Holliday, crew pilot 577th) reported this aircraft as being first hit by flak over the target, hit again at Dunkirk (return route) and having lost a propeller with the plane going down in a spin and believed to have crashed, 3 chutes seen. A German report #KU2368, 23 June at 2130, Airdrome Command at Lille, stated that this aircrew of ten were recovered with six dead: Larsen, Stratton, Robinson, Prazak, Cristofaro and Whitt, and four members captured. The men taken prisoner were identified positively and sent for interrogation at Oberursel/Frankfurt on 27 June.

Individual Accounts: The Fate of the Crew

One crew survivor, O'Neill, later gave information in a 'Casualty Questionnaire' to US authorities after his repatriation from POW status. He stated that their ship had left the Group formation about five miles north of the target after bombing (and took a more direct route returning to England); and about 10 miles south-east of Dunkirk some of the crew began to bail out starting at about 10,000 feet down to 3–4,000 feet due to the plane being in a spin (after being hit by flak again). He also stated that the pilot, copilot, and engineer were in their respective flight positions when the plane took a direct flak hit into the flight deck, and that was the last seen of these members; that the ship had crashed about 10 miles south-east of Dunkirk between a railroad, canal, and a road near a house there, and it burned with no surviving crew members able to get back to it. He noted further that the pilot and copilot were killed instantly, he believed, and the engineer perished before he could bail out since the plane, immediately after the AA hit, went into a right-hand spiral spin and no abandon ship signal was given.

Another report from Lt Hiller, bombardier, stated that he and the radio operator bailed out through the bomb bays after the ship stopped spinning momentarily around 10,000 feet, followed by the navigator and nose gunner who jumped through the nose escape way. (Escape had to be through the nose wheel doors as this exit was the only way from the nose section, and quite difficult to accomplish if wearing a parachute, back or chest pack).

Roll of Honour: 392nd Bombardment Group

Abshier, H. L., S/Sgt, Top Turret, KIA, 02-Aug-44
Ackerman, James M., 2Lt, Copilot, POW, 23-Jun-44
Adago, D. R., S/Sgt, Aerial Gunner, KIA, 09-Apr-44
Adams, B., S/Sgt, Aerial Gunner, KIA, 06-Mar-44
Adams, Richard S., S/Sgt, Top Turret, POW, 08-Oct-43
Adams junr, John H., 1Lt, Navigator, POW, 13-Nov-43
Alexander, Richard W., 2Lt, Bombardier, RTD, 11-Sep-44
Allen, R, T/Sgt, Voice Interrupter, KIA, 14-Apr-45
Allen, James E., S/Sgt, Left Waist Gunner, POW, 24-Feb-44
Allred, Edward L., S/Sgt, Waist Gunner, RTD, 11-Sep-44
Altemus, Charles V., S/Sgt, Right Waist Gunner, POW, 23-Jun-44
Altschaft, William L., S/Sgt, Waist Gunner, POW, 11-Sep-44
Amenta, George S., Sgt, Left Waist Gunner, POW, 06-Aug-44
Ammon, Robert H., S/Sgt, Radio Operator, KIA, 23-Jun-44
Amodeo, Frank A., Pfc, Top Turret, KIA, 02-Mar-45
Amoss, Ralph T., Capt, Bombardier, KIA, 05-Aug-44
Anderson, Thomas, T/Sgt, Nose Turret, POW, 05-Nov-43
Anderson, Charles A., 2Lt, Navigator, KIA, 29-May-44
Anderson, Carl A., S/Sgt, Left Waist Gunner, POW, 18-Mar-44
Anderson, Ellsworth F., 2Lt, Pilot, POW, 18-Mar-44
Anderson, John B., 2Lt, Copilot, KIA, 11-Apr-44
Anderson, T. L., 2Lt, Pilot, KIA, 08-Apr-44
Andrews, William E., T/Sgt, Waist Gunner, POW, 22-Apr-44
Andrews, Harold L., S/Sgt, Right Waist Gunner, POW, 29-Apr-44
Apgar, David R., S/Sgt, Ball Turret, POW, 18-Mar-44
Appert, Donald A., Maj., Mission Pilot, KIA, 04-Oct-43
Apple junr, Odis L., S/Sgt, Radio Operator, KIA, 13-Sep-44
Archambeau, Alfred R., Sgt, Tail Turret, KIA, 29-Apr-44
Archibald, David, Sgt, Left Waist Gunner, POW, 24-Feb-44
Argast, Ray F., 2Lt, Bombardier, POW, 24-Feb-44
Arnold, Leroy D., S/Sgt, Waist Gunner, KIA, 11-Dec-43
Asch, Howard W., S/Sgt, Left Waist Gunner, INT, 20-Jun-44
Ashcraft, Blaine, T/Sgt, Top Turret, INT, 11-Jul-44
Astleford, Charles E., 2Lt, Navigator, KIA, 02-Dec-44
Augninbaugh, Clayton L., S/Sgt, Top Turret, KIA, 27-Apr-44
Axvig, Willard E., Sgt, Tail Gunner, POW, 04-Jan-44
Backus, Donald G., T/Sgt, Top Turret, KIA, 19-May-44
Baetz, Robert E., 2Lt, Pilot, KIA, 28-Dec-44
Bailey, Ralph V., S/Sgt, Ball Turret, POW, 24-Feb-44
Baker, Morton, T/Sgt, Radio Operator, KIA, 22-Mar-45
Baker, Edmund R., S/Sgt, Tail Gunner, INT, 04-Jan-44
Baldwin, Charles L., S/Sgt, Ball Turret, POW, 24-Feb-44
Baldwin junr, William L., 2Lt, Navigator, KIA, 04-Nov-44
Bandura, Norbert A., 2Lt, Copilot, KIA, 18-Mar-44
Barber, K. A., 2Lt, Copilot, KIA, 29-Apr-44
Barnes, Glenn M., T/Sgt, Top Turret, RTD, 15-Jun-44
Barnes, Glenn M., T/Sgt, Top Turret, POW, 18-Sep-44
Barnes, Leonard J., Maj., Command Pilot, KIA, 22-Mar-45
Barnett, Joseph V., 2Lt, Pilot, KIA, 24-Feb-44
Bartholomew, Daniel, S/Sgt, Ball Turret, KIA, 18-Nov-43
Bartnowski, Matthew A., S/Sgt, Mickey Operator, KIA, 28-Jan-45
Barton, James C., Sgt, Left Waist Gunner, INT, 20-Jun-44
Barton, Harold T., Sgt, Tail Gunner, KIA, 21-Feb-44
Barton, P. F., 2Lt, Pilot, KIA, 04-Aug-44
Bass, L. F., 2Lt, Pilot, KIA, 21-Apr-44
Bass junr, R.T., S/Sgt, Right Waist Gunner, KIA, 20-Feb-44
Bassett, Byron E., T/Sgt, Top Turret, KIA, 29-Apr-44
Bassett, Earl T., 1Lt, Navigator, POW, 29-May-44
Batko, Edward L., 2Lt, Navigator, POW, 08-Sep-44
Batts, Malford H., 2Lt, Bombardier, POW, 06-Mar-44
Bauer, Herbert P., T/Sgt, Top Turret, KIA, 18-Nov-43
Baum, William J., Sgt, Left Waist Gunner, KIA, 21-Feb-44
Bayer, Herbert P., T/Sgt, Top Turret, KIA, 18-Nov-43
Bean, Norton M., 2Lt, Navigator, INT, 20-Jun-44
Beard, James W., T/Sgt, Radio Operator, POW, 22-Apr-44
Beatty, James H., 2Lt, Pilot, POW, 06-Aug-44
Becker, John A., 1Lt, Pilot, POW, 04-Jan-44
Becker, John L., 2Lt, Navigator, KIA, 21-Feb-44
Bedore, C.E., 2Lt, Navigator, KIA, 29-Dec-44
Belden, D.C., S/Sgt, Aerial Gunner, KIA, 04-Jan-44
Belitz, Hans C., 1Lt, Pilot, POW, 21-Jun-44

Bell, Roger W., S/Sgt, Right Waist Gunner, POW, 18-Mar-44
Bell, Charles L., 2Lt, Pilot, RTD, 12-Apr-44
Bell, Charles L., 1Lt, Pilot, INT, 20-Jun-44
Bellerine, Richard O., T/Sgt, Radio Operator, POW, 18-Mar-44
Beltz, Gerald E., S/Sgt, Right Waist Gunner, POW, 07-Jul-44
Benadum, Thomas E., S/Sgt, Top Turret, RTD, 11-Sep-44
Bender, John W., 2Lt, Navigator, POW, 24-Feb-44
Bennett, Charles E., S/Sgt, Radio Operator, POW, 08-Apr-44
Bennett, Frank A, Sgt, Right Waist Gunner, POW, 29-Apr-44
Bennett, Fred W., 2Lt, Navigator, POW, 24-Feb-44
Bennett, Lloyd G., T/Sgt, Toggle, INT, 18-Mar-44
Benson, Robert J., 2Lt, Copilot, KIA, 11-Sep-44
Benz, Robert F., 2Lt, Copilot, KIA, 04-Nov-44
Berezoysky, Alex , T/Sgt, Radio Operator, KIA, 11-Sep-44
Berg, Ben D., 2Lt, Navigator, POW, 11-Sep-44
Berger, Robert M., 2Lt, Copilot, POW, 18-Mar-44
Berkise, John A., S/Sgt, Left Waist Gunner, POW, 08-Apr-44
Berlin, William, 2Lt, Navigator, KIA, 18-Nov-43
Bernard, Leo E., S/Sgt, Right Waist Gunner, KIA, 08-Oct-43
Berquist, Earl J., Sgt, Radio Operator, KIA, 06-Aug-44
Bertsch, Paul J., S/Sgt, Tail Gunner, KIA, 03-Mar-44
Beseda, John F., S/Sgt, Tail Gunner, POW, 22-Apr-44
Betterley, E.O., T/Sgt, Radio Operator, KIA, 09-Apr-44
Bettis, Roy W., S/Sgt, Toggler, KIA, 09-Sep-44
Beutler, Kenneth L., Sgt, Left Waist Gunner, KIA, 06-Jul-44
Biakis, Michael J., 2/Lt, Copilot, KIA, 18-Jan-45
Billingsley, Glenn R., 2Lt, Pilot, KIA, 02-Dec-44
Billman, Vernon E., FO, Bombardier, POW, 21-Jul-44
Bingham, Milford O., 2Lt, Pilot, KIA, 11-Dec-43
Birch, Veral J., S/Sgt, Ball Turret, INT, 18-Mar-44
Birnbaum, Stanford I., 2Lt, Toggler, KIA, 23-Jun-44
Bishop, Robert R., 2Lt, Pilot, KIA, 29-Apr-44
Bishop, Charles R., 2Lt, Navigator, INT, 20-Jun-44
Bixby, Gerald C., Sgt, Tail Gunner, KIA, 18-Mar-44
Blackford, Lloyd M., T/Sgt, Radio Operator, POW, 21-Jul-44
Blaida, John M., S/Sgt, Right Waist Gunner, KIA, 29-May-44
Blake, Belden G., 2Lt, Copilot, POW, 24-Feb-44
Blakely, Willis G., 2Lt, Pilot, KIA, 02-Mar-45
Blakut, Joseph P., S/Sgt, Left Waist Gunner, POW, 20-Dec-43
Blanc, Alex D., Sgt, Tail Gunner, POW, 05-Nov-43
Blanco, James W., S/Sgt, Top Turret, INT, 20-Jun-44
Blanco, James W., Sgt, Ball Turret, RTD, 12-Apr-44
Bleckenk, J. H., S/Sgt, Aerial Gunner, KIA, 09-Apr-44
Bleichart, Frank G., S/Sgt, Voice Interpreter, KIA, 28-Jan-45
Blong, James T., Sgt, Top Turret, KIA, 29-Apr-44
Board, Harold J., Sgt, Tail Gunner, KIA, 21-Jul-44
Bobb junr, Lonnie L., 2Lt, Bombardier, KIA, 19-May-44
Bodoh, Allan E., T/Sgt, Top Turret, POW, 07-Jul-44
Bogardus, Levan I., Sgt, Toggler, KIA, 02-Dec-44
Bogie, Walter W., 2Lt, Bombardier, INT, 20-Jun-44
Bogie, Walter W., 2Lt, Bombardier, RTD, 12-Apr-44
Bolick junr, Henry R., 1Lt, Pilot, KIA, 26-Nov-43
Bond, James W., 2Lt, Navigator, KIA, 21-Jul-44
Bondar, Nicholas D., 2Lt, Copilot, KIA, 13-Nov-43
Bonnassiolle, John R., Sgt, Left Waist Gunner, KIA, 29-Apr-44
Books, Dallas O., 1Lt, Pilot, KIA, 18-Mar-44
Boord, Wayne M., S/Sgt, Tail Gunner, KIA, 18-Mar-44
Borick, Paul M., S/Sgt, Top Turret, POW, 08-Apr-44
Bosworth, Benjamin L., S/Sgt, Tail Gunner, POW, 05-Nov-43
Bowman, Frederic N., S/Sgt, Top Turret, KIA, 06-Jul-44
Bowyer junr, Dewey C., Sgt, Right Waist Gunner, KIA, 08-Sep-44
Boyce, Ernie L., S/Sgt, Right Waist Gunner, KIA, 09-Sep-44
Boyd, Jimmie C., S/Sgt, Tail Gunner, KIA, 18-Mar-44
Boyle, Edward W, 2Lt, Bombardier, POW, 30-Dec-43
Braccioforte junr, John F., S/Sgt, Right Waist Gunner, POW, 15-Jun-44
Bradford, T.M., S/Sgt, Aerial Gunner, KIA, 29-Dec-44
Brandes, Arnoy H., 2Lt, Bombardier, KIA, 18-Mar-44
Bratcher, Carey E., 2Lt, Navigator, KIA, 04-Oct-43
Breithrupt, H.A., S/Sgt, Aerial Gunner, KIA, 09-Apr-44
Bremer, Adolph F., 2Lt, Bombardier, EVD, 18-Sep-44
Brettum, R.B., Capt., Pilot, KIA, 22-Mar-45

Bridson, George L., 1Lt, Pilot, INT, 11-Jul-44
Brink, Benjamin E., S/Sgt, Right Waist Gunner, POW, 18-Sep-44
Brockway, Gilbert S., Sgt, Tail Gunner, INT, 20-Jun-44
Brooks, Lee M., 2Lt, Copilot, KIA, 02-Dec-44
Brown, John T., Sgt, Ball Turret, KIA, 18-Mar-44
Brown, James S., T/Sgt, Radio Operator, KIA, 04-Jan-44
Brown, Elmer, S/Sgt, Ball Turret, KIA, 18-Apr-44
Brown, Kenneth O., T/Sgt, Radio Operator, KIA, 13-Nov-43
Brown, Gilbert A., S/Sgt, Waist Gunner, KIA, 29-May-44
Brown, Edmund J., 2Lt, Bombardier, KIA, 18-Mar-44
Brown, Robert T., S/Sgt, Left Waist Gunner, KIA, 19-May-44
Brown, Jan, S/Sgt, Tail Gunner, POW, 24-Feb-44
Brownfelder, Allan R., 2Lt, Navigator, POW, 21-Jul-44
Bryan, Walter F., S/Sgt, Right Waist Gunner, KIA, 13-Dec-43
Bryant, Harold A., S/Sgt, Top Turret, KIA, 24-Apr-44
Buaas, Walter C., 2Lt, Pilot, KIA, 02-Dec-44
Buchert, William L., S/Sgt, Ball Turret, KIA, 04-Jan-44
Buchheit, Edward L., S/Sgt, Top Turret, KIA, 04-Oct 43
Buchols, Roy D., Sgt, Right Waist Gunner, POW, 24-Feb-44
Buecheler, John F., 2Lt, Pilot, POW, 12-Sep-44
Burdette, Joe L., S/Sgt, Left Waist Gunner, INT, 11-Jul-44
Burke, J.E., T/Sgt, Radio Operator, KIA, 25-Mar-45
Burnett, W.H., Sgt, Aerial Gunner, KIA, 21-Apr-44
Burns, Lloyd J., S/Sgt, Tail Gunner, POW, 24-Feb-44
Buschman, John G., Capt., Pilot, POW, 08-Oct-43
Buzzi, Harold G., 2Lt, Bombardier, KIA, 29-Apr-44
Byers, Allen C., Sgt, Right Waist Gunner, KIA, 28-Dec-44
Byler, Harvey J., T/Sgt, Radio Operator, KIA, 19-May-44
Byrd, Jimmie C., S/Sgt, Tail Turret, KIA, 18-March-44
Cable, J.V., Sgt, Aerial Gunner, KIA, 12-Aug-44
Cade junr, George W., T/Sgt, Radio Operator, KIA, 02-Dec-44
Cage, Ralph, Sgt, Left Waist Gunner, KIA, 29-May-44
Cagle, William C., S/Sgt, Right Waist Gunner, KIA, 18-Mar-44
Callaghan, George P., 2Lt, Copilot, KIA, 11-Apr-44
Callejas, Francisco N., S/Sgt, Tail Gunner, KIA, 02-Dec-44
Campbell junr, George L., T/Sgt, Radio Operator, KIA, 26-Nov-43
Candido, Cosomo D., T/Sgt, Radio Operator, RTD, 11-Sep-44
Cannistraro, Pietro A., 2Lt, Bombardier, POW, 18-Mar-44
Cannon, Leslie F., S/Sgt, Top Turret, KIA, 02-Dec-44
Carey, Richard J., 2Lt, Pilot, POW, 21-Jul-44
Carey, Harry V., 2Lt, Copilot, RTD, 11-Sep-44
Carley, Raymond J., 2Lt, Navigator, POW, 06-Mar-44
Carrinton, W.E., S/Sgt, Aerial Gunner, KIA, 13-Jul-44
Carris, Peter, T/Sgt, Radio Operator, POW, 30-Dec-43
Carroll, Joyce B., S/Sgt, Tail Gunner, KIA, 11-Apr-44
Carroll junr, William J., T/Sgt, Radio Operator, POW, 02-Dec-44
Carter, Henry C., S/Sgt, Top Turret, KIA, 29-May-44
Carter junr, Calvin J., FO, Navigator, POW, 15-Feb-45
Carusone, Nicholas M., Sgt, Top Turret, EVD, 30-Dec-43
Cashen, Edward J., 2Lt, Navigator, KIA, 18-Mar-44
Cashman, Claire A., S/Sgt, Top Turret, KIA, 26-Mar-44
Casstevens, Ralph C., 2Lt, Copilot, EVD, 22-Feb-45
Castaneda, Jose A., S/Sgt, Right Waist Gunner, KIA, 07-Oct-44
Castiglione, Joseph S., S/Sgt, Tail Gunner, KIA, 04-Jan-44
Castor, James R., Sgt, Right Waist Gunner, KIA, 18-Apr-44
Cattano, Joseph V., 2Lt, Bombardier, KIA, 18-Nov-43
Caufield, John J., 2Lt, Navigator, KIA, 29-Apr-44
Causey, Warren W., S/Sgt, Gunner, KIA, 05-Jul-44
Cavell, Dominick F., S/Sgt, Right Waist Gunner, KIA, 08-Oct-43
Cechowski, Casimer E., 2Lt, Bombardier, INT, 20-Jun-44
Chamblin, Jean N., T/Sgt, Radio Operator, POW, 05-Nov-43
Chaplinsky, W.A., S/Sgt, Aerial Gunner, KIA, 29-May-44
Chapman, Lorn E., S/Sgt, Top Turret, KIA, 02-Feb-44
Chatterton, G.A., S/Sgt, Aerial Gunner, KIA, 22-Mar-45
Cheairs junr, William T., 2Lt, Copilot, POW, 24-Feb-44
Chenet, James H., 2Lt, Copilot, POW, 13-Nov-43
Chichetto, Anthony F., 2Lt, Navigator, KIA, 18-Apr-44
Chick, Anthony P., Sgt, Tail Gunner, POW, 07-Jul-44
Childers, James E., Pvt, Tail Gunner, POW, 21-Sep-44
Childress, W.J., Sgt, Aerial Gunner, KIA, 29-Apr-44
Chinchilla, Francis P., 1Lt, Bombardier, KIA, 21-Sep-44
Chiodo, Michael A., Sgt, Ball Turret, KIA, 29-Apr-44
Chojecki, John M., T/Sgt, Radio Operator, KIA, 07-Jul-44
Christian, N.R., 2Lt, Bombardier, KIA, 29-Apr-44
Church, Clarence A., Cpl, Radio Operator, POW, 14-Oct-44

Cicora, Anthony F., 2Lt, Copilot, KIA, 11-Sep-44
Cieply, Edward J., 2Lt, Pilot, KIA, 02-Dec-44
Cihon, John A., 2Lt, Bombardier, POW, 24-Feb-44
Cinquina, E., S/Sgt, Aerial Gunner, KIA, 02-Mar-45
Claffey, Curtis F., S/Sgt, Nose Turret, KIA, 11-Dec-43
Clapp junr, Roger E., T/Sgt, Radio Operator, POW, 11-Sep-44
Clapper, Elwin E., 2Lt, Pilot, KIA, 06-Jul-44
Clark, Frank C., T/Sgt, Radio Operator, KIA, 03-Mar-44
Clark junr, James V., S/Sgt, Radio Operator, KIA, 26-Mar-44
Clifford, Richard R., 2Lt, Copilot, POW, 18-Apr-44
Clifford, William W., 1Lt, Pilot, KIA, 08-Oct-43
Clifford, Hayden H., 1Lt, Pilot, POW, 04-Nov-44
Clover, Donald K., 1Lt, Pilot, POW, 18-Mar-44
Cobb junr, Calvin J., S/Sgt, Right Waist Gunner, KIA, 02-Feb-44
Coble, Aubrey D., S/Sgt, Top Turret, KIA, 24-Apr-44
Coday, D.S., S/Sgt, Aerial Gunner, KIA, 09-Apr-44
Coe, Jacque D., T/Sgt, Gunner, POW, 08-Oct-43
Coe, J.D., 2Lt, Radar Navigator, KIA, 05-Aug-44
Cohen, Jack M., 2Lt, Navigator, KIA, 09-Apr-44
Cole, Morrell A., S/Sgt, Ball Turret, KIA, 29-May-44
Coleman, Edward B., S/Sgt, Tail Gunner, POW, 29-May-44
Coleman, Vincent B., 2Lt, Navigator, KIA, 04-Jan-44
Coleman, Roy G., S/Sgt, Right Waist Gunner, POW, 02-Dec-44
Coleman junr, Alvin D., 2Lt, Navigator, KIA, 15-Mar-45
Collins, John M., 2Lt, Copilot, POW, 20-Dec-43
Comeau junr, Eugene L., 1Lt, Pilot, KIA, 02-Dec-44
Conley, Erwin D., S/Sgt, Radio Operator, KIA, 18-Mar-44
Coogan, Alphonsus J., S/Sgt, Right Waist Gunner, EVD, 18-Sep-44
Cook, Joseph M., 2Lt, Copilot, POW, 07-Oct-44
Cook, Ervan J., S/Sgt, Top Turret, POW, 29-May-44
Cook, Bill J., FO, Copilot, KIA, 02-Dec-44
Cooke, Albert R., T/Sgt, Top Turret, POW, 24-Feb-44
Coolidge, Donald R., T/Sgt, Radio Operator, KIA, 29-May-44
Cooper, Joe R., T/Sgt, Radio Operator, KIA, 12-Sep-44
Cooper junr, Samuel L., S/Sgt, Nose Turret, KIA, 08-Apr-44
Copeland, Jack N., S/Sgt, Right Waist Gunner, POW, 13-Nov-43
Coplin, Guy R., S/Sgt, Top Turret, KIA, 19-May-44
Cothran, James W., Sgt, Top Turret, KIA, 07-Jul-44
Coudriet, Frederick G., S/Sgt, Waist Gunner, KIA, 04-Jan-44
Cound, Arthur L., 2Lt, Copilot, KIA, 04-Jan-44
Coveney, Clarence M., S/Sgt, Ball Turret, POW, 18-Mar-44
Cowley, John C., T/Sgt, Top Turret, KIA, 07-Jul-44
Cox, Robert R., 2Lt, Navigator, KIA, 12-Aug-44
Cox, Robert L., Maj., Observer, KIA, 22-Apr-44
Cox, Thomas J., 2Lt, Pilot, POW, 24-Feb-44
Coyle, Quentin M., 2Lt, Copilot, POW, 24-Apr-44
Cozza, Dominick, T/Sgt, Radio Operator, POW, 11-Sep-44
Crabbe, Charles W., T/Sgt, Top Turret, KIA, 02-Dec-44
Craig, James D., S/Sgt, Tail Gunner, KIA, 26-Nov-43
Crawford junr, Earl G., S/Sgt, Left Waist Gunner, POW, 18-Mar-44
Crenshaw, Thomas O., 2Lt, Pilot, POW, 14-Oct-44
Cristofaro, Gus J., S/Sgt, Left Waist Gunner, KIA, 23-Jun-44
Crouch junr, Marshall C., 1Lt, Observer, POW, 29-Jan-44
Cuervo, Frederick J., Sgt, Waist Gunner, KIA, 19-May-44
Cugini, Michael W., S/Sgt, Right Waist Gunner, POW, 18-Mar-44
Culbertson, Leonard D., 2Lt, Copilot, POW, 05-Nov-43
Cullins, Thomas F., S/Sgt, Radio Operator, KIA, 29-May-44
Cumming, Robert B., Sgt, Gunner, KIA, 21-Jul-44
Cummings, Francis J., 2Lt, Navigator, KIA, 18-Mar-44
Cunningham, William A., S/Sgt, Ball Turret, KIA, 13-Nov-43
Cusick, Harrison R., S/Sgt, Radio Operator, POW, 21-Jul-44
D'Ambrosio junr, Marshall J., Sgt, Toggler, RTD, 15-Mar-45
D'Aoust, Wallace W., 1Lt, Pilot, KIA, 05-Nov-43
Dahl, Charles R., S/Sgt, Bombardier, KIA, 29-May-44
Dahlen, Russell E., T/Sgt, Radio Operator, KIA, 05-Nov-43
Dalton, Gerald M., 2Lt, Pilot, KIA, 18-Mar-44
Danford, Robert W., S/Sgt, Ball Turret, POW, 29-Apr-44
Darling, L., T/Sgt, Radio Operator, KIA, 06-Mar-44
Darnall, Robert W., 2Lt, Copilot, POW, 07-Jul-44
Davenport, Bobby J., Sgt, Radio Operator, KIA, 28-Dec-44
Davis, William F., 1Lt, Pilot, POW, 02-Dec-44
Davis, William A., 2Lt, Copilot, KIA, 02-Dec-44
Davis, Edward T., Pvt, Aerial Gunner, POW, 23-Jun-44
Davis, Roy W., T/Sgt, Ball Turret, KIA, 18-Mar-44
Davis, Ray W., S/Sgt, Ball Turret, POW, 08-Oct-43

Davis, Robert, T/Sgt, Radio Operator, POW, 29-May-44
Dawson, Jennings B., 2Lt, Navigator, KIA, 11-Sep-44
Day, Walter, S/Sgt, Tail Gunner, KIA, 04-Jan-44
Deal junr, Fred F., S/Sgt, Left Waist Gunner, KIA, 04-Jan-44
Deaton, James A., Cpl, Radio Operator, KIA, 24-Mar-45
Deck, Glenn A., Sgt, Tail Gunner, KIA, 20-Jun-44
Decker, Jack C., 2Lt, Pilot, KIA, 18-Jan-45
Decker, Chester D., T/Sgt, Top Turret, INT, 18-Mar-44
Delaney, Paul E., S/Sgt, Ball Turret, KIA, 26-Mar-44
Della Beta, Prosdocno J., S/Sgt, Radio Operator, KIA, 15-Mar-44
Dellaughter, William G., S/Sgt, Tail Gunner, POW, 24-Feb-44
Dellitt, John J., 2Lt, Bombardier, KIA, 04-Jan-44
Demery, Robert F., S/Sgt, Engineer, KIA, 18-Jan-45
Democh, Thadoeus, T/Sgt, Radio Operator, KIA, 18-Mar-44
Demontlier, H.E., 2Lt, Bombardier, KIA, 20-Feb-44
Derrick, Pete E., S/Sgt, Left Waist Gunner, KIA, 04-Oct-43
DeSimone, Peter P., S/Sgt, Right Waist Gunner, KIA, 13-Nov-43
Devoe, Charles N., S/Sgt, Tail Gunner, INT, 18-Mar-44
Dewitt, Norman D., Sgt, Right Waist Gunner, POW, 07-Jul-44
Dickison, William G., Sgt, KIA, 13-Feb-44
Dickson, James W., 1Lt, Pilot, KIA, 08-Apr-44
Digman junr, Thomas, 2Lt, Bombardier, KIA, 29-Apr-44
Dinda, Bernard F., S/Sgt, Tail Gunner, KIA, 18-Mar-44
Dinsmore, Robert S., 2Lt, Navigator, KIA, 31-Dec-43
Dinsmore, Walter F., S/Sgt, Right Waist Gunner, KIA, 07-Jul-44
Dobson, Odell F., S/Sgt, Left Waist Gunner, POW, 11-Sep-44
Dodd, James R., 2Lt, Pilot, KIA, 28-Jan-45
Donaldson, Claude D., Lt, Navigator, KIA, 11-Apr-44
Donlon, Maurice A., 2Lt, Navigator, POW, 08-Oct-43
Donohue, John J., Lt, Navigator, EVD, 22-Feb-45
Doolittle, David R., T/Sgt, Radio Operator, KIA, 11-Sep-44
Dorgan, William J., S/Sgt, Tail Gunner, POW, 18-Mar-44
Dorn, Walter A., 2Lt, Copilot, RTD, 12-Apr-44
Dorn, Walter A., Lt, Copilot, INT, 20-Jun-44
Doty, Amos E., S/Sgt, Top Turret, KIA, 19-May-44
Doub junr, Harry G., S/Sgt, Right Waist Gunner, KIA, 18-Mar-44
Dougherty junr, Thomas V., 2Lt, Copilot, KIA, 28-Jan-45
Dowell junr, Armpha E., Sgt, Tail Gunner, POW, 06-Aug-44
Doyle junr, Charles C., 2Lt, Copilot, KIA, 24-Feb-44
Draher, John F., S/Sgt, Right Waist Gunner, KIA, 19-May-44
Drake, Chester W., 2Lt, Bombardier, INT, 11-Jul-44
Draper, James W., S/Sgt, Ball Turret, KIA, 11-Apr-44
Dudley, W.F., S/Sgt, Aerial Gunner, KIA, 06-Mar-44
Dudziak, Teddy, 2Lt, Pilot, KIA, 18-Nov-43
Duerr, Elmer E., S/Sgt, Tail Gunner, EVD, 22-Feb-45
DuFour, Joseph L., Pvt, Right Waist Gunner, KIA, 02-Dec-44
Duggan, James J., T/Sgt, Top Turret, POW, 04-Jan-44
Dunlop, V. N., S/Sgt, Aerial Gunner, KIA, 29-Jan-44
Dunphy, James J., Sgt, Right Waist Gunner, POW, 06-Aug-44
Durrance, Edward E., 2Lt, Copilot, KIA, 04-Jan-44
Dykes, James R., T/Sgt, Radio Operator, EVD, 29-Jan-44
Eckert, James A., S/Sgt, Tail Gunner, EVD, 23-Jun-44
Edwards, Demur S., S/Sgt, Ball Turret, KIA, 19-May-44
Egan, Arthur J., S/Sgt, Tail Gunner, INT, 20-Jun-44
Egan, Arthur J., Sgt, Tail Gunner, RTD, 12-Apr-44
Egler, Martin G., S/Sgt, Left Waist Gunner, RTD, 11-Sep-44
Egler, M.C., S/Sgt, Aerial Gunner, KIA, 22-Mar-45
Eisermann, Gilbert O., Lt, Pilot, POW, 29-May-44
Ellinger, Carl F., 2Lt, Pilot, KIA, 24-Apr-44
Elliott, Malcolm L., T/Sgt, Top Turret, KIA, 05-Nov-43
Eloranto, Toivo E., 2Lt, Pilot, POW, 08-Apr-44
Elsleger, Joseph, Sgt, Right Waist Gunner, POW, 23-Jun-44
Ely, Loyce E., S/Sgt, Left Waist Gunner, EVD, 18-Sep-44
Emerson junr, Herbert B., S/Sgt, Left Waist Gunner, KIA, 13-Nov-43
Engel, Russell W., 2Lt, Navigator, WIA, 06-Sep-43
Englebrecht, Louis C., Sgt, Right Waist Gunner, KIA, 28-Jan-45
Epstein, Morris, Sgt, Radio Operator, KIA, 28-Jan-45
Erickson, Clifford W., S/Sgt, Right Waist Gunner, KIA, 08-Apr-44
Etheridge, Mart T., 2Lt, Bombardier, KIA, 05-Nov-43
Euwer junr, Charles T., 2Lt, Navigator, KIA, 07-Jul-44
Evans, G.B., S/Sgt, Tail Gunner, KIA, 19-May-44
Everhart, Wyreth C., Capt, Pilot, POW, 22-Apr-44
Faas, John E., 2Lt, Copilot, KIA, 07-Jul-44
Farlow, Leland C., 2Lt, Bombardier, POW, 28-Dec-44
Farlow, Lynn B., S/Sgt, Right Waist Gunner, KIA, 26-Mar-44

Farnwalt, W.H., S/Sgt, Aerial Gunner, KIA, 05-Aug-44
Farrar, Robert E., S/Sgt, Toggler, KIA, 08-Sep-44
Farrell, E.E., Cpl, Ground Personnel, KIA, 03-Mar-45
Farren, Emil L., S/Sgt, Top Turret, POW, 18-Mar-44
Farris, Alvin J., S/Sgt, Right Waist Gunner, POW, 11-Sep-44
Feldman, Alfred, Lt, Bombardier, KIA, 24-Feb-44
Feller, Leonard, Lt, Navigator, POW, 04-Jan-44
Felsenthal, Charles L., 2Lt, Pilot, KIA, 19-May-44
Feran, John E., 2Lt, Pilot, KIA, 18-Mar-44
Ferrari, Victor J., 2Lt, Navigator, EVD, 13-Nov-43
Feuerstacke, James A., Lt, Pilot, KIA, 04-Oct-43
Fiebig, Paul E., 2Lt, Bombardier, POW, 12-Sep-44
Fife, R.M., 2Lt, Navigator, KIA, 16-Jan-45
Filkel, Paul E., 2Lt, Bombardier, POW, 05-Aug-44
Fink, Bernard, Sgt, Ball Turret, KIA, 27-Apr-44
Finley, George E., S/Sgt, Top Turret, POW, 06-Mar-44
Finley, Ray, T/Sgt, Radio Operator, INT, 18-Mar-44
Finney, Herbert H., Sgt, Top Turret, RTD, 24-Mar-45
Fisher, Frank A., 2Lt, Copilot, KIA, 07-Jul-44
Fitzgerald, P.M., 2Lt, Copilot, KIA, 05-Jul-44
Fleege, John F., Sgt, Waist Gunner, KIA, 12-Apr-44
Fleming, Kenneth V., 2Lt, Navigator, KIA, 28-Jan-45
Flesny, Robert J., S/Sgt, Right Waist Gunner, POW, 02-Mar-45
Fletcher, Edgar B., S/Sgt, Left Waist Gunner, POW, 13-Nov-43
Floyd, Carlos M., Pvt, Air Transportation Tech., KIA, 18-Sep-44
Floyd, L.G., S/Sgt, Right Waist Gunner, KIA, 13-Sep-44
Floyd, C.E., 2Lt, Bombardier, KIA, 29-Jan-44
Fogarty, Davis M., 2Lt, Pilot, INT, 18-Nov-43
Folda, George, T/Sgt, Radio Operator, POW, 06-Mar-44
Forde, William J., 2Lt, Navigator, 15-Jun-44
Forde, William I., 2Lt, KIA, 13-Jul-44
Forsberg, Bruce F., 2Lt, Bombardier, KIA, 13-Sep-44
Forsythe, William M., 2Lt, Pilot, INT, 20-Jun-44
Fothergill, Clarence E., 2Lt, Copilot, POW, 29-May-44
Fought, Robert C., Sgt, Right Waist Gunner, KIA, 06-Jul-44
Fowler, Robert G., S/Sgt, Left Waist Gunner, POW, 22-Apr-44
Fox, Henry H., T/Sgt, Radio Operator, POW, 23-Jun-44
Franke, Douglas N., 2Lt, Navigator, 29-Apr-44
Frederick, John E., Cpl, Right Waist Gunner, POW, 14-Oct-44
Freeborn, Duane E., Lt, Bombardier, KIA, 13-Nov-43
Freeman, G.W., T/Sgt, Top Turret, KIA, 29-Jun-44
Freshner, William I., S/Sgt, Top Turret, POW, 13-Nov-43
Friesen, Orlando H., S/Sgt, Top Turret, POW, 29-Apr-44
Fross, Horton L., 2Lt, Bombardier, POW, 24-Feb-44
Fryman, B., 2Lt, Pilot, KIA, 29-Apr-44
Fulton, Lester R., T/Sgt, Radio Operator, EVD, 18-Sep-44
Gahm, K.L., 2Lt, Copilot, KIA, 21-Apr-44
Gallagher, Richard, S/Sgt, Left Waist Gunner, KIA, 18-Mar-44
Galler, Isadore, T/Sgt, Radio Operator, POW, 18-Mar-44
Gallo, F.E., T/Sgt, Top Turret, KIA, 06-Oct-44
Gallup, Eugene M., Sgt, Left Waist Gunner, KIA, 24-Apr-44
Garbeff, Theodore J., 2Lt, Navigator, POW, 06-Aug-44
Garvey, James A., T/Sgt, Radio Operator, KIA, 07-Jul-44
Gates, John S., 2Lt, Navigator, INT, 11-Jul-44
Gellis, Leon, Sgt, Waist Gunner, KIA, 12-Apr-44
Gentry, Lester E., 2Lt, Bombardier, KIA, 29-Jan-45
Gerbing, Thomas M., 2Lt, Copilot, EVD, 23-Jun-44
Gerow, James A., 2Lt, Pilot, POW, 18-Sep-44
Gerrard, R.W., T/Sgt, Top Turret, KIA, 09-Apr-44
Gienko, Edward J., S/Sgt, Tail Gunner, POW, 29-Apr-44
Giles, Harold R., S/Sgt, Ball Turret, KIA, 04-Oct-43
Gillian, Edward L., S/Sgt, Ball Turret, KIA, 20-Dec-43
Gilman, Jack P., 2Lt, Navigator, RTD, 05-Mar-44
Gilmore, Elbert E., Sgt, Top Turret, RTD, 12-Apr-44
Gilmore, E.E., T/Sgt, Top Turret, KIA, 28-May-44
Glass, Richard D., S/Sgt, Toggler, KIA, 16-Jan-45
Glassman, Paul S., Cpl, Tail Gunner, POW, 15-Feb-45
Glickman, Bertram, Sgt, Left Waist Gunner, KIA, 21-Jul-44
Godfrey, Herbert M., Lt, Bombardier, KIA, 04-Jan-44
Goodman, E., T/Sgt, Radio Operator, KIA, 22-Jan-44
Gordon, Archie M., 2Lt, Bombardier, KIA, 18-Apr-44
Gorka, Walter T., Sgt, Ball Turret, KIA, 21-Feb-44
Gott, Edwin J., T/Sgt, Radio Operator, KIA, 04-Oct-43
Gragg, Sunny J., 2Lt, Navigator, POW, 11-Apr-44
Graham, John F., 2Lt, Bombardier, KIA, 11-Dec-43

Graham, George E., 2Lt, Copilot, POW, 29-Apr-44
Graham, Gerard R., 2Lt, Navigator, KIA, 29-May-44
Grandon, David P., 2Lt, Navigator, POW, 18-Sep-44
Graper, Melvin H., Capt., Mission Pilot, KIA, 23-Jun-44
Gray, Harry E., 2Lt, Copilot, KIA, 18-Mar-44
Gray, C.T., Maj., Mission Pilot, KIA, 29-Jan-44
Gray, Roy G., S/Sgt, Right Waist Gunner, KIA, 04-Oct-43
Green, James A., 2Lt, Copilot, INT, 11-Jul-44
Green, Robert J., 2Lt, Bombardier, KIA, 08-Oct-43
Green, Carson A., 2Lt, Copilot, KIA, 06-Jul-44
Green, Leroy A., Sgt, Left Waist Gunner, KIA, 11-Apr-44
Green, Harry J., 2Lt, Bombardier, RTD, 15-Jun-44
Green, Harry J., 2Lt, Bombardier, RTD, 13-Jul-44
Greene, Donald R., 2Lt, Bombardier, KIA, 18-Mar-44
Gregory, George , 2Lt, Navigator, KIA, 20-Feb-44
Gressler, Edward J., T/Sgt, Radio Operator, POW, 24-Feb-44
Greetum, R.B., Capt., Pilot, KIA, 22-Mar-45
Griel, John B., 2Lt, Navigator, POW, 24-Apr-44
Griesar, Otto J., 2Lt, Navigator, KIA, 02-Dec-44
Griffin, Edward F., S/Sgt, Right Waist Gunner, KIA, 04-Jan-44
Griffin, Travis W., 2Lt, Pilot, POW, 24-Apr-44
Griggs, Robert H., 2Lt, Pilot, KIA, 09-Apr-44
Grimes, J.T., S/Sgt, Right Waist Gunner, RTD, 05-Mar-44
Grisell, R., 2Lt, Copilot, KIA, 09-Apr-44
Grossi, R.H., Sgt, Aerial Gunner, KIA, 29-Apr-44
Grybos, Theodore J., S/Sgt, Left Waist Gunner, KIA, 11-Apr-44
Guest, Thomas C., 2Lt, Navigator, POW, 02-Dec-44
Guillot, Oliver B., Sgt, Right Waist Gunner, POW, 29-Apr-44
Guion, Walter A., T/Sgt, Radio Operator, KIA, 02-Dec-44
Gustavson, Ralph I., S/Sgt, Right Waist Gunner, POW, 11-Sep-44
Gyure, Fred, Pvt, Tail Gunner, KIA, 18-Mar-44
Haland, Milton L., S/Sgt, Tail Gunner, INT, 18-Mar-44
Hadley, Marcus W., S/Sgt, Radio Operator, KILD, 18-Jan-45
Haffermehl, George T., Lt, Pilot, POW, 18-Mar-44
Haglund, Guy L., 2Lt, Bombardier, KIA, 24-Feb-44
Hahn junr, John E., 2Lt, Engineer, KIA, 21-Jul-44
Haines, Frank W., 2Lt, Pilot, POW, 11-Sep-44
Hall, Ross H., 2Lt, Bombardier, KIA, 24-Apr-44
Hall, Norman L., S/Sgt, Ball Turret, POW, 29-May-44
Halpern, Herbert M., S/Sgt, Voice Interpreter, POW, 02-Mar-45
Halsne, Milton O., S/Sgt, Right Waist Gunner, INT, 18-Mar-44
Halsworth, Robert J., 2Lt, Copilot, POW, 24-Feb-44
Hamann, Lloyd A., 2Lt, Bombardier, POW, 02-Dec-44
Hammond, James W., 2Lt, Bombardier, POW, 05-Nov-43
Hammond, Gordon L., Lt, Copilot, POW, 22-Apr-44
Hampton, Oscar L., T/Sgt, Top Turret, KIA, 02-Dec-44
Hampton, Thomas L., Sgt, Ball Turret, POW, 29-Apr-44
Hampton, Robert G., Sgt, Ball Turret, KIA, 18-Mar-44
Hampton junr, William R., S/Sgt, Right Waist Gunner, KIA, 18-Mar-44
Hancock, Leon G., T/Sgt, Ball Turret, KIA, 18-Mar-44
Haney, Paul W., T/Sgt, Radio Operator, KIA, 02-Dec-44
Hankins, James P., Sgt, Ball Turret, POW, 24-Apr-44
Hanna, Walter W., S/Sgt, Tail Gunner, POW, 11-Apr-44
Hanrahan, Daniel J., S/Sgt, Tail Gunner, POW, 08-Oct-43
Hanson, Floyd B., Pvt, Tail Gunner, KIA, 09-Apr-44
Harbaugh, David E., S/Sgt, Tail Gunner, 29-Apr-44
Hardic, Andrew M., S/Sgt, Left Waist Gunner, KIA, 18-Mar-44
Hardy, Elmer C., S/Sgt, Toggler, KIA, 23-Jun-44
Harrell, Ora L., S/Sgt, Right Waist Gunner, KIA, 18-Mar-44
Harringer junr, John J., Sgt, Right Waist Gunner, KIA, 29-Apr-44
Harris, Melvin C., Sgt, Right Waist Gunner, POW, 11-Dec-43
Harris, Dalton W., S/Sgt, Ball Turret, KIA, 26-Nov-43
Harris junr, John D., Lt, Pilot, POW, 13-Nov-43
Harrod junr, Charles, S/Sgt, Left Waist Gunner, INT, 18-Nov-43
Harron, Robert J., FO, Navigator, KIA, 28-Jan-45
Hartong, Robert R., Sgt, Top Turret, KIA, 28-Jan-45
Hartwick, Edwin J., 2Lt, Bombardier, POW, 21-Jul-44
Harwick, Michael G., S/Sgt, Left Waist Gunner, POW, 18-Mar-44
Hasenfratz, Merle J., Sgt, Tail Gunner, POW, 24-Apr-44
Haskins, Billy D., S/Sgt, Tail Gunner, INT, 18-Nov-43
Hassett, Byron H., T/Sgt, Top Turret, 29-Apr-44
Hathaway, Eugene O., S/Sgt, Radio Operator, KIA, 14-Apr-45
Hatton, Hyman J., Sgt, Right Waist Gunner, POW, 29-Apr-44
Haussmann, Frederick A., S/Sgt, Right Waist Gunner, POW, 24-Feb-44
Haviland junr, Archie F., Lt, Copilot, KIA, 04-Jan-44

Hawkins, Grover H., T/Sgt, Right Waist Gunner, KIA, 20-Dec-43
Hay, S.N., 2Lt, Copilot, KIA, 06-Mar-44
Hay, William R., T/Sgt, Toggler, KIA, 04-Jan-44
Hayden, Ralston, T/Sgt, Top Turret, RTD, 11-Sep-44
Hayden, Quinton R., Sgt, Tail Gunner, KIA, 19-May-44
Hayes, Francis N., 2Lt, Copilot, KIA, 18-Mar-44
Head, William T., 2Lt, Copilot, KIA, 02-Dec-44
Heaslet, Worth W., S/Sgt, Right Waist Gunner, KIA, 03-Mar-44
Heater, Edwin J., S/Sgt, Top Turret, POW, 29-Apr-44
Hebert, Normand B., S/Sgt, Tail Gunner, POW, 18-Sep-44
Hebron junr, Walter T., Lt, Pilot, INT, 18-Mar-44
Heckendorn, George F., S/Sgt, KIA, 13-Nov-43
Heilman, J.A., 2Lt, Bombardier, KIA, 06-Mar-44
Heinemann, Donald L., Lt, Copilot, POW, 04-Jan-44
Helbing, Richard H., S/Sgt, Tail Gunner, KIA, 24-Feb-44
Helmes, Curtis F., S/Sgt, Top Turret, KIA, 11-Dec-43
Helmke, Elton F., S/Sgt, Right Waist Gunner, KIA, 24-Apr-44
Henderson, Milton A., 2Lt, Copilot, POW, 24-Feb-44
Henderson, Dewain J., 2Lt, Navigator, KIA, 24-Feb-44
Henkendorn, George F., S/Sgt, Radio Operator, KIA, 13-Nov-43
Herzig, Herbert, 2Lt, Bombardier, RTD, 11-Sep-44
Hess, Donald W., 2Lt, Navigator, KIA, 29-Apr-44
Hession, W.J., 2Lt, Navigator, KIA, 13-Jul-44
Hestad, Erling A., Lt, Pilot, POW, 06-Mar-44
Hester, C.L., S/Sgt, Left Waist Gunner, POW, 13-Sep-44
Hicks, Allan W., S/Sgt, Top Turret, POW, 22-Feb-45
Hickson junr, Dick, 2Lt, Navigator, POW, 04-Jan-44
Higgins, John P., Sgt, Waist Gunner, KIA, 21-Jul-44
Higgs, Otis C., T/Sgt, Top Turret, POW, 11-Sep-44
Hight, John P., S/Sgt, Radio Operator, KIA, 24-Feb-44
Hildebrand, Robert H., S/Sgt, Ball Turret, INT, 18-Mar-44
Hill, T.J., S/Sgt, Counter Measures, KIA, 25-Mar-45
Hiller, Thomas B., 2Lt, Bombardier, POW, 23-Jun-44
Hinshaw, Hugh M., T/Sgt, Top Turret, POW, 18-Mar-44
Hirshberg, Jack H., 2Lt, Copilot, KIA, 28-Dec-44
Hoffman, Richard H., S/Sgt, Ball Turret, POW, 05-Nov-43
Hoffman, Ralph R., T/Sgt, Top Turret, KIA, 18-Mar-44
Hoganson, Harvey G., S/Sgt, Right Waist Gunner, KIA, 11-Sep-44
Hollenbeck junr, Charles E., S/Sgt, Right Waist Gunner, KIA, 21-Sep-44
Holliday, Lt, Pilot, 03-Aug-44
Holling, J.H., T/Sgt, Radio Operator, KIA, 12-Aug-44
Holmes, G.F., S/Sgt, Top Turret, KIA, 11-Dec-43
Holmes, Homer W., S/Sgt, Top Turret, KIA, 18-Mar-44
Holm, Howard J., 2Lt, Copilot, KIA, 18-Mar-44
Holmes, Jack G., 2Lt, Copilot, POW, 21-Jul-44
Holton, Quinton F., S/Sgt, Right Waist Gunner, POW, 21-Jul-44
Hoover, J.T., T/Sgt, Top Turret, KIA, 08-Oct-43
Hoover, A. L., S/Sgt, Tail Gunner, KIA, 05-Aug-44
Hopple, Harry G., 2Lt, Bombardier, KIA, 03-Mar-44
Horey, Elmer N., Sgt, Toggler, POW, 11-Apr-44
Horn, J.E., S/Sgt, Aerial Gunner, KIA, 25-Mar-45
Horowitz, G., S/Sgt, Aerial Gunner, KIA, 29-Jan-44
Hotle, David J., 2Lt, Bombardier, INT, 20-Jun-44
Houser, Byron M., T/Sgt, Top Turret, EVD, 23-Jun-44
Howard, R.E., T/Sgt, Top Turret, KIA, 29-Jan-44
Howard, J.B., S/Sgt, Aerial Gunner, KIA, 25-Mar-45
Hubbartt, Gene O., 2Lt, Pilot, POW, 15-Feb-45
Hughes, Claude H., Sgt, Ball Turret, KIA, 19-May-44
Hughes, Richard J., 2Lt, Bombardier, POW, 13-Dec-43
Hulbert, Leonard D., Sgt, Tail Gunner, KIA, 28-Jan-45
Hull, Robert L., Lt, Pilot, KIA, 04-Jan-44
Hull, W.W., S/Sgt, Top Turret, KIA, 18-Mar-44
Hultengren, C.W., S/Sgt, Aerial Gunner, KIA, 12-Aug-44
Hummel junr, John R., 2Lt, Pilot, RTD, 24-Mar-45
Hunt, N.J., Lt, Pilot, KIA, 13-Jul-44
Hunter, Robert M., Lt, Bombardier, KIA, 18-Mar-44
Hunter, Clifford J., 2Lt, Pilot, KIA, 05-Mar-44
Hunter, E.R., S/Sgt, Toggler, KIA, 25-Mar-45
Hurd, J.S., Lt, Copilot, KIA, 05-Aug-44
Hurley, William F., T/Sgt, Toggler, KIA, 11-Apr-44
Huston, Clarence F., S/Sgt, Tail Gunner, KIA, 02-Dec-44
Huston, Paul N., 2Lt, Copilot, KIA, 05-Mar-44
Hynes junr, James J., 2Lt, Navigator, KIA, 26-Mar-44
Iannotta, Joseph S., 2Lt, Copilot, KIA, 05-Jul-44
Indahl, Jack M., T/Sgt, Top Turret, KIA, 24-Feb-44

Irvine junr, John S., 2Lt, Bombardier, KIA, 04-Oct-43
Isbell, Kenneth L., S/Sgt, Tail Gunner, KIA, 26-Mar-44
Issenberg, Milton, 2Lt, Bombardier, POW, 23-Jun-44
Italia, Samto, Lt, Toggler, INT, 11-Jul-44
Jackson, Benjamin F., S/Sgt, Ball Turret, POW, 24-Feb-44
Jackson, L.A., S/Sgt, Aerial Gunner, KIA, 13-Jul-44
Jackson, Charles H., S/Sgt, Right Waist Gunner, POW, 24-Feb-44
Jacobs, J., 2Lt, Navigator, KIA, 08-Apr-44
Jacobson, Coleman, 2Lt, Bombardier, POW, 11-Sep-44
Jaffe, Arthur J., 2Lt, Bombardier, INT, 20-Jun-44
Jamar junr, James L., Sgt, Left Waist Gunner, KIA, 09-Feb-45
Janes, Calvin W., Sgt, Right Waist Gunner, KIA, 07-Jul-44
Jankowski, S.F., T/Sgt, Top Turret, KIA, 12-Aug-44
Jarratt, C.W., T/Sgt, Top Turret, KIA, 05-Aug-44
Jasinski, Raymond, S/Sgt, Toggler, POW, 02-Dec-44
Jeans, Roy G., T/Sgt, Radio Operator, KIA, 05-Nov-43
Jenkins, Richard N., S/Sgt, Left Waist Gunner, POW, 29-May-44
Jereb, John F., S/Sgt, Ball Turret, POW, 05-Nov-43
Johns, Mervyn T., 1Lt, Pilot, POW, 24-Feb-44
Johnson, Robert H., 2Lt, Pilot, POW, 07-Oct-44
Johnson, James F., T/Sgt, Radio Operator, KIA, 04-Jan-44
Johnson, Nevin J., Cpl, Passenger, KIA, 18-Sep-44
Johnson, Rex L., 2Lt, Pilot, KIA, 18-Mar-44
Johnson, Robert G., 2Lt, Navigator, KILD, 18-Jan-45
Johnson, Delmar C., 2Lt, Navigator, POW, 18-Mar-44
Johnson, Paul D., S/Sgt, Left Waist Gunner, KIA, 09-Sep-44
Johnston, John V., 2Lt, Pilot, KIA, 24-Feb-44
Jones, Daniel C., Sgt, Bombardier, KIA, 18-Mar-44
Jones, Orley R., 2Lt, Navigator, POW, 18-Mar-44
Jones, Allen V., 2Lt, Navigator, POW, 21-Jun-44
Jones, John P., 2Lt, Copilot, POW, 14-Oct-44
Jones, Robert R., S/Sgt, Right Waist Gunner, POW, 02-Dec-44
Jones, George E., 1Lt, Pilot, POW, 07-Jul-44
Jones, Harold E., 2Lt, Pilot, KIA, 11-Sep-44
Jones junr, Nixon J.E., S/Sgt, Ball Turret, POW, 18-Mar-44
Joslin, Gordon D., S/Sgt, Left Waist Gunner, POW, 02-Dec-44
Joynt, Albert E., 2Lt, Pilot, KIA, 13-Sep-44
Jurgens, Henry F., S/Sgt, Left Waist Gunner, POW, 12-Sep-44
Kahn junr, John E., S/Sgt, Top Turret, KIA, 21-Jul-44
Kaiser, Phillip, 2Lt, Pilot, KIA, 25-Mar-45
Kale, William A., 1Lt, Pilot, INT, 18-Mar-44
Kalionzes, Harry A., 2Lt, Bombardier, INT, 18-Mar-44
Kamanke, Alexander, Sgt, Tail Gunner, KIA, 28-Dec-44
Kamenitsa, William T., 2Lt, Pilot, POW, 29-Apr-44
Kane, Fred J., 2Lt, Bombardier, KIA, 29-Apr-44
Kane, Francis M., T/Sgt, Top Turret, POW, 21-Sep-44
Kaplan, Jacob, 2Lt, Navigator, POW, 24-Feb-44
Kaplan, Murray, S/Sgt, Radio Operator, KIA, 06-Jul-44
Kapp, Rudolph A., Lt, Navigator, KIA, 04-Jan-44
Karaso, Joseph J., S/Sgt, Radio Operator, KIA, 29-Apr-44
Kary, William W., 2Lt, Navigator, POW, 05-Nov-43
Kaufman, Burdette B., S/Sgt, Left Waist Gunner, KIA, 04-Jan-44
Keagle, Paul E., Pvt, Left Waist Gunner, RTD, 24-Mar-45
Kearns, Louis L., 2Lt, Copilot, POW, 13-Nov-43
Kearns, Hiatt H., S/Sgt, Right Waist Gunner, KIA, 02-Dec-44
Kelleher, Daniel P., 2Lt, Copilot, KIA, 24-Feb-44
Kellerman, Robert B., S/Sgt, Top Turret, KIA, 20-Jun-44
Kelly, John B., 1Lt, Pilot, RTD, 15-Mar-45
Kelly, John L., Sgt, Right Waist Gunner, POW, 24-Apr-44
Kelly, Tracy M., S/Sgt, Ball Turret, POW, 24-Feb-44
Kelly, William E., 2Lt, Navigator, POW, 13-Dec-43
Kempker, Edward J., 2Lt, Bombardier, KIA, 05-Nov-43
Kennett, Roy L., S/Sgt, Radio Operator, POW, 29-Apr-44
Kenney junr, Joseph A., S/Sgt, Left Waist Gunner, KIA, 26-Mar-44
Kenyon, John C., FO, Copilot, POW, 15-Feb-45
Kenyon, Charles L., S/Sgt, Ball Turret, POW, 24-Feb-44
Kielblock, Albert L., S/Sgt, Voice Interpreter, KIA, 07-Oct-44
Kieras, Eugene J., S/Sgt, Top Turret, KIA, 18-Sep-44
Kiger, Jerome E., Sgt, Tail Gunner, KIA, 21-Jul-44
Kight, Donald A., S/Sgt, Toggler, KIA, 14-Apr-45
Killea, Kevin B., S/Sgt, Aerial Gunner, KIA, 25-Mar-45
Kilpatrick, H.K., S/Sgt, Aerial Gunner, KIA, 05-Aug-44
Kimball, Robert A., S/Sgt, Left Waist Gunner, KIA, 18-Mar-44
Kimball, Burleigh A., S/Sgt, Left Waist Gunner, KIA, 02-Dec-44
Kinsinger, William D., S/Sgt, Left Waist Gunner, KIA, 02-Dec-44

Kintana, Frank T., S/Sgt, Right Waist Gunner, INT, 11-Jul-44
Kitlan, Richard K., 2Lt, Copilot, POW, 08-Apr-44
Klinchok, John J., S/Sgt, Left Waist Gunner, KIA, 26-Nov-43
Knight, Joseph S., T/Sgt, Radio Operator, KIA, 23-Jun-44
Knight, Joseph S., Sgt, Radio Operator, RTD, 12-Apr-44
Knudson, Bernard L., 2Lt, Navigator, KIA, 24-Mar-45
Koch junr, William J., S/Sgt, Ball Turret, KIA, 18-Mar-44
Kochenash, Charles, S/Sgt, Radio Operator, KIA, 07-Jul-44
Koenig, William S., FO, Bombardier, POW, 14-Oct-44
Kohn, Frank A., Sgt, Radio Operator, POW, 28-Jan-45
Kornman, Harold C., 2Lt, Navigator, EVD, 22-Apr-44
Kost, Peter, S/Sgt, Left Waist Gunner, POW, 24-Feb-44
Koswan, Joseph, 2Lt, Navigator, POW, 02-Dec-44
Kowalchik, Edward C., S/Sgt, Right Waist Gunner, INT, 20-Jun-44
Kramer, Alton W., T/Sgt, Left Waist Gunner, POW, 11-Apr-44
Krapf, Norman C., S/Sgt, Radio Operator, KIA, 19-May-44
Krause, Thomas J., 2Lt, Navigator, POW, 21-Jul-44
Krause, Harold L., S/Sgt, Left Waist Gunner, POW, 02-Dec-44
Krejci, Jack J., Sgt, Right Waist Gunner, POW, 29-Apr-44
Krek, Bailey R., T/Sgt, KIA, 18-Mar-44
Kresser, Fred M., S/Sgt, Radio Operator, KIA, 09-Apr-44
Krogh, Svend A., S/Sgt, Right Waist Gunner, KIA, 26-Nov-43
Krugh, Glenn L., Sgt, Left Waist Gunner, KIA, 08-Sep-44
Krushas, Vitold P., S/Sgt, Top Turret, POW, 29-Apr-44
Kubale, Edward W., 2Lt, Copilot, KIA, 08-Apr-44
Kudej, Robert W., Sgt, Right Waist Gunner, KIA, 09-Feb-45
Kurkomelis, Gus C., S/Sgt, Right Waist Gunner, INT, 18-Nov-43
Kuttner, F. F., 2Lt, Bombardier, KIA, 09-Apr-44
Kuykendall, Lewis E., S/Sgt, Left Waist Gunner, KIA, 04-Nov-44
Kuziora, Walter F., S/Sgt, Top Turret, KIA, 04-Oct-43
Kvorjak, Michael B., 2Lt, Copilot, KIA, 04-Oct-43
LaBonte, Felix J., S/Sgt, Tail Gunner, KIA, 02-Feb-44
Lacey, N.J., T/Sgt, Aerial Gunner, KIA, 04-Aug-44
Lambert, Raymond P., 1Lt, Pilot, KIA, 04-Jan-44
Lamer, Marvin, 1Lt, Copilot, KIA, 11-Apr-44
Lamma, Ralph E., 1Lt, Pilot, KIA, 13-Nov-43
Lampe, Maurice, S/Sgt, Left Waist Gunner, POW, 23-Jun-44
Landry, Gerald E., T/Sgt, Top Turret, INT, 11-Jul-44
Landry, Louis H., S/Sgt, Tail Gunner, POW, 18-Mar-44
Lane, Tommie, S/Sgt, Waist Gunner, POW, 07-Jul-44
Lang, Robert J., 2Lt, Pilot, KIA, 19-May-44
Lang, Charles F., T/Sgt, Top Turret, POW, 07-Oct-44
Lang, William S., 2Lt, Navigator, RTD, 11-Sep-44
Lange, Donald H., S/Sgt, Tail Gunner, RTD, 11-Sep-44
Lanier, Ralph, S/Sgt, Tail Gunner, KIA, 13-Nov-43
Lankford, Woodrow D., S/Sgt, Ball Turret, POW, 24-Feb-44
Larsen, Neil R., 1Lt, Pilot, KIA, 23-Jun-44
Larson, Lawrence E., 2Lt, Pilot, KIA, 29-May-44
Larson, Robert N., 2Lt, Bombardier, KIA, 29-May-44
Lasater, Jerome R., Sgt, Left Waist Gunner, KIA, 07-Jul-44
Laskowski, Raymond, Cpl, Radio Operator, POW, 15-Feb-45
Lauger, Lloyd, T/Sgt, Radio Operator, POW, 07-Oct-44
Laurin, Paul A., S/Sgt, Radio Operator, KIA, 02-Dec-44
LaVick, K.D., S/Sgt, Left Waist Gunner, KIA, 20-Feb-44
Law, John L., S/Sgt, Left Waist Gunner, POW, 02-Mar-45
Lawler, David J., Cpl, Tail Gunner, POW, 14-Oct-44
Lawrence, Howard F., T/Sgt, Top Turret, POW, 18-Mar-44
Lawson, Earl J., T/Sgt, Radio Operator, POW, 29-Apr-44
Lechliesche, Charles L., T/Sgt, Top Turret, KIA, 08-Oct-43
Leidl, Barvin E., 2Lt, Navigator, POW, 24-Feb-44
Leigh, Robert H., Sgt, Tail Gunner, EVD, 18-Sep-44
Lemily, Gerard P., S/Sgt, Tail Gunner, KIA, 15-Mar-44
Lentz, Bernard J., S/Sgt, Left Waist Gunner, POW, 11-Sep-44
Lessey, John E., 2Lt, Bombardier, KIA, 04-Jan-44
Levine, G.S., 2Lt, Navigator, KIA, 05-Jul-44
Levine, Samuel J., 2Lt, Navigator, KIA, 07-Jul-44
Lidgard, Willard V., Lt, Copilot, KIA, 18-Mar-44
Lindley, George W., Sgt, Waist Gunner, KIA, 21-Jul-44
Lindlow, Ronald R., 2Lt, Navigator, KIA, 29-Jan-44
Lindsay, Edward L., S/Sgt, Ball Turret, KIA, 09-Apr-44
Lingle, John A.H., S/Sgt, Left Waist Gunner, POW, 22-Feb-45
Linn, Raymond L., S/Sgt, Toggler, KIA, 07-Jul-44
Linzey, J.D., 2Lt, Bombardier, KIA, 18-Mar-44
Liston, Leonard M., S/Sgt, Tail Gunner, POW, 11-Sep-44
Loar, Robert, 2Lt, Copilot, POW, 21-Jun-44

Lockhart, Kenneth T., S/Sgt, Tail Gunner, POW, 11-Sep-44
Lofresto, Henry C., 2Lt, Pilot, POW, 20-Dec-43
Long, Albert L., 1Lt, Navigator, POW, 18-Mar-44
Long, William S., 2Lt, Navigator, RTD, 11-Sep-44
Longacre, Harold N., S/Sgt, Tail Gunner, POW, 12-Sep-44
Longchamps, Alfred L., S/Sgt, Ball Turret, INT, 18-Mar-44
Longo, Robert J., S/Sgt, Ball Turret, POW, 29-Apr-44
Losey, James C., T/Sgt, Top Turret, POW, 18-Mar-44
Losse, Roy W., 2Lt, Navigator, KIA, 06-Jul-44
Louizedes, S., T/Sgt, Radio Operator, KIA, 25-Mar-45
Louizides, Solomon, T/Sgt, Radio Operator, INT, 18-Nov-43
Lousha, Carl C., S/Sgt, Toggler, KIA, 02-Dec-44
Love, Joseph W., S/Sgt, Radio Operator, POW, 21-Jul-44
Love, David C., 2Lt, Bombardier, KIA, 07-Jul-44
Love, William E., T/Sgt, Top Turret, KIA, 26-Nov-43
Lowder, Leonard L., 2Lt, Navigator, KIA, 06-Mar-44
Lowensteim, Alfred C., Lt, Navigator, KIA, 02-Dec-44
Lowry, Walter F., 2Lt, Pilot, KIA, 26-Mar-44
Luce, Arthur W., 2Lt, Copilot, KIA, 29-Apr-44
Luchak, Alexander, S/Sgt, Left Waist Gunner, POW, 08-Apr-44
Luciano, Robert E., S/Sgt, Tail Gunner, POW, 24-Feb-44
Luetzow, Wilbur H., 2Lt, Bombardier, KIA, 21-Feb-44
Luniewicz, Theodore E., Sgt, Radio Operator, KIA, 09-Feb-45
Luttrell, William T., 2Lt, Navigator, POW, 12-Sep-44
Lynch, James M., S/Sgt, Top Turret, KIA, 15-Mar-44
Lyroid, Walter A., 2Lt, Navigator, INT, 18-Mar-44
Maben, Jack F., 2Lt, Copilot, KIA, 18-Mar-44
Maccarone, Angelo A., Pvt, Toggler, KIA, 28-Jan-45
MacDonald junr, George E., T/Sgt, Top Turret, KIA, 29-May-44
Maceyra, Edward, 2Lt, Navigator, KIA, 25-Mar-45
Machak, John C., 2Lt, Bombardier, POW, 20-Dec-43
MacKenzie, Walter B., S/Sgt, Left Waist Gunner, KIA, 05-Nov-43
MacMullen, Donald H., 2Lt, Copilot, INT, 18-Mar-44
MacPherson, Albert J., S/Sgt, Aerial Gunner, KIA, 04-Jan-44
Macuzick, Harrison R., S/Sgt, Radio Operator, POW, 21-Jul-44
Madden, Tim E., FO, Copilot, POW, 06-Mar-44
Magee, William H., 2Lt, Navigator, KIA, 05-Nov-43
Magee junr, John H., S/Sgt, Ball Turret, KIA, 04-Jan-44
Mahon, Jack F., 2Lt, Copilot, KIA, 18-Mar-44
Mahoney, John E., T/Sgt, Top Turret, KIA, 06-Mar-44
Malavasic, Anthony F., S/Sgt, Tail Gunner, POW, 31-Dec-43
Malek, Alovaius J., T/Sgt, Radio Operator, POW, 13-Dec-43
Maloney, Eugene V., 2Lt, KIA, 30-Aug-43
Maloy, Joe B., Sgt, Left Waist Gunner, POW, 29-Apr-44
Mandell, Nicholas, Sgt, Radio Operator, EVD, 13-Nov-43
Mardis, Kenneth A., 2Lt, Copilot, POW, 18-Mar-44
Marfia, Frank, 1Lt, Pilot, KIA, 13-Nov-43
Marinelli, Nicholas R., S/Sgt, Left Waist Gunner, POW, 28-Jan-45
Markuson, C.O., 1Lt, Pilot, KIA, 25-Mar-45
Maroun, Nader P., 2Lt, Navigator, POW, 21-Sep-44
Marshall, Charles R., Sgt, Right Waist Gunner, KIA, 21-Jul-44
Marshall, James W., 2Lt, Copilot, KIA, 05-Nov-43
Martell, Floyd P., T/Sgt, Radio Operator, KIA, 04-Jan-44
Martin, Charles D., S/Sgt, Left Waist Gunner, POW, 05-Nov-43
Martin, John W., 2Lt, Copilot, 15-Jun-44
Martin, Arlias V., FO, Navigator, INT, 20-Jun-44
Martin, Marvin C., T/Sgt, Top Turret, POW, 24-Feb-44
Martin, Earl M., T/Sgt, Radio Operator, INT, 18-Mar-44
Martin junr, Louis J., S/Sgt, Top Turret, POW, 24-Feb-44
Marvin, Henry E., S/Sgt, Right Waist Gunner, POW, 07-Jul-44
Marx, Isaac S., 2Lt, Pilot, POW, 13-Nov-43
Massimiani, Orlando A., Sgt, Radio Operator, KIA, 11-Dec-43
Masteka, George F., S/Sgt, Radio Operator, POW, 18-Mar-44
Masters, Enoch E., S/Sgt, Left Waist Gunner, KIA, 18-Mar-44
Matracia, August A., S/Sgt, Toggler, KIA, 11-Sep-44
Matta, I.D., S/Sgt, Aerial Gunner, KIA, 29-Jan-44
Matthews, Avila D., S/Sgt, Right Waist Gunner, POW, 02-Dec-44
Mattson, William R., T/Sgt, Top Turret, EVD, 29-Jan-44
Matusky, Paul P., Cpl, Left Waist Gunner, POW, 15-Feb-45
Maupin, Jesse C., 2Lt, Navigator, KIA, 26-Nov-43
Mayer, Henry T., S/Sgt, Right Waist Gunner, KIA, 15-Mar-44
Mayer junr, Randell S., FO, Navigator, POW, 07-Jul-44
Maylander, Nathan, S/Sgt, Tail Gunner, KIA, 18-Mar-44
Maynard, Claiborne R., T/Sgt, Top Turret, KIA, 11-Sep-44
Mazzei, Anthony P., T/Sgt, Top Turret, POW, 13-Dec-43

McAdams, Ralph E., T/Sgt, Radio Operator, POW, 07-Jul-44
McAfee, Stewart P., FO, Navigator, RTD, 11-Sep-44
McAllaster, Robert W., T/Sgt, Radio Operator, KIA, 11-Sep-44
McAnn, Henry W., S/Sgt, Left Waist Gunner, POW, 18-Mar-44
McBrayer, James N., 2Lt, Bombardier, KIA, 05-Mar-44
McBrayer junr, Henry G., S/Sgt, Right Waist Gunner, POW, 18-Mar-44
McCalicher, Robert L., T/Sgt, Top Turret, POW, 29-Apr-44
McCarthy, Clarke G., 1Lt, Pilot, EVD, 23-Jun-44
McCormick, John E., S/Sgt, Right Waist Gunner, EVD, 22-Feb-45
McCormick, J.J., 2Lt, Copilot, KIA, 22-Mar-45
McCormick, S.G., Sgt, Aerial Gunner, KIA, 05-Jul-44
McCrary, Joe E., S/Sgt, Right Waist Gunner, EVD, 29-Jan-44
McDade, John J., 2Lt, Navigator, KIA, 08-Apr-44
McDonald, Paul R., 1Lt, Bombardier, POW, 18-Mar-44
McDonald, Leo F., 1Lt, Navigator, INT, 18-Mar-44
McDonald, Ralph L., S/Sgt, Tail Gunner, KIA, 29-Apr-44
McElroy, Virgil E., Sgt, Radio Operator, KIA, 15-Mar-45
McEwan, D.L., S/Sgt, Aerial Gunner, KIA, 13-Jul-44
McGee junr, Oliver W., S/Sgt, Top Turret, KIA, 14-Apr-45
McGinley, William C., S/Sgt, Tail Gunner, EVD, 29-Jan-44
McGlinn, Matthew J., S/Sgt, Right Waist Gunner, POW, 29-May-44
McGowan, William J., S/Sgt, Right Waist Gunner, KIA, 11-Apr-44
McGowen, Robert L., 2Lt, Copilot, INT, 18-Mar-44
McGrew, Cecil C., S/Sgt, Left Waist Gunner, POW, 02-Dec-44
McGuire, William C J., 2Lt, Navigator, KIA, 18-Mar-44
McKee, Thomas R., 1Lt, Pilot, KIA, 31-Dec-43
McKinzie, W.L., T/Sgt, Top Turret, KIA, 13-Jul-44
McLamore, Paul L., 2Lt, Navigator, KIA, 08-Oct-43
McMillan, William J., 2Lt, Navigator, POW, 18-Mar-44
McNamara, Paul E., S/Sgt, Left Waist Gunner, POW, 24-Feb-44
McNamara, Roger C., T/Sgt, Radio Operator, POW, 04-Jan-44
McNichol, Thomas F., 2Lt, Pilot, KIA, 11-Apr-44
McShane, W.F., 2Lt, Navigator, KIA, 05-Aug-44
McSweeney, John D., 2Lt, Navigator, EVD, 23-Jun-44
Meehan, John L., 2Lt, Pilot, RTD, 11-Sep-44
Mehtala, Arvid, S/Sgt, Right Waist Gunner, KIA, 18-Nov-43
Melton, James A., FO, Bombardier, KIA, 04-Nov-44
Menard, John F., 2Lt, Pilot, POW, 21-Jul-44
Merrill, James R., 2Lt, Navigator, KIA, 28-Dec-44
Meshon, Martin, S/Sgt, Left Waist Gunner, KIA, 24-Feb-44
Metz, William, T/Sgt, Radio Operator, KIA, 29-May-44
Metz, Louis, 2Lt, Navigator, KIA, 03-Mar-44
Michel, George W., T/Sgt, Radio Operator, INT, 11-Jul-44
Mihalso, Clarence M., T/Sgt, Top Turret, KIA, 04-Jan-44
Mikalian, Charles W., S/Sgt, Radio Operator, POW, 24-Apr-44
Milchak, Elmer A., Sgt, Right Waist Gunner, KIA, 24-Mar-45
Miller, Bert D., 2Lt, Pilot, KIA, 15-Mar-44
Miller, D.C., S/Sgt, Aerial Gunner, KIA, 24-Feb-44
Miller, Dewitt A., 1Lt, Bombardier, POW, 04-Jan-44
Miller, Gene A., 2Lt, Bombardier, KIA, 29-Apr-44
Miller junr, Herman H., 1Lt, Pilot, KIA, 21-Feb-44
Miller junr, John A., 2Lt, Copilot, KIA, 18-Nov-43
Miller, Joseph R., S/Sgt, Tail Gunner, POW, 02-Dec-44
Miller, Samson, S/Sgt, Right Waist Gunner, INT, 20-Jun-44
Milliken, Ellsworth W., S/Sgt, Right Waist Gunner, POW, 18-Mar-44
Milliken, William M., 2Lt, Pilot, KIA, 07-Jul-44
Mills, Elwood J., Sgt, Left Waist Gunner, KIA, 05-Mar-44
Minick junr, Frank, S/Sgt, Aerial Gunner, KIA, 12-Aug-44
Mislinski, George J., S/Sgt, Tail Gunner, KIA, 05-Nov-43
Mitchell, Jewell M., S/Sgt, Ball Turret, INT, 18-Mar-44
Mitchell, Ray , 2Lt, Toggler, POW, 18-Mar-44
Mitchell, Robert J., T/Sgt, Radio Operator, POW, 24-Feb-44
Mizenberg, W.O., FO, Navigator, KIA, 05-Jul-44
Modlin, Richard E., S/Sgt, Toggler, KIA, 11-Sep-44
Moffat, John E., 2Lt, Copilot, POW, 29-Jan-44
Mohr, Donald C., T/Sgt, Radio Operator, POW, 11-Apr-44
Monoghan, T. D., S/Sgt, Aerial Gunner, KIA, 25-Mar-45
Monroe, Robert W., S/Sgt, Radio Operator, KIA, 29-Apr-44
Montez, Arthur G., S/Sgt, Right Waist Gunner, KIA, 02-Dec-44
Moor, James W., 2Lt, Bombardier, KIA, 13-Nov-43
Moore, J. T. P., S/Sgt, Tail Gunner, INT, 11-Jul-44
Moore, John H., Sgt, Right Waist Gunner, KIA, 09-Apr-44
Moore, Robert L., S/Sgt, Radio Operator, INT, 20-Jun-44
Moore, Lawrence R., Lt, Bombardier, KIA, 04-Oct-43
Moore, H.B., S/Sgt, Aerial Gunner, KIA, 06-Mar-44

Moorehead junr, James C., 2Lt, Navigator, POW, 18-Mar-44
Morgan, Lenard S., T/Sgt, Left Waist Gunner, INT, 20-Jun-44
Morgan, Lark C., Sgt, Tail Gunner, POW, 29-Apr-44
Moriarty, Maurice, T/Sgt, Radio Operator, KIA, 04-Oct-43
Morphew, Orval S., 2Lt, Pilot, KIA, 04-Oct-43
Morris, Jack C., Lt, Navigator, POW, 07-Jul-44
Morris, Marvin O., Sgt, Tail Gunner, POW, 29-Apr-44
Morris, John A., S/Sgt, Left Waist Gunner, POW, 23-Jun-44
Morris, Everette N., S/Sgt, Top Turret, KIA, 18-Mar-44
Morrison, Thomas C., T/Sgt, Radio Operator, KIA, 31-Dec-43
Morrow, Wallace L., S/Sgt, Tail Gunner, RTD, 05-Mar-44
Morse, Ellis H., Sgt, Toggler, RTD, 24-Mar-45
Morton, Neil H., 2Lt, Copilot, KIA, 24-Apr-44
Mosteka, George F., S/Sgt, Radio Operator, POW, 18-Mar-44
Mucklin, Cecil D., S/Sgt, Top Turret, RTD, 05-Mar-44
Muka, John J., Sgt, Right Waist Gunner, POW, 28-Jan-45
Mulder, Robert L., Sgt, Toggler, POW, 06-Aug-44
Muldoon junr, James E., Lt, Pilot, RTD, 18-Mar-44
Mulhern, Robert T., S/Sgt, Radio Operator, POW, 21-Jun-44
Munford, Ben, Sgt, Waist Gunner, KIA, 27-Apr-44
Murphy, William F., T/Sgt, Left Waist Gunner, POW, 13-Nov-43
Murphy, Edward R., S/Sgt, Aerial Gunner, KIA, 04-Jan-44
Murphy, Walter F., KILD, 30-Aug-43
Murphy junr, Horace G., S/Sgt, Right Waist Gunner, KIA, 31-Dec-43
Murray, John R., 2Lt, Bombardier, KIA, 06-Jul-44
Musum, Marion E., Sgt, Waist Gunner, KIA, 31-Dec-43
Myers, J.W., S/Sgt, Radio Operator, KIA, 29-Apr-44
Nagle, Francis J., Sgt, Radio Operator, POW, 22-Feb-45
Naters, Edmond R., S/Sgt, Tail Gunner, KIA, 18-Nov-43
Negri, John D., S/Sgt, Left Waist Gunner, POW, 18-Sep-44
Negus, J.V., S/Sgt, Tail Gunner, KIA, 02-Nov-44
Nelson, Arch W., S/Sgt, Right Waist Gunner, POW, 24-Feb-44
Nelson, Verne A., S/Sgt, Ball Turret, RTD, 05-Mar-44
Nemeth, John L., Sgt, KIA, 11-Dec-43
Neuman, William E., 2Lt, Bombardier, KIA, 02-Dec-44
Neuman, Howard L., Cpl, Toggler, POW, 15-Feb-45
Newberry, Wando D., S/Sgt, KIA, 08-Oct-43
Newell, Roger V., 2Lt, Copilot, KIA, 08-Sep-44
Nicholson, William P., 2Lt, Pilot, POW, 05-Nov-43
Nilsen, Arnold V., S/Sgt, Top Turret, POW, 04-Nov-44
Nixon, Alton D., S/Sgt, Tail Gunner, KIA, 18-Mar-44
Norton junr, Walter J., S/Sgt, Left Waist Gunner, KIA, 03-Mar-44
Nurrell, R. E., Sgt, Aerial Gunner, KIA, 21-Apr-44
Nuzum, Marion E., Sgt, Left Waist Gunner, KIA, 31-Dec-43
O'Neill, Thomas J., 2Lt, Navigator, POW, 23-Jun-44
O'Neill, Francis L., S/Sgt, Tail Gunner, KIA, 08-Apr-44
O'Neill, Christ D., S/Sgt, Right Waist Gunner, KIA, 05-Nov-43
O'Reilly, Charles E., S/Sgt, Ball Turret, POW, 13-Nov-43
Ofenstein, Leo E., 2Lt, Pilot, KIA, 29-Apr-44
Okon, Martin A., Sgt, Radio Operator, KIA, 11-Apr-44
Olivas, Maclovio, Cpl, Left Waist Gunner, POW, 28-Jan-45
Olive, William E., 2Lt, Copilot, INT, 20-Jun-44
Olsen, William, 2Lt, Navigator, EVD, 30-Dec-43
Olsen, Erling A., T/Sgt, Top Turret, POW, 05-Nov-43
Olson, Ralph, S/Sgt, Radio Operator, KIA, 24-Apr-44
Oppenheim, Alfred M., 2Lt, Navigator, POW, 11-Sep-44
Opshal, Roland C., Sgt, Right Waist Gunner, POW, 18-Mar-44
Orenbach, David, 2Lt, Navigator, INT, 20-Jun-44
Orenbach, David, 2Lt, Navigator, RTD, 12-Apr-44
Orlando, Frank J., Sgt, Tail Gunner, KIA, 07-Jul-44
Ortiz, Joseph C., Sgt, Ball Turret, POW, 13-Nov-43
Osterheldt, James J., S/Sgt, Right Waist Gunner, KIA, 11-Apr-44
Ott, J.W., 2Lt, Navigator, KIA, 25-Mar-45
Ott, John W., 2Lt, Navigator, INT, 18-Nov-43
Ouerve, Frederick J., Sgt, Left Waist Gunner, KIA, 19-May-44
Overton, David J., S/Sgt, Right Waist Gunner, POW, 24-Feb-44
Pace, John W., S/Sgt, Tail Gunner, KIA, 02-Dec-44
Padolski, Paul D., S/Sgt, Toggler, KIA, 29-May-44
Page, Robert E., Sgt, Toggler, KIA, 28-Jan-45
Page, Leander, 2Lt, Pilot, INT, 20-Jun-44
Page junr, Leander, 2Lt, Pilot, POW, 04-Jan-44
Paine, Albert E., 2Lt, Copilot, KIA, 29-May-44
Painter, Richard E., S/Sgt, Ball Turret, KIA, 31-Dec-43
Palmer, Royal D., 2Lt, Copilot, KIA, 04-Jan-44
Palumbo, Anthony P., Pvt, Top Turret, POW, 08-Sep-44

Paolantonio, Anthony L., S/Sgt, Ball Turret, EVD, 29-Jan-44
Paolucci, Umberto, T/Sgt, Radio Operator, INT, 11-Jul-44
Parish, John K., 2Lt, Bombardier, INT, 18-Nov-43
Parish, John K., 2Lt, Bombardier, KIA, 25-Mar-45
Parker, Earl S., T/Sgt, Top Turret, POW, 18-Mar-44
PAR, Kenneth C., 2Lt, Navigator, INT, 18-Mar-44
Parr junr, Clarence A., 2Lt, Bombardier, POW, 24-Apr-44
Patterson, Joseph B., 2Lt, Pilot, POW, 24-Feb-44
Patterson, Maurice J., T/Sgt, Radio Operator, POW, 04-Nov-44
Patterson junr, Henry C., T/Sgt, Top Turret, KIA, 04-Jan-44
Patterson junr, Earl A., S/Sgt, Nose Turret, KIA, 18-Nov-43
Patzmann, R.O.E., S/Sgt, Aerial Gunner, KIA, 05-Jul-44
Paules, Russell E., 2Lt, Copilot, KIA, 18-Mar-44
Payne, Charles F., Sgt, Left Waist Gunner, KIA, 18-Mar-44
Payton, Josephine B., T/Sgt, Top Turret, KIA, 24-Feb-44
Peacock, Clyde E., S/Sgt, Right Waist Gunner, INT, 18-Mar-44
Pearson, Bryan T., S/Sgt, Left Waist Gunner, KIA, 19-May-44
Pederson, Fredrick M., S/Sgt, Waist Gunner, POW, 12-Nov-43
Pedrotta, Charles H., 2Lt, Copilot, POW, 02-Dec-44
Pellecchia, Raymond W., Sgt, Top Turret, KIA, 28-Jan-45
Pendergraft, John C., S/Sgt, Tail Gunner, KIA, 02-Dec-44
Peppard, J.M., 2Lt, Navigator, KIA, 14-Apr-45
Pergande, Bradford E., Sgt, Top Turret, KIA, 09-Feb-45
Perry, Elda L., S/Sgt, Ball Turret, KIA, 05-Nov-43
Perry, R., 2Lt, Copilot, KIA, 25-Mar-45
Perry, Raymond A., S/Sgt, Right Waist Gunner, POW, 05-Nov-43
Peters, James F., Sgt, Tail Gunner, POW, 24-Apr-44
Peters, Henry J., Sgt, Toggler, POW, 21-Jun-44
Peterson, George H., T/Sgt, Top Turret, KIA, 24-Feb-44
Peterson, Clifford L., 1Lt, Pilot, POW, 18-Mar-44
Peterson, Carl L., T/Sgt, Top Turret, KIA, 23-Jun-44
Peterson, Lynn, Lt, Pilot, KIA, 18-Mar-44
Petrozzella, Benjamin C., 2Lt, Navigator, KIA, 18-Mar-44
Pettigrew, William B., 2Lt, Bombardier, POW, 02-Dec-44
Pettigrew, William R., 2Lt, Bombardier, POW, 04-Jan-44
Peyton, John B., 2Lt, Pilot, KIA, 20-Feb-44
Pfeifer, Ambrose R., S/Sgt, Left Waist Gunner, KIA, 04-Jan-44
Phillips, William H., Sgt, Left Waist Gunner, POW, 07-Jul-44
Phillips, Harry E., Sgt, Ball Turret, KIA, 24-Apr-44
Phipps junr, Homer H., 2Lt, Navigator, POW, 13-Sep-44
Pitts, Jimmie B., S/Sgt, Tail Gunner, INT, 20-Jun-44
Place, Robert K., S/Sgt, Tail Gunner, KIA, 11-Sep-44
Plank, Gerald , Sgt, Right Waist Gunner, INT, 20-Jun-44
Plucket, Joseph F., S/Sgt, Waist Gunner, POW, 20-Dec-43
Plude, Robert W., S/Sgt, Right Waist Gunner, POW, 04-Nov-44
Polochan, J., T/Sgt, Aerial Gunner, KIA, 24-Feb-44
Poppel, Samuel B., 1Lt, Bombardier, INT, 18-Mar-44
Poremba, Stanley J., Cpl, Right Waist Gunner, KIA, 15-Mar-45
Porter, Clifford T., S/Sgt, Right Waist Gunner, KIA, 18-Mar-44
Porter, Lawrence M., 2Lt, Copilot, POW, 11-Sep-44
Pose, Harold E., T/Sgt, Top Turret, POW, 13-Nov-43
Potts junr, Benjamin F., S/Sgt, Top Turret, POW, 12-Sep-44
Pounds, Raymond L., 2Lt, Pilot, POW, 07-Jul-44
Powell, Marvin L., Sgt, Left Waist Gunner, KIA, 29-May-44
Powell, Hollis, Sgt, Tail Gunner, RTD, 24-Mar-45
Powers, George, S/Sgt, Tail Gunner, INT, 11-Jul-44
Prazak, Stanley J., S/Sgt, Tail Gunner, KIA, 23-Jun-44
Prell, Donald D., 2Lt, Pilot, KIA, 19-May-44
Price, Donald E., Sgt, Tail Gunner, POW, 08-Apr-44
Propst, Earl J., S/Sgt, Mickey Operator, KIA, 13-Sep-44
Prouse, Harold W., 2Lt, Pilot, POW, 07-Jul-44
Prudhoume, Elroy J., T/Sgt, Top Turret, POW, 13-Nov-43
Pryce, Richard J., S/Sgt, Right Waist Gunner, KIA, 24-Feb-44
Prys, John, 2Lt, Copilot, KIA, 29-May-44
Przeniczny, William, S/Sgt, Left Waist Gunner, POW, 24-Feb-44
Purdy, Robert F., 2Lt, Copilot, KIA, 04-Oct-43
Purner, David J., 2Lt, Navigator, POW, 29-Apr-44
Puryear, Ronnie R., 2Lt, Copilot, KIA, 21-Jul-44
Quagliano, Frank A., S/Sgt, Right Waist Gunner, POW, 04-Jan-44
Qualey, Leroy F., 2Lt, Copilot, INT, 20-Jun-44
Quick, Lowell I., S/Sgt, Left Waist Gunner, POW, 07-Jul-44
Quigley, Edward J., 2Lt, Navigator, POW, 08-Apr-44
Ralston, Gerald J., S/Sgt, Left Waist Gunner, POW, 11-Sep-44
Randall, Stafford R., 2Lt, Copilot, KIA, 02-Feb-44
Rankin, Jack H., S/Sgt, Left Waist Gunner, POW, 18-Mar-44

Ranta, Eino J., 2Lt, Bombardier, POW, 24-Feb-44
Raschke, Walter C., Lt, Pilot, KIA, 18-Mar-44
Rasmussen, M. D., S/Sgt, Aerial Gunner, KIA, 05-Jul-44
Rathburn, Earl E., S/Sgt, Tail Gunner, KIA, 11-Apr-44
Ratko, Edward L., 2Lt, Navigator, POW, 08-Sep-44
Razo, Enrico G., S/Sgt, Left Waist Gunner, INT, 20-Jun-44
Reardon, Patrick M., Sgt, Left Waist Gunner, POW, 13-Nov-43
Reddy, Willis J., 2Lt, Copilot, POW, 04-Jan-44
Reardon junr, Daniel J., Sgt, Tail Gunner, KIA, 15-Mar-45
Redman junr, Gaines A., S/Sgt, Left Waist Gunner, POW, 21-Jul-44
Reed IV, J.W., 2Lt, Pilot, KIA, 29-Apr-44
Reese, William J., T/Sgt, Top Turret, KIA, 04-Jan-44
Reese, R.L., Lt, Pilot, KIA, 05-Jul-44
Reeves, W.E., Sgt, Aerial Gunner, KIA, 21-Apr-44
Rehill junr, James, Sgt, Ball Turret, INT, 20-Jun-44
Reid, Henry, T/Sgt, Top Turret, INT, 20-Jun-44
Reiffer, A.P., 2Lt, Copilot, KIA, 20-Feb-44
Reilly, Bernard A., S/Sgt, Ball Turret, KIA, 08-Apr-44
Reily, C.J., Sgt, Aerial Gunner, KIA, 29-Apr-44
Reinoch, Wilbur T., 2Lt, Navigator, KIA, 19-May-44
Reljac, Joseph G., S/Sgt, Tail Gunner, KIA, 13-Dec-43
Repley, Charles A., Sgt, Waist Gunner, POW, 11-Apr-44
Replogle, Wendall G., 2Lt, Bombardier, KIA, 26-Mar-44
Reynolds, James E., 2Lt, Copilot, RTD, 24-Mar-45
Reynolds, James J., S/Sgt, Radio Operator, RTD, 15-Jun-44
Reynolds, Hugh D., S/Sgt, Waist Gunner, KIA, 18-Mar-44
Ricci, Joseph A., 2Lt, Copilot, KIA, 29-May-44
Rice, Thomas L., S/Sgt, Ball Turret, KIA, 15-Mar-44
Rich, Clarence B., 2Lt, Navigator, EVD, 23-Jun-44
Rich, Nicholas R., Sgt, Waist Gunner, KIA, 27-Apr-44
Richards, Thomas I., 2Lt, Navigator, POW, 07-Jul-44
Richards, William J., 2Lt, Navigator, KIA, 18-Sep-44
Richards, E.B., Sgt, Top Turret, KIA, 08-Apr-44
Richards junr, Robert, S/Sgt, Right Waist Gunner, POW, 12-Sep-44
Richardson, Frank E., 2Lt, Bombardier, KIA, 18-Mar-44
Richter, Ernest R., S/Sgt, Tail Gunner, KIA, 19-May-44
Richmond junr, Thomas C., S/Sgt, Tail Gunner, KIA, 14-Apr-45
Riddleberger, William I., 2Lt, Copilot, POW, 09-Sep-44
Rigby, Clyde W., 1Lt, Pilot, KIA, 04-Jan-44
Riley junr, Albert J., S/Sgt, Waist Gunner, POW, 19-May-44
Rinke, Alfred P., T/Sgt, Top Turret, POW, 22-Apr-44
Roberts, Truman F., S/Sgt, Left Waist Gunner, KIA, 15-Mar-44
Roberts junr, Omar E., 2Lt, Bombardier, POW, 13-Nov-43
Robertson, Sieguart J., Lt, Pilot, INT, 11-Jul-44
Robinson, James W., S/Sgt, Top Turret, KIA, 21-Feb-44
Robinson, William F., T/Sgt, Top Turret, KIA, 23-Jun-44
Robson, Nicholas B., Lt, Copilot, POW, 13-Nov-43
Roddy, Willis H., 2Lt, Copilot, POW, 04-Jan-44
Rodiwicz, Norman W., T/Sgt, Top Turret, POW, 24-Feb-44
Rodnitsky, Bud E., S/Sgt, Bombardier, KIA, 19-May-44
Roetzel, P. R., 1Lt, Copilot, KIA, 13-Jul-44
Rogers junr, Charles J., S/Sgt, Tail Gunner, KIA, 04-Nov-44
Rogers, Gerald E., 2Lt, Pilot, KIA, 29-Apr-44
Rogillio junr, Douglas S., 2Lt, Pilot, POW, 13-Dec-43
Rooney, George W., T/Sgt, Radio Operator, KIA, 04-Oct-43
Roper, Donald W., S/Sgt, Ball Turret, KIA, 18-Apr-44
Roper, Jack A., 2Lt, Navigator, POW, 29-Apr-44
Rorer, Frank, T/Sgt, Top Turret, KIA, 04-Oct-43
Rosati, Louis, S/Sgt, Left Waist Gunner, EVD, 29-Jan-44
Rosenfeld, Carl B., T/Sgt, Waist Gunner, KIA, 11-Apr-44
Rosko, Eugene M., T/Sgt, Radio Operator, POW, 18-Mar-44
Ross, Eli D., T/Sgt, Radio Operator, POW, 20-Dec-43
Ross, Herbert J., S/Sgt, Ball Turret, KIA, 04-Jan-44
Ross, Jack R., T/Sgt, Ball Turret, POW, 22-Apr-44
Ross, James M., S/Sgt, Tail Gunner, POW, 18-Mar-44
Ross, John A., 2Lt, Bombardier, KIA, 27-Apr-44
Ross, Leon K., S/Sgt, Ball Turret, POW, 11-Apr-44
Ross, Robert F., 2Lt, Copilot, KIA, 04-Nov-44
Rossi, Vincent H., S/Sgt, Tail Gunner, POW, 07-Jul-44
Rowe, George F., 2Lt, Bombardier, KIA, 09-Apr-44
Rowlett, Robert W., Sgt, Tail Gunner, KIA, 29-Apr-44
Royal, Clarence K., S/Sgt, Ball Turret, POW, 18-Mar-44
Rubenstein, Stanley J., S/Sgt, Tail Gunner, POW, 02-Mar-45
Rudd, Charles, 1Lt, Pilot, KIA, 11-Sep-44
Rudnitsky, Bud E., S/Sgt, Nose Turret, KIA, 19-May-44

Rupp junr, Paul, Cpl, Top Turret, POW, 14-Oct-44
Rush, William A., Sgt, Right Waist Gunner, POW, 08-Apr-44
Ruvolis junr, Lee, 1Lt, Pilot, POW, 07-Jul-44
Ryan, Patrick J., 2Lt, Navigator, POW, 29-Apr-44
Ryan junr, James D., 2Lt, Navigator, KIA, 13-Nov-43
Sabaca, Joseph J., Sgt, Tail Gunner, KIA, 06-Jul-44
Sablitz, Paul, Sgt, Tail Gunner, KIA, 28-Jan-45
Sabota, Roman A., Sgt, Left Waist Gunner, POW, 28-Dec-44
Sackal, Ward M., T/Sgt, Top Turret, KIA, 31-Dec-43
Sackeli, Angelo, T/Sgt, Top Turret, KIA, 09-Apr-44
Saltzman, Robert L., S/Sgt, Left Waist Gunner, KIA, 02-Dec-44
Sambanis, George, S/Sgt, Tail Gunner, KIA, 20-Dec-43
Sanchez, Ismael V., S/Sgt, Tail Gunner, POW, 24-Feb-44
Sanders junr, Lewis L., 2Lt, Navigator, KIA, 09-Feb-45
Sands, Ralph D., S/Sgt, Ball Turret, KIA, 02-Feb-44
Sands, John E., 2Lt, Bombardier, POW, 22-Apr-44
Sanna, Mario G., S/Sgt, Nose Turret, POW, 13-Nov-43
Satterly junr, Everett F., Sgt, Engineer, POW, 30-Dec-43
Savage, Charles C., 2Lt, Bombardier, KIA, 18-Mar-44
Scalet, Joseph, T/Sgt, Top Turret, KIA, 02-Dec-44
Scarpine, Pasquale, 1Lt, Copilot, POW, 21-Sep-44
Schad, Richard, Cpl, Right Waist Gunner, POW, 15-Feb-45
Schaefer, Creighton E., S/Sgt, Observer, KIA, 09-Sep-44
Schaefer, Lee A., Sgt, Ball Turret, KIA, 19-May-44
Schearer, Martin O., 2Lt, Navigator, KIA, 04-Oct-43
Schafer, Wesley A., 1Lt, Pilot, INT, 20-Jun-44
Schaumberg, Gunther, S/Sgt, Voice Interpreter, KIA, 28-Dec-44
Schenkenberger, Jacob, S/Sgt, Left Waist Gunner, KIA, 07-Jul-44
Schiffer, James L., S/Sgt, Right Waist Gunner, KIA, 04-Oct-43
Schilling, John, 2Lt, Copilot, KIA, 03-Mar-44
Schilter, Norman J., S/Sgt, Tail Gunner, KIA, 04-Jan-44
Schlossberg, Marvin E., 2Lt, Pilot, POW, 24-Feb-44
Schmeizle, Oliver G., Sgt, Radio Operator, KIA, 29-Apr-44
Schmidt, Arthur N., Sgt, Tail Gunner, KIA, 08-Sep-44
Schmidt, Elmer A., S/Sgt, Aerial Gunner, KIA, 08-Apr-44
Schmid, Frank F., S/Sgt, Top Turret, KIA, 07-Jul-44
Schmidt, Fred I., Sgt, Tail Gunner, EVD, 30-Dec-43
Schoelerman, Harold A., 2Lt, Copilot, KIA, 02-Mar-45
Schoolmaster, Clinton F., Maj., Pilot, KIA, 25-May-44
Schroeder, Harold R., 2Lt, Copilot, KIA, 08-Oct-43
Schultz, George T., 2Lt, Navigator, POW, 11-Dec-43
Schuster, William N., 2Lt, Pilot, KIA, 28-Jan-45
Schwartz, Edward S., 1Lt, Bombardier, POW, 18-Mar-44
Scudder, Monroe A., Sgt, Top Turret, KIA, 28-Dec-44
Sederquist, Donald L., 2Lt, Copilot, KIA, 04-Oct-43
Seery, James B., S/Sgt, Right Waist Gunner, INT, 11-Jul-44
Seifert, Robert B., S/Sgt, Tail Gunner, KIA, 04-Oct-43
Sekevac, Roy, T/Sgt, Top Turret, KIA, 13-Nov-43
Sekal, John, S/Sgt, Top Turret, POW, 21-Jun-44
Selden, Frederick, Sgt, Right Waist Gunner, KIA, 29-May-44
Senk, John J., S/Sgt, Tail Gunner, KIA, 04-Oct-43
Serafine, John M., T/Sgt, Top Turret, POW, 18-Mar-44
Serrette, Robert L., Sgt, Tail Gunner, KIA, 09-Sep-44
Sewell, Wade, 2Lt, Pilot, EVD, 18-Sep-44
Sexton, Philip S., S/Sgt, Tail Gunner, POW, 24-Feb-44
Seymour, Alden, S/Sgt, Right Waist Gunner, INT, 20-Jun-44
Shafer, J.D., S/Sgt, Aerial Gunner, KIA, 12-Aug-44
Sharpe, William G., 1Lt, Pilot, KIA, 18-Mar-44
Shea, P.F., 1Lt, Pilot, KIA, 06-Mar-44
Shea, Harold A., S/Sgt, Toggler, POW, 22-Feb-45
Sheaver, Martin G., 2Lt, Navigator, KIA, 04-Oct-43
Shelley, Joe H., 1Lt, Pilot, KIA, 21-Sep-44
Shelton, William L., 1Lt, Copilot, KIA, 24-Feb-44
Shelton junr, Orville W., 1Lt, Toggler, KIA, 11-Sep-44
Sheppard, William B., S/Sgt, Ball Turret, KIA, 03-Mar-44
Sheres junr, Fred C., 2Lt, Pilot, KIA, 29-Apr-44
Sheridan, James J., 2Lt, Navigator, KIA, 11-Apr-44
Sheridan, Theodore V., S/Sgt, Tail Gunner, POW, 07-Jul-44
Sherman, Phillip , 2Lt, Navigator, KIA, 18-Mar-44
Sherwood, Walter B., 1Lt, Pilot, KIA, 11-Apr-44
Shiffer, James L., S/Sgt, Right Waist Gunner, KIA, 04-Oct-43
Sholander, Carl T., 2Lt, Copilot, KIA, 28-Jan-45
Sibley, James M., 2Lt, Pilot, POW, 30-Dec-43
Sicard, Norman L., S/Sgt, Ball Turret, POW, 24-Feb-44
Sichau, Walter R., S/Sgt, Radio Operator, RTD, 05-Mar-44

Sichau, Walter R., T/Sgt, Radio Operator, POW, 18-Apr-44
Siggs, Peter S., 2Lt, Navigator, KIA, 20-Dec-43
Silvasy, Frank A., 2Lt, Navigator, POW, 24-Feb-44
Similia, Wilber, S/Sgt, Bombardier, KIA, 19-May-44
Simons, Les, 2Lt, Bombardier, KIA, 31-Dec-43
Simpson, James F., S/Sgt, Tail Gunner, KIA, 13-Nov-43
Simpson, V. A., S/Sgt, KIA, 25-Mar-45
Skaggs, Robert L., 2Lt, Copilot, KIA, 19-May-44
Slack, George E., T/Sgt, Radio Operator, KIA, 18-Mar-44
Slagle, Charles I., S/Sgt, Right Waist Gunner, POW, 06-Mar-44
Slama, Alex, T/Sgt, Top Turret, KIA, 25-Mar-45
Slama, Alex R., T/Sgt, Top Turret, INT, 18-Nov-43
Slowick, John E., Capt., Navigator, KIA, 18-Mar-44
Smith junr, Alonzo C., S/Sgt, Left Waist Gunner, POW, 18-Mar-44
Smith, Arthur M., S/Sgt, Waist Gunner, POW, 29-Apr-44
Smith, Brian T., 1Lt, Pilot, KIA, 04-Oct-43
Smith, Clifford E., FO, Bombardier, KIA, 09-Sep-44
Smith, C.L., T/Sgt, Top Turret, KIA, 20-Feb-44
Smith, Herbert J., 2Lt, Copilot, KIA, 26-Nov-43
Smith, James E., 2Lt, Copilot, KIA, 14-Apr-45
Smith, James W., 2Lt, Navigator, POW, 29-May-44
Smith, Loren B., Cpl, Top Turret, POW, 15-Feb-45
Smith, Paul E., Pfc, Radio Operator, POW, 21-Sep-44
Smith, R.E., T/Sgt, Radio Operator, KIA, 05-Aug-44
Smith, Richard E., 1Lt, Pilot, KIA, 03-Mar-44
Smith junr, Roy A., T/Sgt, Top Turret, POW, 13-Sep-44
Smith, William W., S/Sgt, Ball Turret, INT, 18-Nov-43
Smith, William H., S/Sgt, Right Waist Gunner, POW, 21-Jun-44
Smith, Willis H., Sgt, Tail Gunner, KIA, 29-May-44
Smittle, Floyd D., 2Lt, Bombardier, KIA, 04-Oct-43
Soda, Manuel J., T/Sgt, Top Turret, KIA, 09-Sep-44
Sokol, Alexander R., S/Sgt, Radio Operator, KIA, 19-May-44
Somerhalder, Walter R., FO, Bombardier, KIA, 09-Feb-45
Sooy, Bruce L., 1Lt, Pilot, POW, 18-Mar-44
Sooy, Harry B., S/Sgt, Top Turret, POW, 11-Apr-44
Sopchak, John, S/Sgt, Aerial Gunner, KIA, 18-Mar-44
Sopha, Bernhardt E., T/Sgt, Top Turret, POW, 02-Dec-44
Sorrells, John F., Sgt, Ball Turret, KIA, 29-Apr-44
Southwell, Elton E., S/Sgt, Radio Operator, POW, 18-Sep-44
Spades, Richard J., S/Sgt, Radio Operator, POW, 02-Mar-45
Spaulding, Robert E., S/Sgt, Right Waist Gunner, KIA, 05-Nov-43
Spencer, William A., 2Lt, Bombardier, KIA, 11-Sep-44
Sporry, Richard F., 2Lt, Copilot, KIA, 05-Nov-43
Silver, Eugene R., 2Lt, Bombardier, POW, 24-Feb-44
Stafford, Jacob A., Sgt, Left Waist Gunner, INT, 11-Jul-44
Stalsby, S.C., FO, Copilot, KIA, 12-Aug-44
Stancik, Martin, T/Sgt, Top Turret, KIA, 18-Mar-44
Stankan, Paul C., 1Lt, Navigator, KIA, 24-Feb-44
Stanley, Charles E., 2Lt, Copilot, POW, 02-Dec-44
Stark junr, Elmer O., Sgt, Ball Turret, KIA, 29-May-44
Stauder, James B., Capt., Pilot, KIA, 25-Nov-44
Steele, W.M., 2Lt, Navigator, KIA, 21-Apr-44
Steinetz, Douglas R., 2Lt, Pilot, KIA, 05-Nov-43
Stells, George F., Sgt, Radio Operator, KIA, 07-Jul-44
Stephens, Louis M., 2Lt, Pilot, POW, 09-Sep-44
Stephens, Dale J., Sgt, Ball Turret, POW, 08-Apr-44
Stetson, Harvey E., 2Lt, Navigator, POW, 19-May-44
Stevens, Hirschall M., S/Sgt, Left Waist Gunner, KIA, 08-Oct-43
Stewart, Jack O., S/Sgt, Waist Gunner, POW, 13-Nov-43
Stewart, James M., 2Lt, Pilot, KIA, 02-Feb-44
Stewart, Stanley A., S/Sgt, Left Waist Gunner, POW, 21-Sep-44
Stickley, Fred F., S/Sgt, Left Waist Gunner, POW, 07-Oct-44
Still, Joe T., S/Sgt, Radio Operator, POW, 11-Apr-44
Stoltz, Charles W., 2Lt, Pilot, KIA, 29-May-44
Storey, Harold D., 2Lt, Copilot, KIA, 18-Mar-44
Stover, A.R., 2Lt, Bombardier, KIA, 21-Apr-44
Stratton junr, Charles R., 2Lt, Copilot, KIA, 23-Jun-44
Stricker, Donald A., T/Sgt, Radio Operator, KIA, 02-Feb-44
Strickler, Chester C., S/Sgt, Left Waist Gunner, POW, 18-Mar-44
Strother, Charles K., Sgt, Tail Gunner, KIA, 29-May-44
Stukus, John, 1Lt, Pilot, POW, 29-Jan-44
Sulkowski, Joseph T., 2Lt, Bombardier, EVD, 18-Sep-44
Sullivan, Edward, Sgt, Waist Gunner, KIA, 18-Apr-44
Sullivan junr, John L., Sgt, Ball Turret, EVD, 30-Dec-43
Surls, David L., S/Sgt, Waist Gunner, KIA, 04-Jan-44

Sutton, Ralph H., S/Sgt, Left Waist Gunner, POW, 05-Nov-43
Swangrin, R.E., Capt., Navigator, KIA, 22-Mar-44
Swanson, Arthur W., Sgt, Right Waist Gunner, KIA, 21-Feb-44
Synder, R.D., 2Lt, Navigator, KIA, 29-Jan-44
Syriod, Walter A., 2Lt, Navigator, INT, 18-Mar-44
Takacs, Alexander, S/Sgt, Waist Gunner, POW, 13-Dec-43
Talley, Edgar, S/Sgt, Toggler, KIA, 02-Mar-45
Tantum, William R., S/Sgt, Right Waist Gunner, KIA, 04-Jan-44
Taylor, Adrian L., Sgt, Tail Gunner, KIA, 18-Mar-44
Taylor, Edward J., 2Lt, Copilot, POW, 13-Sep-44
Taylor junr, Ralph E., 1Lt, Copilot, KIA, 07-Jul-44
Techudy, Evan E., 1Lt, Bombardier, KIA, 21-Jul-44
Telken, Henry F., 2Lt, Pilot, KIA, 21-Jul-44
Telly, Martin T., T/Sgt, Radio Operator, KIA, 24-Feb-44
Teran, Edward J., 2Lt, Pilot, POW, 11-Apr-44
Thom, Fred S., T/Sgt, Top Turret, KIA, 07-Jul-44
Thomas junr, Harry E., 1Lt, Bombardier, POW, 07-Jul-44
Thomas, James W., T/Sgt, Aerial Gunner, KIA, 21-A[r-44
Thomas, William L., 2Lt, Navigator, POW, 14-Oct-44
Thompson, Robert E., Sgt, Right Waist Gunner, 29-Apr-44
Thornton, M., S/Sgt, Aerial Gunner, KIA, 05-Jul-44
Thrall, Leo C., T/Sgt, Top Turret, KIA, 04-Oct-43
Tiefenthal, Dexter E., 1Lt, Pilot, POW, 18-Apr-44
Timm, Henry A., Sgt, Left Waist Gunner, KIA, 29-May-44
Tistraro, Pietro A., 2Lt, Bombardier, POW, 18-Mar-44
Todd, Raymond E., T/Sgt, Top Turret, POW, 11-Apr-44
Todrowski, Henry R., S/Sgt, Radio Operator, POW, 02-Dec-44
Toler, Needham, T/Sgt, Top Turret, INT, 18-Mar-44
Tolken, Henry F., 2Lt, Pilot, KIA, 21-Jul-44
Tollok, R.C., Cpl, Tail Gunner, KIA, 11-Sep-44
Tomak, James E., S/Sgt, Left Waist Gunner, KIA, 09-Apr-44
Tor junr, D., T/Sgt, Radio Operator, KIA, 20-Feb-44
Torres, Edward J., S/Sgt, Waist Gunner, KIA, 29-May-44
Townsend, Edward S., Sgt, Tail Gunner, KIA, 09-Feb-45
Toxel, D.G., S/Sgt, Aerial Gunner, KIA, 29-Jan-44
Trappe, William H., Sgt, Tail Gunner, KIA, 19-May-44
Tremlett, Robert S., S/Sgt, Tail Gunner, KIA, 23-Jun-44
Trivison, Joseph R., S/Sgt, Radio Operator, KIA, 29-Apr-44
Troup, David G., S/Sgt, Tail Gunner, POW, 06-Mar-44
Troutman, Edward A., S/Sgt, Waist Gunner, KIA, 29-May-44
Trumpy, Egidius, T/Sgt, Top Turret, KIA, 11-Apr-44
Tschudy, Evan E., 1Lt, Bombardier, KIA, 21-Jul-44
Tubbs, Herbert L., S/Sgt, Tail Gunner, KIA, 21-Jul-44
Tucker, Herbert L., S/Sgt, Ball Turret, KIA, 04-Oct-43
Tufts, Albert M., 2Lt, Copilot, , 29-Apr-44
Turner, Dwight L., 2Lt, Copilot, KIA, 29-Jan-44
Tweten, Ernest A., S/Sgt, Tail Gunner, KIA, 08-Oct-43
Twitchell, Frederick O., S/Sgt, Ball Turret, POW, 06-Mar-44
Tyler, Ace W., 1Lt, Pilot, KIA, 29-May-44
Tynes junr, David D., T/Sgt, Top Turret, KIA, 08-Oct-43
Usury, W. F., 1Lt, Pilot, KIA, 29-Jan-44
Vallarelli, Frederick J., 2Lt, Copilot, POW, 18-Sep-44
Valley, Wilbur L., 2Lt, Navigator, KIA, 19-May-44
Van Alstine, Nathan O., S/Sgt, Tail Gunner, KIA, 07-Oct-44
Vandervort, E., Sgt, Counter Measures, KIA, 08-Apr-44
Varela, Henry J., 1Lt, Bombardier, POW, 08-Apr-44
Vasques, Raul, S/Sgt, Tail Gunner, KIA, 04-Jan-44
Vaughan, Dieudonne, FO, Copilot, RTD, 15-Mar-45
Vavra, Charles E., S/Sgt, Tail Gunner, KIA, 13-Sep-44
Veronick, Joseph J., T/Sgt, Radio Operator, POW, 13-Nov-43
Verzyl, Rayford R., S/Sgt, Right Waist Gunner, KIA, 19-May-44
Vesey, Edward J., S/Sgt, Radio Operator, POW, 24-Feb-44
Victor, Albert I., 2Lt, Copilot, KIA, 26-Mar-44
Vineall, Bradford H., S/Sgt, Left Waist Gunner, POW, 21-Jun-44
Viosca, Randall C., S/Sgt, Top Turret, KIA, 29-Apr-44
Volet, Leonard, 2Lt, Copilot, POW, 30-Dec-43
Vovos, Alkedee D., T/Sgt, Radio Operator, POW, 04-Jan-44
Vowels, Leroy J., S/Sgt, Top Turret, KIA, 29-May-44
Vrieling, Russell I., 2Lt, Copilot, POW, 18-Mar-44
Wade, Burton L., 2Lt, Pilot, KIA, 09-Feb-45
Wagner, Frederick J., S/Sgt, Right Waist Gunner, KIA, 18-Mar-44
Wagonseller, Robert V., T/Sgt, Top Turret, KIA, 18-Mar-44
Wald, Frederick M., S/Sgt, Left Waist Gunner, POW, 30-Dec-43
Walker, Charles S., 2Lt, Navigator, KIA, 02-Mar-45
Walker junr, Joseph R., 2Lt, Pilot, EVD, 22-Feb-45

Walker, Robert S., 2Lt, Copilot, INT, 18-Nov-43
Walker, Thomas G., 2Lt, Copilot, KIA, 31-Dec-43
Wall, John J., 2Lt, Copilot, KIA, 29-Apr-44
Walla, Mitchell A., S/Sgt, Left Waist Gunner, KIA, 24-Feb-44
Wallace, Frank C., T/Sgt, Radio Operator, KIA, 18-Mar-44
Waller, Clarence R., 2Lt, Copilot, POW, 08-Oct-43
Walley, Henry P., 2Lt, Copilot, KIA, 21-Feb-44
Walsh, Donald A., T/Sgt, Top Turret, POW, 21-Jul-44
Walsh, Frank T., 2Lt, Navigator, KIA, 18-Mar-44
Walton, Raymond T., Cpl, Left Waist Gunner, POW, 14-Oct-44
Wals, Harry R., S/Sgt, Tail Gunner, POW, 21-Jun-44
Ward, Milton K., 1Lt, Bombardier, KIA, 18-Mar-44
Ward, Raymond A., T/Sgt, Radio Operator, INT, 20-Jun-44
Wardell, John A., 2Lt, Copilot, POW, 12-Sep-44
Wargo, Michael A., Lt, Bombardier, KIA, 11-Apr-44
Warner, Charles W., 2Lt, Pilot, KIA, 14-Apr-45
Wasserstein, Hyman, 2Lt, Navigator, KIA, 04-Oct-43
Waters, Joseph F., 2Lt, Navigator, POW, 07-Oct-44
Watkins junr, Howard O., Capt., Pilot, KIA, 02-Dec-44
Watson, Harry Q., T/Sgt, Radio Operator, KIA, 18-Nov-43
Waugh, Colby A., 2Lt, Pilot, KIA, 04-Jan-44
Wear, Hugh L., S/Sgt, Top Turret, POW, 21-Jul-44
Weber, Fred J., 2Lt, Navigator, POW, 22-Apr-44
Weber, Roy C., S/Sgt, Radio Operator, INT, 20-Jun-44
Weeks, Harvey H., Sgt, Ball Turret, KIA, 24-Apr-44
Wehunt, John W., S/Sgt, Tail Gunner, KIA, 15-Jun-44
Weiner, Harry D., S/Sgt, Left Waist Gunner, KIA, 04-Oct-43
Weise, Everett H., 2Lt, Copilot, KIA, 18-Sep-44
Weiss, Daniel B., 2Lt, Copilot, KIA, 19-May-44
Weiss, Jones E., FO, Bombardier, KIA, 07-Oct-44
Weitkemper, Richard C., S/Sgt, Left Waist Gunner, POW, 15-Jun-44
Welch, Roy E., S/Sgt, Tail Gunner, KIA, 20-Feb-44
Wells, Elting H., 2Lt, Copilot, POW, 06-Aug-44
Wells, Virgil W., S/Sgt, Right Waist Gunner, KIA, 04-Oct-43
Wemeth, John L., Sgt, Left Waist Gunner, KIA, 11-Dec-43
Wendorf, Jack A., 2Lt, Navigator, KIA, 04-Jan-44
Wenslaff, Richard L., T/Sgt, Radio Operator, KIA, 24-Feb-44
Westerfault, Frank M., S/Sgt, Waist Gunner, POW, 20-Dec-43
Westerfield junr, Henry B., 2Lt, Bombardier, POW, 13-Nov-43
Whalen, James M., FO, Copilot, KIA, 11-Sep-44
Wheeler, Bernard J., 2Lt, Navigator, KIA, 02-Feb-44
Wheeler, Mervin, S/Sgt, Ball Turret, KIA, 18-Mar-44
White, Edmund J., FO, Pilot, RTD, 11-Sep-44
White, Edward J., 1Lt, Bombardier, KIA, 08-Apr-44
White, James G., 1Lt, Bombardier, INT, 18-Mar-44
White junr, Harry A., 1Lt, Pilot, RTD, 15-Jun-44
White, Ralph L., 1Lt, Navigator, INT, 11-Jul-44
White, Robert K., 2Lt, Pilot, POW, 24-Feb-44
Whitlock, George E., S/Sgt, Tail Gunner, POW, 07-Jul-44
Whitnah, Joseph C., 2Lt, Bombardier, KIA, 08-Oct-43
Whitt, Clyde G., S/Sgt, Right Waist Gunner, KIA, 23-Jun-44
Whittmore, Warren T., 1Lt, Pilot, POW, 23-Jun-44
Wieland, Joe L., 2Lt, Navigator, KIA, 24-Apr-44
Weir, Richard A., 2Lt, Copilot, POW, 29-Apr-44
Wilcox, Delmar R., 2Lt, Bombardier, KIA, 02-Feb-44
Wilcox, Robert W., Sgt, Bombardier, POW, 29-Apr-44
Wilde, Allison H., 2Lt, Copilot, KIA, 09-Apr-44
Wilkinson, H. C., T/Sgt, Radio Operator, KIA, 13-Jul-44
Willemin junr, William W., 2Lt, Bombardier, INT, 11-Jul-44
Willhite, Max R., T/Sgt, Radio Operator, KIA, 08-Oct-43
Williams junr, Arthur L., S/Sgt, Right Waist Gunner, POW, 04-Jan-44
Williams junr, Charles A., 2Lt, Navigator, KIA, 15-Mar-44
Williams, Charles I., Sgt, Tail Gunner, POW, 02-Dec-44
Williams junr, James L., S/Sgt, Top Turret, KIA, 02-Dec-44
Williams, Robert V., T/Sgt, Radio Operator, POW, 24-Feb-44
Willig, Norman K., S/Sgt, Tail Gunner, KIA, 18-Mar-44
Willingham, Nelson H., 2Lt, Copilot, INT, 18-Mar-44
Willis, Vincent C., 2Lt, Copilot, INT, 11-Jul-44
Wilson, Delmar R., 2Lt, Bombardier, KIA, 02-Feb-44
Wilson, Fonzy M., S/Sgt, Radio Operator, KIA, 29-Apr-44
Wilson, James C., S/Sgt, Waist Gunner, KIA, 04-Oct-43
Wilson, Leo, S/Sgt, Left Waist Gunner, POW, 06-Mar-44
Wilson, William E., 2Lt, Copilot, KIA, 15-Mar-44
Wimer, French R., 2Lt, Navigator, KIA, 09-Sep-44
Winans, George L., 2Lt, Copilot, INT, 20-Jun-44

Wind, Frank A., S/Sgt, Right Waist Gunner, KIA, 13-Nov-43
Winkley, Robert D., 2Lt, Copilot, KIA, 11-Dec-43
Winzenburg, George T., 2Lt, Navigator, KIA, 05-Nov-43
Wishbow, Gabriel E., 2Lt, Bombardier, KIA, 15-Mar-44
Wisley, R.D., S/Sgt, Aerial Gunner, KIA, 06-Mar-44
Wohlstrom junr, Theodore C., T/Sgt, Radio Operator, KIA, 18/03/44
Wolfer, Anthony J., S/Sgt, Top Turret, KIA, 18-Mar-44
Woller, Christian S., S/Sgt, Tail Gunner, KIA, 04-Oct-43
Womer, William S., S/Sgt, Toggler, KIA, 29-Apr-44
Woodard, Donald G., 2Lt, Bombardier, POW, 07-Jul-44
Woods, Don R., 2Lt, Pilot, KIA, 08-Sep-44
Wooten, Warren J., T/Sgt, Top Turret, KIA, 03-Mar-44
Worcester, Charles E., T/Sgt, Toggler, KIA, 02-Dec-44
Worker, Lewis R., 2Lt, Copilot, POW, 13-Dec-43
Wrek, Bailey R., T/Sgt, Radio Operator, KIA, 18-Mar-44
Wright, Anthony, T/Sgt, Top Turret, POW, 18-Apr-44
Wright, Garland, T/Sgt, Radio Operator, KIA, 09-Sep-44
Wright, James K., S/Sgt, Radio Operator, INT, 20-Jun-44
Wright, Richard S., S/Sgt, Tail Gunner, POW, 13-Nov-43
Wunderlin, Carl F., 2Lt, Copilot, KIA, 07-Jul-44
Wyatt, Bert W., 2Lt, Pilot, KIA, 29-Apr-44
Wyatt, Raymond L., 2Lt, Navigator, KIA, 13-Nov-43
Yarbrough, William L., S/Sgt, Toggler, KIA, 11-Apr-44
Yarbrough junr, William L., 2Lt, Bombardier, KIA, 26-Nov-43
Yeates, Clyde K., S/Sgt, Radio Operator, POW, 08-Sep-44
Yensho, Edward, Pvt, Air Transportation Tech., KIA, 18-Sep-44
Yocauvone, John R., 2Lt, Bombardier, POW, 29-May-44
York, Roy D., T/Sgt, Top Turret, KIA, 08-Apr-44
Yorra, Marshall S., S/Sgt, Ball Turret, KIA, 13-Dec-43
Yost, Douglas A., Sgt, Top Turret, KIA, 15-Mar-45
Yost, Kenneth E., S/Sgt, Left Waist Gunner, INT, 18-Mar-44
Young, Archie B., Sgt, Left Waist Gunner, POW, 29-Apr-44
Young, Edward , 2Lt, Bombardier, POW, 07-Jul-44
Young, Francis E., T/Sgt, Top Turret, INT, 20-Jun-44
Young junr, Robert L., 2Lt, Navigator, KIA, 29-Apr-44
Zanini, Olympic C., 2Lt, Copilot, KIA, 19-May-44
Zeanah, Tommie, S/Sgt, Ball Turret, INT, 04-Jan-44
Zeigler, Richard H., 2Lt, Copilot, KIA, 09-Feb-45
Zeman, Milan R., FO, Copilot, KIA, 29-Apr-44
Zerangue, Felix A., S/Sgt, Right Waist Gunner, KIA, 24-Feb-44
Ziegenhardt, Donald E., 2Lt, Copilot, POW, 21-Jul-44
Ziehm, Ralph W., S/Sgt, Tail Gunner, RTD, 11-Sep-44
Zielke, Wallace P., Sgt, Left Waist Gunner, RTD, 15-Mar-45
Zimmerman, Seymour, S/Sgt, Radio Operator, KIA, 21-Feb-44
Zimpleman, John R., T/Sgt, Radio Operator, KIA, 08-Apr-44
Zschiesche, Charles E., T/Sgt, Nose Turret, KIA, 08-Oct-44
Zubay, Steve M., S/Sgt, Ball Turret, KIA, 04-Jan-44
Zybort, Stanley C., Sgt, Top Turret, POW, 06-Aug-44

KEY:	
1Lt	First Lieutenant
2Lt	Second Lieutenant
Cpl	Corporal
EVD	Escapee
FO	Flying Officer
INT	Interned in a neutral country
KIA	Killed in action
KILD	Killed in the line of duty
Mickey	Radar operator
Pfc	Private First Class
Pvt	Private
RTD	Returned to depot
S/Sgt	Staff sergeant
T/Sgt	Technical sergeant
Toggler	Bombardier
WIA	Wounded in action

After VE Day

By Dick Mason

The ending of the Second World War was a time of change and to some extent, upheaval. VE Day for us was something of an anti-climax. Most servicemen were still away, some prisoners of war, some awaiting demob, and a few staying on. Many of our prisoners still remained including the Italians, who worked on local farms, a few Germans and the odd Austrian. It seemed to me that the Austrians were even more Nazi than the Nazis – SS material to a man. I heard a story of one who was allowed to plant crocuses in a lawn during his last few days as our guest. These duly emerged in his chosen pattern, spelling HEIL HITLER, by which time our gardener was safely back home!

By contrast the Italians ('Eyeties' we called them) were real gentlemen, civilised and in no way warlike and they became our very good friends. The ones we knew were accommodated unguarded in old cottages where, so far as I know, they did their own cooking and housekeeping whilst having a reasonably successful time with the local ladies. I soon learned Italian for 'do you have a sister', as well as a rather more direct-approach version of it.

'Our' Italians loved to sing; I can remember one song word for word including the tune, to this day. It was about sugar beet, but because it might have some rude bits I shall not repeat it here. I say this because I once recited it to a charming Italian lady who gave the opinion that the accent was Southern Italy, but blushed quite prettily whilst being distinctly reluctant to provide a literal translation. Bong again! Tact and I don't mix very well, which can be considered an unfilled gap in my education to this day.

The Eyeties did however, contribute to our learning process, whilst also playing their part in widening our horizons, and influencing our perception of mankind in general. What a crying shame that Mussolini felt the need to turn these kind, civilised and good-natured people into fierce worriers and no wonder he failed. They were not cowards, just too nice to be turned into cold-blooded killers. As I have gone through life I have realised that these people were not unique in this, more likely representative of thousands of people worldwide who were sent to the killing fields against their will and contrary to their instincts.

This was a time of upheaval and change, even in our rather restricted world, everything and everyone having changed in various ways. Some evacuees from the big cities had returned, others settled locally; servicemen began returning to their roots as very different people from those they had been pre-war and with a very different outlook on life. Marriage had taken people away, the exodus would accelerate as GI brides in their thousands embarked on a new life of sometimes wedded bliss, sometimes bitter disappointment.

Having the opposite effect on the local population in terms of headcount, were the settlers from distant places who married local people and made their homes here, or for other reasons decided to move in, bringing with them their own culture and habits. All this is obvious in retrospect, but the impact on me did not really begin to register until I started work and became closely acquainted with some of them.

And so it was that the war years and its immediate aftermath helped to drag people away from a previously almost feudal environment and into a much broader and more enlightened take on life.

'Jive Bomber'. The crew for this aircraft were: Walter F. Lowry, Albert I. Victor, James J. Hynes, Wendell G. Replogle, James V. Clarke, Claire A. Cashman, Lynn B. Farlow, Joseph A. Kenney, Paul E. Delaney, Kenneth L. Isbell. This plane flew 11 sorties and then was sadly lost with none of the crew surviving, during a mission to bomb Febvin Palfart (Mission No. 57).

'Sally'. This aircraft flew 16 sorties and then crash landed at Horsham St Faith when returning from a poorly executed mission to bomb an armament factory at Magdeburg south-west of Berlin.

PART II: LONGHAM

Chapter 7

Views of Longham

Longham is situated 2 miles north of Wendling and 5 miles north-west of Dereham. It was once a typical thriving village with a wheelwright, thatcher, two public houses and a village store that would supply everything its inhabitants could possibly require. Sadly Longham is still a typical Norfolk village; its school has been closed, the chapel converted into a house and many of the old trades gone as they are no longer required in these modern times. Looking on the brighter side, however, Longham has managed to hang on to its football team, Post Office and the White Horse public house (although this establishment now gets much of its trade from customers who travel into the village for meals and special events).

There follows a collection of photographs which reveal the village and its environs; despite the many changes that have taken place over the years, it is still a beautiful place to live.

Longham village sign.

Aerial view of the White Horse public house taken in 1965.

The White Horse in Longham, c.1950.

Old painting of the White Horse, c.1914.

Wendling Road, 2002.

Chapel Road, Longham, 2002.

Kenny Page taking a bucket of freshly laid eggs to the Post Office, c.1940. At this time the Post Office Stores in Longham was a thriving business with local girls working in the shop. Kenny was employed to do the deliveries and maintain the shop's gardens, which were on the opposite side of the road.

Mrs Abbey with Reenie Sadler, Joan Purple and Phyllis Abbey – three of the girls who worked in the shop, c.1944.

Mr Abbey behind the Post Office, c.1950.

Longham Post Office, c.1950.

Longham Post Office, c.1985.

Chapter 8

Longham Church

St Andrew's Church, Longham.

St Andrew's Church

At the time of the Domesday Book, Hermerus de Farrariis seized the lands of a freeman in 'Lauuingham', Hermerus being the ancestor of the Lords Bardoiph. Only part of Longham is mentioned in the Domesday Book as the rest was held by the King under the manor of Mileham. The first rector was John de Castleacre in 1308 and the Registers date from 1558.

The old manor-house on the road to Wendling was surrounded by a moat, which is still there, and part of it was turned into two cottages. It was an old Tudor mansion pulled down by Thomas William Coke, First Earl of Leicester (1754–1842), who pulled down so many mansions on his estates. The present house called the Hall near the church was built by him c.1840 and is a plain rather unedifying building of white brick, built in true Holkham fashion.

It is recorded that several Celts were unearthed at Longham not far from the Devil's Dyke which lay to the north-west of the church.

The church is approached from the south-east across part of the park, now under cultivation, belonging to the Hall. Starting at the Perpendicular south porch, we will consider the outside of the church, progressing in an easterly direction, before we venture inside.

There are three Perpendicular windows in the south side of the nave. These have embattled transomes in their centre lights and they have the remains of head stops. At the eastern end in the angle of the last buttress can be seen the outside wall of the turret stair leading to the rood-loft. The nave, which was restored and re-roofed in 1898 for £430 raised by subscriptions – is covered with Broseley tiles. A cross on the east end dated 1626 in the brickwork was found to be unsound in 1898. The present cross was placed there in 1965.

The chancel was entirely rebuilt in 1867 by the Earl of Leicester's family. It has a pantile roof and a floriated cross on the east end. On the south side there are two Perpendicular windows which were reset in their present position. The east window is modern in the Perpendicular style. The vestry is situated on the north side with a rather odd buttress on its western end.

In the north side of the nave there are two Perpendicular windows similar to those on the south side and a Perpendicular north door.

The tower has two broad angle buttresses on its eastern corners and two diagonal buttresses on its western corners. This gives it a very powerful squat appearance when seen from the east. The west window is Perpendicular with three lights. It is recorded that the top stage of the tower was taken down in 1788 for the sum of £55 and that the upper stage was added in the nineteenth century by J.S. Hastings (whose memorial is in the chancel). It is thought that the tower used to be higher. There were six bells during the reign of Edward VI (mid-1500s) and a faculty was obtained to sell a badly split bell weighing 7cwt in 1757. Another bell was sold in 1788 and this weighed 14cwt and fetched about £25. Later yet another badly cracked bell inscribed *Thomas Draper me fecit 1583* was sold and replaced by a new one costing £70. This one was cast by John Warner & Sons, London, and is inscribed *Sancti Petri cum voco ad templum venite* AD1888.

Inside the Church

The nave has hammer beams with arch braces. The church was reseated for 100 people when it was re-roofed in 1878. The pulpit of carved oak was erected to the memory of John Sutton Hastings by his daughter. There is a memorial tablet to him on the south wall of the chancel. An interesting stone is set in the very top of the east window on the south side.

This stone must be the drain from an old piscina reset there.

A Perpendicular niche can be seen in the south-east corner of the nave by the rood stair turret and entrance to the rood-loft. These were opened up in 1898. Two interesting stone brackets can be seen in the east windows on the north and south sides of the nave. It is possible that these supported the Bressummer (main beam) of the rood-loft. If this was the case, then the loft would have cut right across the top of the screen. In fact it is believed that the screen was reset here from another church during the 1867 restorations.

The organ was dedicated on 21 December 1919 as a Thanks Offering for Peace after the First World War and the electric blower was dedicated in 1958. The altar rails in the Memorial Chapel in the south-east corner of the nave came from St Peter's Church in Great Yarmouth and the crossed keys of St Peter can be seen on the shields.

The chancel is entirely modern, having been rebuilt in 1867. It 'weeps' to the south, but experts have suggested that this was due more to careless building than to any particular reference to the position of Christ's head on the cross. It has the two reset Perpendicular windows in the south side and a nice seventeenth-century altar table. The wording on the memorial to John Sutton Hastings is also worthy of noting on the south wall.

The plate consists of an inscribed silver chalice dated 1567 and an ancient paten converted into a lid for the chalice. More recently, in the nineteenth century, a plated flagon and paten were obtained.

The screen is late-fifteenth century Perpendicular and was restored in the 1970s by Mr Royal who removed a lot of dark brown paint. Some of the original colouring can still be seen in the lower panels.

The church tower.

The tower arch.

Inside the church.

The church font is Perpendicular with a lead-lined octagonal bowl.

The rood stair, which leads to the rood-loft, a type of balcony.

This bracket once supported the rood-loft.

Chapter 9

People of Longham

No matter where a place may be, how illustrious its history or beautiful its surroundings, at the heart of a community is always its people. This chapter contains a small selection of photographs of people of all ages, at work, play and worship, in order to bring into focus the everyday aspects of the life of the village and to celebrate the people who live here – both past and present.

Left: *Group of local children beside the clay pit in Longham. The picture includes: Joan Purple, Irene Sadler, Pansy Watts, Miss Cross, Eleanor Kemp, Reenie Sadler, Peter English and Sonny Webster.*

Below: *Longham village hall committee, c.1941. Left to right, back row: Bertie Pooley, Bob Hammond, Mr Abbey, Mr Simms, Reverent Toll, Walter Coe, George Webster; front row: Mrs Coe, Quinnie Harwood, Mrs Toll, Mrs Abbey, Mrs Hammond.*

Sport

Longham cricket team, 1926. Included in the photograph are: *Dot Killing-Gray, George Webster, Ernie Pooley, Robert Killing-Gray, Bertie Pooley, Dodger Webster and Jack Webster.*

Above: *Longham cricket team, c.1916.*

Right: *Front cover of the 1926 cricket season programme.*

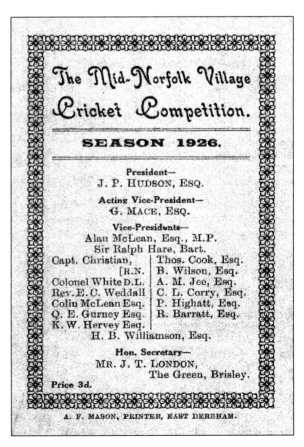

The Mid-Norfolk Village
Cricket Competition.

SEASON 1926.

President—
J. P. HUDSON, ESQ.

Acting Vice-President—
G. MACE, ESQ.

Vice-Presidents—
Alan McLean, Esq., M.P.
Sir Ralph Hare, Bart.

Capt. Christian,	Thos. Cook, Esq.
[R.N.	B. Wilson, Esq.
Colonel White D.L.	A. M. Jee, Esq.
Rev. E. C. Weddall	C. L. Corry, Esq.
Colin McLean Esq.	P. Highatt, Esq.
Q. E. Gurney Esq.	R. Barratt, Esq.
K. W. Hervey Esq.	

H. B. Williamson, Esq.

Hon. Secretary—
MR. J. T. LONDON,
The Green, Brisley.

Price 3d.

A. F. MASON, PRINTER, EAST DEREHAM.

The Pooley Family

Ernie Pooley on a Ford Major, 1945.

John and Rosa Pooley standing at the gates of their home, Rose Cottage, which stands behind the White Horse public house, c.1920.

Right: *Irene Pooley's ID card, first stamped in 1945. She is the daughter-in-law of John and Rosa Pooley.*

Below: *The inside of Irene Pooley's ID card.*

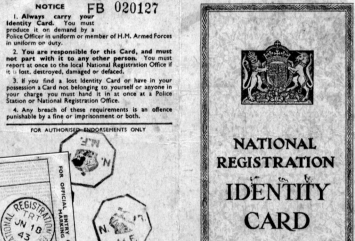

This hand-crafted book-end was made and given to Ralph Pooley by one of the Polish prisoners of war who worked in the area, 1944/45.

Sunday School

Photograph of the Sunday school group taken near the chapel. The Sunday school was held in the chapel and was frequently attended by children from the Abbey, Sadler, Everett, Watts, Purple and Page families.

Sunday school inside the chapel.

Sunday school inside the chapel.

PART III: BEESTON

Chapter 10

Beeston: A Thriving Community

The heart of Beeston (or Beeston next to Mileham as it was once known) was originally clustered around the church but it is now a scattered village with its heart nearly a mile east of the original village. Beeston has been a thriving village with many small businesses recorded throughout its history; in the nineteenth century such tradesmen included a shoemaker, a baker, a blacksmith and a wheelwright. There were also four public houses: The Bell Inn, The Holkham Arms, The Ploughshare and one more unnamed establishment listed in 1836 as a 'beer house & blacksmith' and then later as a 'beer house & School'.

The Second World War brought many changes to the area as a large part of the village was taken over by the American Air Force as they were stationed at neighbouring Wendling Airbase. The Americans built many buildings in and around the village to house the airmen as well as the many different back-up units crucial for the smooth operation of the base. After the war some of these buildings were used to house a number of local families.

Beeston is still a thriving village and one of the few local villages still to have its own school, Post Office and public house. Along with these there has been an influx of larger employers moving into the village during the latter part of the twentieth century to occupy the buildings left by the Americans.

The filming of 'Allo 'Allo! at Beeston Church

This area has been used for a number of different television programmes over the years. A relatively recent example of this is when the Church of St Mary the Virgin at Beeston was used to film a couple of episodes of the BBC comedy series *'Allo 'Allo!*, which was transmitted between 1982 and 1992. Its isolated location made Beeston church ideal for filming such a programme. This was a rather exciting occasion for the village and a number of locals came along to the church to meet the actors and watch the filming.

Beeston Post Office, c.1900.

Village Views

Church Farm House, c.1920.

Beeston Post Office and store, c.1960.

Beeston Post Office and store, 2002.

These small cottages once housed the village school.

The Old Bakery. The lean-to extension beside the road once housed the baker's oven.

The filming of 'Allo 'Allo at Beeston Church

Carmen Silvera (Edith Artois) and Gorden Kaye (René Artois) standing in the doorway of Beeston church. The cast worked in and around the village for one week during June 1989.

Guy Siner as Lieutenant Hubert Gruber, June 1989.

The filming of 'Allo 'Allo at Beeston Church

Clockwise, starting top left:

Roger Kitter (who played Italian officer Captain Bertorelli) with one of the local children (Ben Walthew) who gathered to meet the stars.

Kim Hartman, who played Private Helga Geerhart, signing her autograph.

Derek Royle (who played Leclerc's twin brother), Francesca Conshaw (Maria Recamier) and Rose Hill (Edith's mother Fanny 'Fifi' Lafanne) in the bed. This picture was taken in the church.

Richard Marner as Colonel Von Strohm.

Beeston Hunt

The riders from the West Norfolk Hunt gather outside The Ploughshare public house, c.1982.

The hounds depart for a day of hunting at Beeston and the surrounding area, c.1982.

Chapter 11

Beeston Church and the Music of Worship

A sketch of the church by Mr R.J. Ladbrooke, 1820.

The Church of St Mary the Virgin
Taken from 'Church Tours' by
Richard Butler-Stoney OBE (1992)

This church has retained its complete set of Decorated period windows with a rich variety of designs in flowing tracery. This gives it unsurpassed beauty which is a thrill to find on such a remote site. The church at Great Walsingham, built in 1320, has some similar features but it is without its entire chancel. It seems likely that the same master builder and craftsmen built Beeston church soon afterwards.

The original Decorated period church had clerestory windows (an upper row of windows that appear above the level of the aisle roofs) of quatrefoils within circles. Early in the Perpendicular period, probably 1410, the clerestory walls were raised and eight tall windows replaced the quatrefoils. These windows were the gift of Beeston's Guild of the Virgin Mary.

The tower was also raised by the addition of an extra belfry stage and so we can see a Decorated belfry topped by a Perpendicular belfry, but sadly only one modest bell hangs inside. It seems the other bells were sold to buy a barrel organ and gallery in 1826. The proportions of this church are most elegant and the extra height to the tower would have been in keeping with the taller nave.

The spire was added in 1873 to replace a small spire on a cupola which had been struck by lightning.

The east windows of both aisles have double reticulated tracery. All the windows are particularly tall and have very high pointed arches. Inside we find tall slender piers of clustered columns, which further contribute to the uplifting experience.

The roof is a single hammer beam design with long wall posts decorated by carvings, and showing the appearance of really ancient English oak. The carved figures stand on a pedestal and have a canopy over them, but have been thoroughly defaced. This suggests that they were saints, but sadly they cannot now be identified. The window above the chancel arch must have been added to throw light on these figures. On the hammer beams there is a further row of angels holding shields.

The north aisle roof also has angels holding shields and saints on the wall posts but here the saints are seated and have been even more severely disfigured. The fine medieval oak carpentry includes carvings where the beams cross. On some, traces of their original colouring can still been seen. The external covering was replaced by stainless steel in 1987 following a series of attempts to steal the lead.

Remains of a fifteenth-century sacristy (a room where the vestments and sacred vessels were kept and where the celebrant prepared for the service) can be seen on the south side of the chancel in the form of a row of stone corbels which supported a lean-to roof. The blocked sacristy door shows on the inside next to the priest's door.

When Stephen Barnwell came from Ireland in 1580 to become the new lord of the manor a row ensued, because Beeston's ancient custom of the ploughshare was threatened. As a result a rhyming notice was painted above the door in the porch explaining the custom and ending with the words 'Lord Barnwell see thou keep it.' It was duly kept.

Consecration crosses can be seen on either side of the tower arch. These existed from the time when the Bishop of Norwich first consecrated the building, c.1325.

The font is set in an imposing position with the benches specially arranged to allow space around it. The carved conical font cover, except for the curious ball at the top, dates from the medieval period.

Beeston church with the steeple intact. The steeple was struck by lightning in 1872 and burnt down.

View from the church tower looking towards Beeston village in the distance.

The angel in the roof of the north aisle.

Left: *Inside Beeston church. The stage is being constructed for the concerts held in the church in 1990.*

Below, left: *Inside the church in 1989.*

Below: *Coffin bearer.*

Two views of the church font.

The benches are a complete set dating from the fifteenth century, which have elaborate traceried backs. The quatrefoil within a circle design echoes that of the early clerestory windows. The armrests have been robbed of their wood carvings but the poppy heads survive.

The floor has kept its original level throughout. This is one of few churches that has kept the chancel floor at its original level. Handmade bricks pave the church and contribute to the timeless feel of the interior. A few much-worn glazed Bawsey tiles have been reset around the base of the font. They would have been part of the original floor of this church.

The rood-screen dates from the fifteenth century but sadly it has been badly mutilated and its rood-loft is missing. The painted panels have been defaced with vicious thoroughness, but some saints may be recognised by their symbols. From north to south they are: St Cecilia with a garland of roses; St Agnes with a lamb; St Etheldreda, Abbess with a crosier; St Clement of Rome with an anchor; a bishop, possibly St Thomas of Canterbury; St Leonard with a chain. Above these are beautifully carved animals – look for a monkey, a deer, a unicorn, a boar mauling a man, a fox catching a bird, an eagle and St George slaying a dragon.

The arms of John Fitzalan, Earl of Arundel who married Lady Maltravers represent the patron on the screen. He died in 1434. Their heads feature on the outer doorway of the porch. Also on the screen will be found the ploughshare with 'B' and a tun or barrel, making a pun on the word Beeston.

The parclose screens in both aisles survive almost in their entirety. The screen in the south aisle is the earlier one and was kept by the Guild of St John the Baptist. The north aisle chapel with its lavish Perpendicular tracery was kept by the Guild of the Virgin Mary, and the chancel was kept by the Guild of the Holy Trinity.

The vestry was formed in 1813 in the south aisle where it extends alongside the tower. There is a fireplace there. A similar room exists in the north aisle. It is unusual to have the aisles surrounding the tower, but they were all built at the same time.

A Latin wall plaque with fine calligraphy near the door tells how John Forby refurbished the chancel in 1598. He was rector from 1595 to 1614 and did much to restore the church after the destruction of images in 1548. The seats which he provided lasted until the nineteenth century.

The wall painting above the chancel arch is a frame for the royal arms of James I which was painted by William Roose in John Forby's time. The royal arms near the south door are Hanoverian. Further wall painting was done on the east wall with shields of Cambridge colleges; most of these have been lost, but enough remains to imagine the setting. John Forby was a member of Caius College.

The pulpit was installed in 1592. It had the shape of a wineglass, but then it was greatly restored in the seventeenth century, when it gained the panelling with segmented arches and long pilasters. An iron fixing for its sounding board may be seen in the wall behind.

The organ was made by a blacksmith in West Tofis, near Thetford, who only made four organs, of which this is the last to remain in use. Sycamore wood was used for the organ's interior.

Floor slabs commemorate the Barnwell family of Mileham Hall who were lords of the manor here from the sixteenth to nineteenth centuries. The Revd William Barnwell was a rector here and was buried on the same day as his wife. There are also five small oval slabs to the memory of the infant children of the Revd John Nelson.

A stone cross beside the church path reminds us of Beeston's famous boxer, Jem Mace, who was born near The Ploughshare Inn in 1831 and had a long and distinguished career in professional bareknuckle boxing which he transformed into a more legitimate sport. He died in Liverpool in 1910.

New altar curtains and carpets purchased in 1991.

Above, left and right: *The rood-screen.*

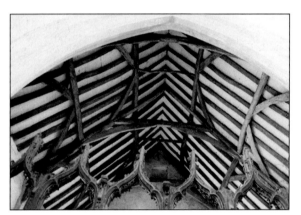

Two views of the church ceiling.

Left: *Church organ. Arthur Dennis Howard was the organist from the early 1970s until the mid-1980s. He was also headmaster at Mileham School.*

Mr and Mrs Dawson, along with Mrs Skipper, decorating Beeston Methodist chapel in Chapel Lane, c.1959.

Beeston church as it stands in 2005.

Music in a Country Church

On 25 May 1990 the Norfolk Churches Trust organised two concerts in Beeston church with Dame Kiri Te Kanawa and the Russian pianist Andrei Gavrilov. The events were attended by a number of local people as well as a very special guest, Prince Charles.

Andrei Gavrilov, Russian pianist.

Dame Kiri Te Kanawa.

Glynis Clampitt, Maddy Shakespeare and Linda Winterbone.

Local people, including Cynthia Potter, Maddy Shakespeare, Vicki Middleton and Peter and Wendy Carter, gathering ready to enter the church.

Above: *Mr and Mrs Carter, Miss Glynis Clampitt and Mr and Mrs Shakespeare.*

Right: *Mr and Mrs Sutton with Mr and Mrs Duffield.*

Mrs Wendy Carter, churchwarden.

Prince Charles was one of the many guests at the church.

Aston Martin belonging to Prince Charles.

✥

Chapter 12

People of Beeston

There follows a collection of photographs of people who live, or have lived, in the village of Beeston. It is the contribution made by them and their friends and families to village life that make Beeston such a special place to be.

The Bolton Family

Edward Gowing Bolton married Ellen May Starling of Great Fransham on 3 July 1893 at Beeston church. They were then graced with the following children: Edward James (1893), Frederick (1895), Grace Margaret (1898), Henry (1902). Ellen died in 1903.

Edward married Kate Margaret Starling of Runcton Holme on 17 December 1903 at Beeston church. The family grew with the birth of Edith Farrow (1904), Violet Ann (1906), Robert Herbert (1909), Frank Starling 'Jack' (1911), Doris Gertrude (1912), Winifred May (1914), Helen Mary (1917). Edward senr died in 1948, followed by Kate in 1952.

Bolton children, c.1910.

The Bolton family.

The Bolton Family

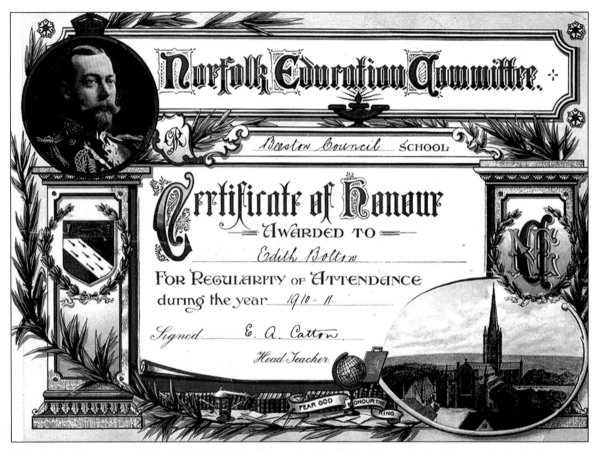

Certificate of honour presented to Edith Bolton for regularity of attendance during the years 1910–11.

Above: *School photograph of Edith Farrow Bolton, c.1910.*

Right: *Garcia and Fred Bolton, c.1918.*

The Hammonds

This wedding photograph was taken by a photographer from the American airbase at a wedding between a member of the Hammond family (Florence Edge) and an American airman (Dale Hanna), September 1944.

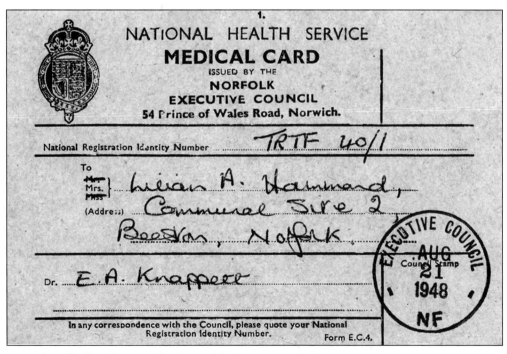

A 1948 medical card. Note the GP at this time was Dr E.A. Knappett.

The Hammonds

Above: *Joy Hammond's baptism certificate, 1934.*

Left: *Joy Hammond aged 12.*

The Hammonds

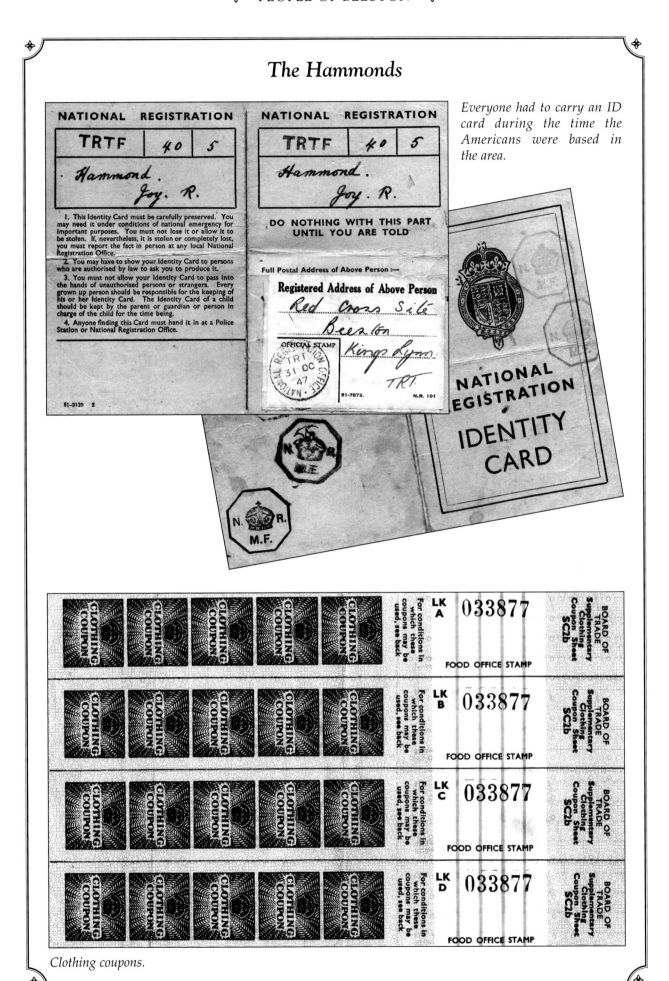

Everyone had to carry an ID card during the time the Americans were based in the area.

Clothing coupons.

Dick Hammond and his Cars

Dick with his Willys Overland 'Four' Tourer, 1972.

Dick Hammond with his early Renault, c.1972.

Dick Hammond and his Cars

Dick Hammond's scrapyard, c.1975.

Dick Hammond's Morris Cowley, 1972.

George Dye and Dick Hammond.

Dick Hammond and his Cars

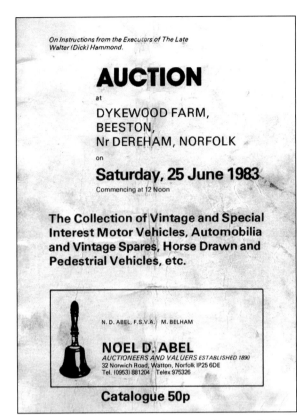

On Instructions from the Executors of The Late
Walter (Dick) Hammond.

AUCTION
at

DYKEWOOD FARM,
BEESTON,
Nr DEREHAM, NORFOLK

on

Saturday, 25 June 1983
Commencing at 12 Noon

The Collection of Vintage and Special Interest Motor Vehicles, Automobilia and Vintage Spares, Horse Drawn and Pedestrial Vehicles, etc.

N. D. ABEL, F.S.V.A.   M. BELHAM

NOEL D. ABEL
AUCTIONEERS AND VALUERS ESTABLISHED 1890
32 Norwich Road, Watton, Norfolk IP25 6DE
Tel. (0953) 881204   Telex 975326

Catalogue 50p

Auction at Dykewood Farm

On Saturday 25 June an auction was held at Dykewood Farm, Beeston, on the instructions of the executors of the will of the late Walter (Dick) Hammond. It was described as an auction of a collection of vintage and special interest motor vehicles, automobilia and vintage spares, plus horse-drawn and pedestrian vehicles. Included in this auction were:

A four wheel open 'Landau type' carriage.

A wagon type market stall with serving flap and shelved and fitted interior on spoked solid rubber wheels, made by The City and Suburban Carriage Co.

A pedestrian fire tender on spoked wheels by Merryweather & Sons, London.

A pedestrian four-wheel hearse.

A 1931 Jowett 'Black Princess' 7h.p. four-door saloon, reg. ED6511.

A 1934 Triumph 'Gloria' four-door saloon with aluminium coachwork, reg. ATV 414.

A 1934 Lanchester drop-head coupe. Its coachwork was done by Martin Walter Ltd of Folkestone, reg. UJ 3329.

A 1937 Austin 'Ruby' two-door saloon, reg. DGY 603.

A 1932 Morris 'Isis' four-door saloon, reg. FH 7927.

A 1936 Austin Seven 'Opel' two seater, reg. BRL 899.

A 1934 Mercedes Benz drop-head two-door coupe, reg. DLY 3.

A 1933 Mercedes Benz drop-head two-door coupe, reg. CZ 7474.

A 1927 Morris 'Cowley' four-seater 'Flat nose' tourer, reg. FH 5144.

On Saturday 25 June 1983 an auction was held at Dykewood Farm to sell a collection of vintage motor vehicles belonging to the late Dick Hammond. Dick died in 1981.

A 1922 Willys Overland 'Four' Tourer (converted to an open truck), reg. BW 5884.

A 1933 Morris 'Ten' fixed-head coupe, reg. CG 2808.

A 1931 Rover four-door saloon, reg. NG 808.

An early 1930s French 'Trend car' coach built box type car trailer.

A rare 1934 aluminium bodied four-door streamline saloon with rear engine built by Crossley Burney of Manchester, reg. AMB 487

A 1938 Austin six 'Norfolk' 18h.p. saloon, reg CNG 574.

A 1932 Ford model 'Y' four door 8h.p. saloon, reg RT 9194.

A 1938 Morris 'Twelve' four-door saloon, reg DBJ 430.

A 1933 Austin 'Ten' four-door saloon, reg GV 334.

A Ford 'Ten' with fibre glass sports body.

A Fordson Platform Commercial, four cylinder petrol, reg. JE 5351.

Some of the late Dick Hammond's cars, c.1970.

The Cross Family

Ray, Russell and Ralph Cross working hard.

Joan and Julie Gray. Julie later married Ralph Cross.

The Cross family all dressed up, c.1958.

The Cross Family

Malcolm and Shirley Cross, c.1967.

Malcolm and Shirley Cross with their grandmother Violet Gray, c.1965.

Mrs Ethel (Dinah) Cross.

A young Ralph Cross, c.1950.

Ralph Cross with his little brother Richard, c.1945.

The Cross family home in Drury Square.

The Cross Family

Ray and Russell Cross, c.1943.

Richard Cross, c.1950.

Ruby Hudson, Joan Cross, Roy Cross and Jean Cross.

The Cross Family

Ralph and Julie Cross on their wedding day, 1 August 1958.

Ralph and Julie Cross, Terry Gray and Ethel (Dinah) Cross, 1 August 1958.

The Walthew Family

The Walthew children, c.1949. Left to right, back row: Frank junr (born 27-8-38), Laurance (born 15-2-40); front row: Elizabeth (born 7-9-42) and Rodney (born 27-9-44).

Frank and Marion Walthew with their family on their wedding day. Frank met Marion when Frank's sister brought Marion to visit her family home; it was love at first sight. After a long courtship they got married on 31 July 1937.

The Walthew Family

Frank Walthew senr aged 21. Frank was born on 2 July 1912 at Windsor Green, Birmingham. His first job was as a baker and confectioner; he worked 60 hours a week, for which he was was paid ten shillings. When war broke out in September 1939 Frank was put in charge of a fire-fighting unit. After the war Frank and his family moved to Leicester where they stayed for two years until Frank was able to buy his own 37½ acre farm in Beeston. On this farm he had a number of large greenhouses from which he ran a greengrocer's round, going to local RAF camps and villages. He later had a shop at the RAF base at Sculthorpe. All this sadly came to an end in January 1975 when severe gales destroyed all but two of Frank's greenhouses and he had to sell most of his land.

Marion Walthew aged 21 (born 24-7-16).

Community Life

Men working at the early gravel pit.

'Skipper', a local man, who delivered bread and groceries.

Community Life

Above: *Beeston WI trip to Wroxham, 1965. Some of the people in the photograph: Charlie Watson, Jack Hudson, Hilda Watson, Fred Roegel, Mrs Hammond, Mrs Bennett, Sylvia Horne, Joe Mann, Charlie Powley, Pearl Horne, Mr Newell, Mrs Laws, Flo Self, Harry Cooper, Cary Hunter, Mrs J. Claxton, Mrs J. Hudson, Mrs A. Betts, Mr Eagle, Mrs L. Dack, Mr Dawson, Mr Gaze, Mr L. Dack, Charlie Elliot, May Burrell, Molly Claxton, Eva Collings, Mrs Rutherford, George Burrell, C. Collings, Mrs Dawson, Mrs Napier, Mrs Frary, Mr Barker and Keith Carter.*

Left: *The unveiling of the village sign, early 1970s. Mrs Symonds is at the front with Tony Wales.*

Community Life

Beeston's football team, 1948–49.

Mr A.H. Mack, chairman of the Dereham and District Football League, presenting the Dereham and District Cup (Division II) to the captain of Beeston FC, Keith Rallison, at Dereham, May 1966. On the right of the group is the league secretary Mr E.H. Coggles. Beeston only had one defeat in 20 games in the league this season. The team members in this photograph are: Guy Littleproud, Maurice Laws, Ralph Cross, Mike Gardener, Dennis Winterbone, Ivan Feeke, Keith Rallison, Colin Skipper, Maurice Skipper, Micky Meen, Nobby Clarke and Eddie Garner. The Journal, reported on Friday 13 May 1966:

> Beeston clinched the Necton and District League championship on Wednesday week with an 8-1 victory over Jentique and Matamec. From Beeston's first four corners they scored four goals, through C. Skipper, R. Cross, G. Littleproud, and D. Winterbone. Midway through the second half they added four in quick succession, through Rallison, Skipper and left-half Mike Gardener (2). Jentique's goal came in a break-away near the end.

Community Life

May Burrell was known to everybody as Auntie May. She lived in Beeston all her life and worked as the local nurse and midwife, delivering many local babies. Although this kept her very busy, she still found time for meetings at the school and church. Such meetings could bring out a different side to this sweet, polite lady, as if she didn't agree with the way things were being done she could be a force to be reckoned with!

Miss Burrell, now Mrs Kemp, with her horse near Point Farm, c.1950.

Ben Burgess

Aerial view of Ben Burgess's tractor business, c.1977. Mr Ben Burgess purchased the old Second World War American airbase at the Dereham Road site from Eric Matthews & Co. in 1976, the site on the edge of Wendling airfield which was home to the 392nd Bomb Group. The main building was the Airbase Headquarters, which eventually became an Agricultural Engineering Works, previously handling the now historical David Brown Tractors.

When Ben Burgess took over the site it became a John Deere tractor dealership. His business, originally selling Marshall tractors, had been established in Norwich in 1936. He sold his first John Deere model 4010 in 1964. This tractor was 100hp, which was rather large in those days, especially as most tractors were still only 35hp.

The first John Deere tractors sold from Beeston, were on average around 75hp and cost about £5,500 (in 2003 the average tractor is nearer 150hp and costs £45,000 with equipment such as 4wd, air conditioning, suspension and a CD player.

The number of staff employed at the dealership has also changed, 24 people worked at Ben Burgess (Beeston) in 1976. The workshop employed 13 mechanics, along with 11 in the sales and admin. Today the depot employs only 17 people.

One of the longest serving employees who had only just started when Ben Burgess's site was opened remembers how different the working conditions were back in 1976. The first thing that Ben Burgess did was to install central heating. The floors, walls and ceilings were all solid concrete and the roof regularly leaked. The building offered no heat retention and he remembers working in a coat for most of the winter months.

Over the years the buildings have been added to, mostly additional storage and a secondary workshop area. The yard has been tidied up with concrete and shingled machinery display areas, whilst trees and hedges have been planted to encourage wildlife. In 1997 the premises enjoyed a complete refurbishment, with floor, wall and roof insulation, double-glazing and a more efficient heating system. At the same time a large barn-style building was put over the top of the office along with stores to protect the building and increase the working area. This has given the company a much larger showroom, enabling the diversification into lawnmowers and small tools, etc.

The company has the privilege of holding the Royal Warrant for the supply of farm machinery and services to the Sandringham estate.

The retention of the original old building has kept the links with former war veterans and their relatives, who still visit the area. They are delighted that the building has been put to good use, especially as John Deere was originally an American company.

Ben Burgess

This photograph was taken when Ben Burgess officially opened the Beeston branch in 1977.

This plaque is proudly on display in the offices at Ben Burgess & Co.

A reception was held for visiting servicemen in one of the workshops at Ben Burgess & Co., 29 July 1990.

These old airbase buildings are now enclosed in a new extension.

Chapter 13

Beeston School

Beeston School, c.1960.

Beeston Primary School
By Mrs Ani Martin

Beeston Primary School was built in 1879 to accommodate over 100 pupils between the ages of 5 and 13 or 14, although it was never anticipated that they would all be there every day! A large detached house stood within the grounds, which was for the head teacher and his or her family and was still in use until the early 1970s. These days it stands derelict and empty, used only for rough storage.

Pupils had to walk to school, sometimes for a very long distance from outlying farms, often with a return journey for the lunch break. The school kept a logbook, which detailed the events of the day, including details such as 'school closed for measles':

Dec. 15 1881: Thin numbers on Friday, owing to a menagerie visiting the neighbourhood.
Nov. 9 1883: Primary teacher excused lessons on two evenings on account of her mother's illness... Had to severely caution the big girls against their habits of non-punctuality.
July 23 1919: Received notices of revised scale of annual salaries as follows: Ellen Catton (head teacher) £170, Bertha Ward (teacher) £85, Edith Jeffries (teacher) £65.

The punishment book also makes very interesting reading and certainly poor behaviour of any kind was not tolerated:

Feb. 7 1928: Florence Burton aged 14 years, received one stroke of the cane on her hand for flouncing into seat when told to move.
Jan. 18 1940: James Wyett aged 9 years, received 4 strokes of the cane, for spitting milk over a girl and making himself a general nuisance.

Our most famous ex-pupil is the indomitable Keith Skipper, who tells the yarn about his first day at school when, aged five, he was unable to find the toilets and so invented them in the middle of the girls' playground!

Another past pupil was Pearl Bailey (née Dawes), who attended the school from 1912, when she was aged 10. She visited us recently, aged 101, to talk to the children about her memories (see the reports written by Molly, Bethany, Catalina and Fred).

Beeston School, mid-1920s.

Beeston School, 1927–28. Left to right, back row: *Violet Massingham, Sid Hudson, Gilbert Wytt, Clifford Claxton, Tom Knock, Victor Skipper, Sid Burton, Will Webb, Joan Barnard;* third row includes: *Miss A. Pyle, Hilda Pyman, Peggy Sporne, Elsie Wyett, Josephine Mason, Doris Abbs, Enid Downes, Molly Claxton, Audrey Eagle, Violet Burton;* second row: *Sylvia Head, Eileen Wales, Joyce Bolton, Mary Burton, Ethel Wyett, Molly Huggins, Annie Dye, Edna Ward, Mary Galer;* front row: *Gordon Garwood, John Galer, Kenneth Hudson, Harry Wyett, Sam Eagle, ? Callaby, Alec Wales, Bertie Wyett, Harold Burton.*

Beeston School, c.1982. Left to right, back row: *Mrs Squires, Wayne Wall, Gary Middleton, Scott Tilbrook, Michelle ?, Mark Roberts, Clive Parke, Mr P. Fenn;* middle: *Jenny Forbes, David Walthew, Jeanette Bush, Calvin Croll, Andrew Brooks, Matthew Walthew, Sharon Adams, Starr Croll, ?, Hector Croll, Robert Walthew, Jill Roberts;* front row: *William Sorrell, Gavin Beales, Richard Wales, Daniel Winterbone, Adam Gould, Karen Codman, Tania Bush.*

Beeston schoolchildren.

Beeston School, c.1960. Left to right, back row: ?, Colin Skipper, Colin Soames, Terry Wales, Peter Rutterford, Keith White, Michael Wilmot, Ben Payne, Mrs Webdale; third row: Dennis Winterbone, ?, Glenville Holland, Jennifer Brown, Christine Burrows, Maisie Bennett, Katherine Halls, Olive Bennett, Carol Payne, ?, Sheila Lane; second row: Linda Lane, Mary Brown, Norma Richardson, Jane Reeve, Pearl Horne, Joy Wright, Denise Wright, Janet Hall; front row: Kathleen Turner, Brenda Willimot, Daphne Halls, Ricky Cross, Mona Turner, Barbara Gage.

Left: *Pearl Bailey age 10, c.1912.*

Below: *Ex-pupil Pearl Bailey aged 101 visits Beeston Primary School, 16 September 2003.*

Work by Molly Gould, aged eight.

24th September

The visit of Mrs Pearl Bailey

On Tuesday the 16th September 2003, we had a visitor who was a witness from 1912, Mrs. Pearl. Bailey. She told us that she was a 101¼. When she came she wasted no time, before she showed us her card from the Queen.

She told us that she left school at 13. In the classroom for lighting they used oil lamps which were on pulleys. They also had coalfires. On a really cold day the teacher would let the children go up in twos and warm themselves.

Untidy or dirty children were sent home for the whole day, because you weren't not allowed in school.

by Molly Gould

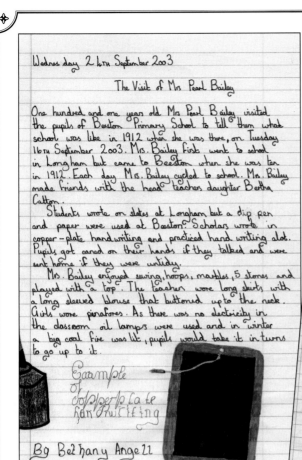

Wednesday 24th September 2003

The Visit of Mrs Pearl Bailey

One hundred and one years old Mrs Pearl Bailey visited the pupils of Beeston Primary School to tell them what school was like in 1912 when she was there, on Tuesday 16th September 2003. Mrs. Bailey first went to school in Longham but came to Beeston when she was ten in 1912. Each day Mrs. Bailey cycled to school. Mrs. Bailey made friends with the head teachers daughter Bertha Cotton.

Students wrote on slates at Longham but a dip pen and paper were used at Beeston. Scholars wrote in copper-plate hand writing and practiced hand writing alot. Pupils got caned on their hands if they talked and were sent home if they were untidy.

Mrs. Bailey enjoyed sewing, hoops, marbles, 5 stones and played with a top. The teacher wore long skirts with a long sleeved blouse that buttoned up to the neck. Girls wore pinafores. As there was no electricity in the classroom oil lamps were used and in winter a big coal fire was lit, pupils would take it in turns to go up to it.

Example of copperplate handwriting

By Bethany Angell

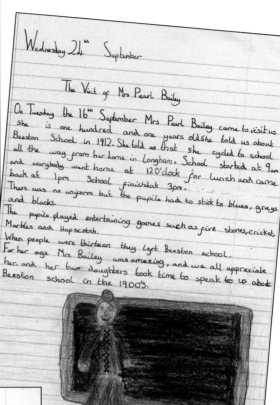

Wednesday 24th September

The Visit of Mrs Pearl Bailey

On Tuesday the 16th September Mrs Pearl Bailey came to visit us she is one hundred and one years old she told us about Beeston School in 1912. She told us that she cycled to school all the way from her home in Longham. School started at 9am and everybody went home at 12 o'clock for lunch and came back at 1pm School finished at 3pm.
There was no uniform but the pupils had to stick to blues, greys and blacks.
The pupils played entertaining games such as five stones, cricket, Marbles and Hopscotch.
When people were thirteen they left Beeston school.
For her age Mrs Bailey was amazing, and we all appreciate her and her two daughters took time to speak to us about Beeston school in the 1900's.

By Catalina Burks

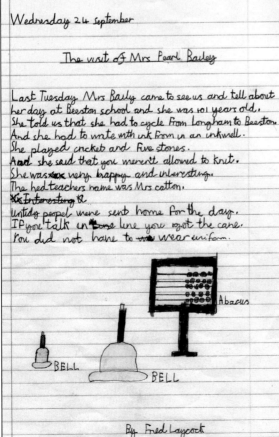

Wednesday 24 September

The visit of Mrs Pearl Bailey

Last Tuesday Mrs Baily came to see us and tell about her day at Beeston school and she was 101 years old.
She told us that she had to cycle from Longham to Beeston.
And she had to write with ink from in an inkwell.
She played cricket and five stones.
And she said that you weren't allowed to knit.
She was very happy and interesting.
The head teachers name was Mrs cotton.
Interesting
Untidy people were sent home for the day.
If you talk in line you got the cane.
You did not have to wear uniform.

BELL   BELL   Abacus

By Fred Laycock

Clockwise, starting top left:
Work by Bethany Angell, aged nine.

Work by Catalina Burks, aged nine.

Work by Fred Laycock, aged eight.

Peggy as a nurse, c.1935.

Peggy Norris (née Sporne)
By Jill Scott and Diane Walthew

Peggy and her family at Crossway Farm, Beeston. Peggy, born in 1917, was the much-loved only child of Frederick and Lottie Sporne. When she was very young they moved from Haveringland to Crossways Farm in Beeston. The crossroads there are still known by some as Sporne Corner!

A thinking child, at age five she decided that there were boy and girl pigs because God had made some and Jesus the others. When told, at six years of age, to come back and shut the hall door she replied, 'Alright, I must wear out the stair carpet then!' The character was fast developing!

After school at Beeston and at the King's Lynn High School, she began her nursing training at the Norfolk and Norwich Hospital on 1 January 1936, becoming a State Registered Nurse in June 1939. During the 1940s she worked in hospitals across the country, including two spells back in Norwich, one as a midwife at the N&N, and from June 1941 to September 1942 at the Jenny Lind Hospital for Sick Children.

Having gained her diploma in nursing in 1946 she became a Registered Sister Tutor in 1947. Those nurses whose tutor she was could not have had a better introduction to nursing, nor a better mentor. She showed compassion and understanding while at the same time instilling into those girls (they would all have been girls then!) the high standards as she, herself, lived by, especially with regard to the care of others.

Many will not know that during the 1950s she studied in Switzerland, and attended the International Council of Nurses in Rome. Nor that she was the co-author of a nursing manual, and revised another to bring it up-to-date. She was a woman of many talents! She retired from nursing in 1970.

While learning to drive she met Joseph (Joe) Norris. They married in 1972 and lived first in Poynton. As so often with girls born in Norfolk, wherever they travel – and live – they eventually return to Norfolk with their husbands! Peggy and Joe spent four very happy years together in Beeston, until Joe passed away.

During the 26 years that Peggy lived at 'Halfacre' she contributed a great deal to the life of the village; she was a driver for the Church Community Car Service, a parish councillor and a school governor.

She became a member of the Parochial Church Council in March 1983, and secretary in April of that year. As secretary she was instrumental in obtaining grants, and dealt with all the paperwork that was necessary so that the church could be re-roofed and the inside cleaned and redecorated.

While in Beeston she kept up her hobbies of reading, walking, swimming, bird watching (there was always a pair of field glasses on the window-sill beside her favourite chair) and gardening; she knew not only the English names of plants and flowers, cultivated and wild, but also the Latin ones! And she could pronounce them correctly!

There is so much more that could be said about Peggy, including her love of dogs, but she will certainly be remembered for her often wicked sense of humour.

AT THE COURT AT WINDSOR,

The 15th day of July 1881.

PRESENT,

THE QUEEN'S MOST EXCELLENT MAJESTY IN COUNCIL.

WHEREAS the School Board of Beeston All Saints and Little Bittering, appointed under "The Elementary Education Act, 1870," have, in virtue of the powers conferred upon them by the 74th section of that Act, as amended by the "Elementary Education Act, 1876," with the approval of the Education Department, made certain Byelaws, numbered 4742:

And whereas all the conditions in regard to the said Byelaws, which are required to be fulfilled by the said Acts, have been fulfilled, and the said Byelaws have been submitted for the sanction of Her Majesty in Council: NOW, THEREFORE, Her Majesty, having taken the said Byelaws (copy whereof is hereunto annexed) into consideration, is pleased, by and with the advice of Her Privy Council, to declare, and doth hereby declare, Her sanction of the same.

BYELAWS REFERRED TO IN THE FOREGOING ORDER.

No. MMMMDCCXLII.

BYE LAWS made under Section 74 of the Elementary Education Act, 1870, as amended by the Elementary Education Act, 1876, for the PARISH OR TOWNSHIP of BEESTON ALL SAINTS and LITTLE BITTERING by the BEESTON ALL SAINTS and LITTLE BITTERING SCHOOL BOARD.

Definitions.

1. In these Bye-Laws

The term "district" means the Parish or Township of Beeston All Saints and Little Bittering.

The term "child" means a child residing in the district.

The term "school" means a certified efficient school.

"Attendance" means an attendance at a morning or afternoon meeting as defined by the Code of 1876.

The "Code of 1876" means the Code of Minutes of the Education Department made in the year 1876 with respect to the Parliamentary Grant to Public Elementary Schools in England.

The term "Local Authority" means the Local Authority for the district acting for the time being under the Elementary Education Act, 1876.

Children to attend School.

2. The parent of every child of not less than 5, nor more than 13, years of age, shall cause such child to attend school, unless there be a reasonable excuse for non-attendance.

Reasonable Excuses.

Any of the following reasons shall be a reasonable excuse, namely :—

(a) That the child is under efficient instruction in some other manner.

(b) That the child has been prevented from attending school by sickness or any unavoidable cause.

(c) That there is no Public Elementary School open which the child can attend within 2 miles, measured according to the nearest road from the residence of such child.

Time of Attendance.

3. The time during which every child shall attend school shall be the whole time for which the school selected shall be open for the instruction of children of similar age, including the day fixed by Her Majesty's Inspector for his annual visit.

Proviso as to Religion and Labour Acts.

4. Provided always that nothing in these Bye Laws—

(a) Shall prevent the withdrawal of any child from any religious observance or instruction in religious subjects :

(b) Shall require any child to attend school on any day exclusively set apart for religious observance by the religious body to which its parent belongs ; or

(c) Shall have any force or effect in so far as it may be contrary to anything contained in any Act for regulating the education of children employed in labour.

Proviso as to Standard for Exemption.

5. And provided always that—

(a) A child between ten and thirteen years of age shall not be required to attend school if such child has received a certificate from one of Her Majesty's Inspectors of Schools that it has reached the Fourth Standard prescribed by the Code of 1876.

(b) A child between ten and thirteen years of age shown to the satisfaction of the Local Authority to be beneficially and necessarily employed shall not be required to attend school for more than 150 attendances in each year if such child has received a certificate from one of Her Majesty's Inspectors of Schools that it has reached the Third Standard prescribed by the Code of 1876.

Penalty.

6. Every parent who shall not observe, or shall neglect or violate these Bye Laws, or any of them, shall, upon conviction, be liable to a penalty not exceeding, with the costs, five shillings for each offence.

Revocation.

7. Any Bye Laws heretofore made under Section 74 of the Elementary Education Act, 1870, or under that Section as amended by the Elementary Education Act, 1876, are hereby revoked as from the day on which the present Bye Laws shall come into operation.

The above Bye Laws were made by the Beeston All Saints and Little Bittering School Board at a meeting held on the 7th day of October 1880.

In witness whereof the School Board have hereunto set their common seal this 7th day of October 1880.

L.S.

John Lovett Clerk

Printed by GEORGE EDWARD EYRE and WILLIAM SPOTTISWOODE,
Printers to the Queen's most Excellent Majesty. 1881.

Clockwise, starting top left:
Front page of School Charter, dated 15 July 1881.

School Charter page 2.

School Charter page 3.

Pupil Admissions, 13 November 1945 – 21 April 1947

Date Of Admission	Child's Full Name	Address	Parent/Guardian's First Name
13-11-45	Pooley, Phyllis	Herne Hill Farm, Beeston	Everson
26-11-45	Pooley, Rose	Herne Hill Farm, Beeston	Everson
28-1-46	Hammond, Patricia	The Cottage, Beeston	Thomas Henry
16-9-46	Reeve, Patricia	Water End Farm, Beeston	Reginald Frank
16-9-46	Hammond Wendy	The Cottage, Beeston	Thomas Henry
17-9-46	Margarson, Margaret	Post Office, Beeston	Edward John
17-9-46	Reeve, Grace	Water End Farm, Beeston	Arthur
6-11-46	Carpenter, Alan	Near Mrs Hammond, Beeston	Frederick William
7-1-47	Seymour, Keith	c/o The Bungalow, Beeston	Cynthia Wright
7-1-47	Cowles, Raymond	The Hut, RAF Station, Beeston	Ruby Mildred
7-1-47	Whitehead, Julia	Beeston	Edward Dennis
7-1-47	Powley, Winston	7 Council Houses, Beeston	Charles
7-1-47	Wyett, Pamela	RAF Station, Beeston	Thomas Gilbert
11-11-46	Carpenter, Barry	Beeston	Frederick William
17-3-47	Evens, Ronald	Beeston	Dudley Courtney
17-3-47	Evens, David	Beeston	Dudley Courtney
17-3-47	Howe, Pamela	Beeston	Reuben Ernest
24-3-47	Betts, Carole	2 Council Houses, Beeston	Henry Albert
24-3-47	Betts, Raymond	2 Council Houses, Beeston	Henry Albert
15-4-47	Holland, Marlene	Near School, Beeston	Herbert
12-5-47	Walthew, Frank	Fransham Road Farm, Beeston	Frank Bernard
12-5-47	Walthew, Laurence	Fransham Road Farm, Beeston	Frank Bernard
14-7-47	Mackenzie, Maureen	Hospital Site, RAF Beeston	Donald William
21-7-47	Symonds, Sylvia	RAF Beeston	Ernest
28-7-47	Chambers, Margaret	The Bungalow, Beeston	-
15-9-47	Howe, Reuben	RAF Site, Beeston	Ernest
15-9-47	Skipper, Malcolm	Holmdene Cottage, Beeston	Victor
15-9-47	Walthew, Elizabeth	Fransham Road Farm, Beeston	Frank Bernard
15-9-47	Scott, Robert	c/o Mrs Laws, Beeston	George
15-9-47	Winterbone, Brian	1 Council Houses, Beeston	Cyril
13-10-47	Futter, David	RAF Site, Beeston	Arthur
13-10-47	Futter, Daphne	RAF Site, Beeston	Arthur
13-10-47	Futter, Glenda	RAF Site, Beeston	Arthur
24-11-47	Leggett, Brian	RAF Site, Beeston	Wallace
27-11-47	Thacker, Jean	RAF Site, Beeston	-
27-11-47	Thacker, Sheila	RAF Site, Beeston	Marjorie
27-11-47	Thacker, Muriel	RAF Site, Beeston	Marjorie
8-12-47	Palmer, Patricia	Beeston	Marjorie
8-12-47	Palmer, Anthony	Beeston	Peggy
13-1-48	Reeder, Joan	RAF Site, Beeston	George
16-2-48	Kemp, Sylvia	2 WAAF Site, Beeston	John
1-3-48	Parker, Jean	1 WAAF Site, Beeston	Martin
12-4-48	Ames, Maureen	9 WAAF Site, Beeston	Frederick
12-4-48	Whitehead, Ann	RAF Station, Beeston	Charles
19-4-48	Elliott, George	6 Officers Mess, Beeston	Harry
19-4-48	Elliott, Daphne	6 Officers Mess, Beeston	Harry
19-4-48	Elliott, Doreen	6 Officers Mess, Beeston	Harry
19-4-48	Matless, Pauline	4 Officers Mess, Beeston	Charlie Elliott
19-4-48	Hudson, Ernest	5 Sergeants Mess, Beeston	George Arthur
19-4-48	Hudson, George	5 Sergeants Mess, Beeston	-
19-4-48	Shrimpling, Ernest	3 WAAF site, Beeston	-
19-4-48	Gilbert, John	1 Officers Mess, Beeston	John
19-4-48	Gilbert, David	1 Officers Mess, Beeston	-
21-4-47	Osborne, Sheila	3 Water Tower site, Beeston	Arthur
21-4-47	Osborne, Dorothy	3 Water Tower Site, Beeston	Arthur

Pupil Admissions, 28 April 1947 – 12 September 1949

Date Of Admission	Child's Full Name	Address	Parent/Guardian's First Name
28-4-47	Osborne, Ronald	3 Water Tower Site, Beeston	Arthur
10-5-48	Smith, Sylvia	2 Medical Site, Beeston	Charles
10-5-48	Butcher, Clive	1 Officers Mess, Beeston	Albert
24-5-48	Smith, David	2 Medical Site, Beeston	Charles
24-5-48	Chapman, Jennifer	PX Site, Beeston	Reginald Arthur
24-5-48	Chapman, Terrence	PX Site, Beeston	Reginald Arthur
25-5-48	Emery, June	Red Cross Site, Beeston	Herbert
27-5-48	Emery, Margaret	Red Cross Site, Beeston	Herbert
31-5-48	Ward, David	7 Sergeants Mess, Beeston	George
8-6-48	Simpson, Terrence	6 Sergeants Mess, Beeston	Geof James Robert
14-7-48	Everett, Rosemary	1 Water Tower, Beeston	Henry
14-7-48	Everett, Iris	1 Water Tower, Beeston	Henry
14-7-48	Everett, Gladys	1 Water Tower, Beeston	Henry
28-6-48	Bowden, Alan	RAF Camp, Beeston	-
13-9-48	Mitchell, Pamela	Ploughshare, Beeston	Hedley
13-9-48	Bunting, William	RAF, Beeston	William
13-9-48	Bunting, Edith	RAF, Beeston	William
13-9-48	Reeder, Audrey	RAF, Beeston	George
13-9-48	Emery, Peter	RAF, Beeston	Herbert
14-9-48	Fraser, Gordon	Church Farm Cottages, Beeston	Alexander Nelson
14-9-48	Sherlock, Ronald	Church Farm Cottages, Beeston	Dr Barnado's Home
27-9-48	Cross, Roy	Drury Square, Beeston	Wilfred
27-9-48	Hammond, Walter	RAF Camp, Beeston	Walter
4-10-48	Dack, Brian	6 Airmen's Site, Beeston	Robert
11-10-48	Star, Sheila	8 Airmen's Site, Beeston	-
11-10-48	Jorden, Mervyn	1 Airmen's Site, Beeston	Jabez Hugh
8-11-48	Uda,l David	3 Airmen's Site, Beeston	John Harold
11-1-49	Elliott, Aubrey	RAF Beeston	Harry
11-1-49	Lacey, Roderick	Rectory Cottage, Beeston	Frederick Stanley
2-3-49	Beale, Shirley	5 Sergeants Mess, Beeston	Charles William
2-3-49	Beale, Bridget	5 Sergeants Mess, Beeston	Charles William
14-3-49	Palmer, Pauline	Dykewood Farm, Beeston	Henry
14-3-49	Palmer, Roy	Dykewood Farm, Beeston	Henry
2-5-49	Cook, Lilian	Bate's Square, Beeston	George Edward
2-5-49	Kemp, Barbara	WAAF Site, Beeston	John
2-5-49	Thacker, Michael	RAF Site, Beeston	Margorie
2-5-49	Skipper, Keith	Holmdene Cottages, Beeston	Victor
2-5-49	Chapman, Wendy	PX Site, Beeston	Reginald
2-5-49	Gray, Rosemary	Communal Site, Beeston	Russell
20-6-49	Tuck, Linda	Point House, Beeston	Charles
20-6-49	Smith, Reginald	1 Naafi Site, Beeston	-
20-6-49	Smith, Gwendoline	1 Naafi Site, Beeston	-
20-6-49	Smith, Michael	1 Naafi Site, Beeston	-
20-6-49	Smith, Doreen	1 Naafi Site, Beeston	-
12-9-49	Bennett, Neville	8 WAAF Site, Beeston	Reginald
12-9-49	Claxton, Veronica	Beeston	Miss Claxton
12-9-49	Barrell, June	Holkham House, Beeston	Miss E. Barrell
12-9-49	Walthew, Rodney	Fransham Road, Farm, Beeston	Frank
12-9-49	Symons, Brenda	WAAF Site, Beeston	Ernest
12-9-49	Attewell, John	WAAF Site, Beeston	Leonard
12-9-49	Rogerson, Ann	Ration Stores, Beeston	James
12-9-49	Rogerson, James	Ration Stores, Beeston	James
12-9-49	Hawes, Brian	Beeston	Martin
12-9-49	Tann, Philip	School House, Beeston	Frank

Date.	Name of Child.	Age.	Offence.	Punishment Inflicted.	Signature of Teacher inflicting the Punishment.
	Peter webdale 27.1.38	9 yrs.	Writing an indecent note & passing round class.	2 strokes, 1st being faulty.	Ivy W Burgess.
28.1.38	Enid Deacon	11 yrs.	Unpunctuality	2 strokes of cane	Ivy W Burgess.
	Evelyn Cook.	12 yrs.	For jeering at the Hd. Teacher		Ivy W Burgess.
12.5.38	Susan Pattison	11 yrs.	For continual inattention and making herself a general nuisance	2 strokes of cane	Ivy W Burgess.
1.11.38	Vera Burton	12 yrs	Unseemly laughter	1 stroke	Ivy W Burgess

Extract from punishment book.

PART IV: BITTERING

Chapter 14

Views of Bittering and the Woodland Shrine

Bittering, also known as Bittering Parva or Little Bittering, is situated 5½ miles north-west of East Dereham. It is composed of a scattering of farms and associated housing covering approximately 392 acres and a small but delightful church set back from the road, which has to be accessed by a narrow track between two fields. Bittering's largest employer is a sand and gravel works where Bittering Hall once stood.

Bittering Hall. This building was demolished in 1981 and a tarmac plant now occupies this site.

Kenny Page, John Warner, Don Pooley and Ralph Pooley taking a break from poaching in Bittering.

The front of the Woodland Shrine. It can be accessed via the main drive to the tarmac plant and then turning right, so that you double back on yourself. The chapel, just inside the woods, is dedicated to the Virgin Mary and was built by Paul Hodac, a soldier from Czechoslovakia. His military career began in March 1938 when the young forestry worker enlisted to defend his homeland from the Nazis. When Hitler's troops invaded Czechoslovakia, Mr Hodac escaped to Poland, having first prayed to the Virgin Mary for help to cross safely. As the invading army advanced across Europe, he fought on the front line and ended up in England when France was taken by the Germans.

After the war, he never forgot his escape from the Nazis and decided to build a shrine as a gesture of thanks to the Virgin Mary, where people could come and pray. He bought Spread Oak Wood, an isolated and peaceful site, for this purpose. Mr Hodac then taught himself joinery and bricklaying, and took seven years to build the chapel, mainly during weekends and holidays, with help from local people who donated items for the chapel such as the wrought-iron gates at the entrance to the grounds, the medieval wooden door, and the internal furniture and religious adornments.

The stone arch around the door came from Kempstone Church, near Litcham. A cross-stitch picture of roses in an urn was made by soldiers in the trenches during the First World War.

The shrine opened in 1983 and mass is held there annually. People from all denominations are welcome. For the rest of the year, the chapel stands alone in its quiet woodland surroundings, as a fitting memorial to the Czech airmen based at Wretham Airfield during the war.

The north side of the Woodland Shrine.

Chapter 15

Bittering Church

The east end of Bittering church.

The west and south walls of Bittering church.

The Church of St Peter and St Paul

Taken from 'Church Tours' by Hugh Holbeach and
Richard Butler-Stoney OBE (1985)

This church claims to be the smallest Parish Church in regular use in the Diocese of Norwich; it measures 17 x 6 yards.

At first sight there appears to be no division between nave and chancel, but a close inspection of the exterior masonry reveals a join in the flintwork near the west edge of the south-west square-headed window and the same on the north side. The walls are just slightly thicker to the west of this line, moreover the west corners of the nave were constructed with large flints.

From this, it is thought that the nave end was constructed first, say before 1200. It could have had an apse for its chancel at the beginning, but the whole building was so small that it could only have been intended for the moated manor-house and its environs, which was sited to the north-west of the church. The font also belongs to this date.

The next building phase was in the Early English period (the first stage of English Gothic, which began in the late-twelfth and into the thirteenth century) when the walls were continued on the same lines and the east window, with its three very narrow stepped lancets, were made. The double-light south-east window and its exquisite angel piscina and simple sedilia (stone seats for priests in the south wall of the chancel) are of the the same date, c.1250.

A third phase was the addition of the square-headed windows in the Perpendicular period (fifteenth century). There are three of them, and the walls were made higher with the addition of more flint work. Two buttresses were added on the north side, and inside the screen was made between nave and chancel.

The bell turret with space for two bells shows in Ladbrooke's drawing, c.1820, but Blomefield in 1808 describes the church as decayed with no bell. In 2005 it has one bell in a crudely reconstructed turret. Whether there ever was a tower remains a matter of speculation. So far no evidence of one has been found, although there is a list of church goods dated October 1547 mentioning 'too greate bells wt the roopes and certen leade that lay abowte the bells'. Could there have been a detached timber belfry?

On entering the church through the narrow high-pointed doorway one steps down into a hallowed house of prayer of enormous antiquity. Very close to the door is the font, which is shaped like a Norman font with its circular bowl standing on a large round column with four lesser shafts. However, the bowl is decorated modestly with a trefoil design, which is more like thirteenth-century work, and so it has been concluded that it is contemporary with the walls at about 1200.

The interior west wall has two shallow blank arcades with a high pointed shape, which must have been a development of the Norman custom for

Arches in the church wall.

The bell turret.

The font.

The east window.

decorating the church walls. Higher up on the west wall, near the apex, is a lancet window filled with early Victorian glass.

The little pipe-organ came from Wicklewood Church, near Wymondham. It was reconditioned and installed by Messrs W. & A. Boggis in 1967.

The church organ.

The calor gas lights have been converted to electricity and make an attractive feature. A round plaque on the north wall is in memory of Rosemary Heather Napier who lived in Bittering Hall and was a lifelong benefactor who helped in the restoration of this church in 1961. At that time, the church was inside the park, but the Hall has since been totally demolished. The park has been ploughed up, and the gravel pit has been extended towards the church.

The squire's pew has the most delightful Jacobean carving along the front. The pulpit also has more such carving and is adjacent to the reading desk. There is no lectern.

In the chancel there is more nice oak carving, and a wonderful old parish chest on short legs. The sanctuary rails came from St Peter's Church in Great Yarmouth and were installed here in 1966. Close to the walls are three old coffin stones believed to mark the graves of three of Bittering's early rectors.

The reredos is a picture of our Lord presiding at the Last Supper, which was given in memory of Barbara Napier who died in 1926, aged 26.

The grave of a three-year-old boy who died in 1733 is marked by a stone under the squire's pew, and that of a one-month-old boy who died in 1757 lies near the reading desk. This latter one has its inscription simply cut onto two flooring bricks.

The chancel flooring slabs are interesting, because a descendant of William Wilberforce (the English politician and social reformer who campaigned to outlaw slavery across the British Empire, and brought about the 1833 Slavery Abolition Act) had to change his name to Puleston when he married Catherine T.F. Puleston, lady of the manor. She was a great local character who died in 1942. Her grave is in the centre with the beautiful stained glass in the east window dedicated to her memory. Her husband, the Revd R.W. Puleston lies on the south side of the chancel, and he was rector here for 50 years. On the north side is Barbara F. Puleston, daughter of Revd and Catherine Puleston, who died in 1926, aged 26. Barbara's son William and his wife Rosemary lived and eventually died in Spain. Their son, Barbara's grandson, Leonard, still lives in Spain.

Bittering Parva has always been a small place with little over 300 acres and under 50 people at most. The number of houses has continued to decline over the years and the gravel working has expanded. The church here closed in the 1950s for a short period and grazing animals threatened to ruin it, but in 1958 restoration work began under the leadership of Canon Robert Dodson and it was reinstated as a Parish Church in 1961. Since then it has always had well-attended services once a month.

No trace of the Roman road survives here, but it once passed on the south side of the site of the church and its line is clear from a study of the map. A moated site just north-west of the church is clearly visible. It had a further enclosure near the church which is now only a crop mark.

It is a credit to the faith of the people of Bittering down through the centuries that this little Parish Church is still standing and is still well supported.

The church altar.

Above: *The old wooden parish chest.*

Right: *The pulpit.*

Below: *Napier & Anderson's lorry. Mr Napier, a farmer, was one of the last people to live in Bittering Hall before it was demolished, c.1948. The family also ran a gravel pit in Bittering.*

Right, top: *Plaque to the memory of Rosemary Heather Napier, a local lady who gave generously to the church. She was married to William Napier, son of Barbara Puleston.*

Right: *Plaque to the memory of William Napier.*

Wendling Registers and Census

Wendling Registers

The following information has been gleaned from various registers, which recorded certain facts and figures about Wendling over the years. A selection of material has been included here to give a taste of life across the centuries.

1539: First baptism, 13 February.
1615: Edward Raxon (minister), Edmond Holland, Robert Deli (churchwardens).
1624: Thomas Byrd (curate), Roger Brett, Thomas Craske (churchwardens).
1628, 1632, 1635: Thomas Byrd (curate).
1628: Haman Ferrour, Henry Blanche (churchwardens).
1638–39: Nicholas Hammond (curate), Christopher Spratt, Thomas Markon (churchwardens), Nicholas Hammond occurs to 1653.

The entries of marriage are but a few, but in 1646 there were 27 marriages and in 1647 there were 25 (the average being three or four). Between 1649 and 1660 there are no records of any marriages.

Prominent names during first half of seventeenth century are Haye, Hovell, Periall, Blanche, Crane, Crowe, Ferrour, Mathew, Stalworthe, Bailie, Bayfield, Kitmear, Dexter, Large, Stanforth, Armstrong, Hanson, Grenhoe.

Crowe

Baptisms
1540: Agnes Crowe, Filia Xp'hen Crowe (10 December).
1544: Thomas Crowe, 7 March.
1550: John Crowe, 19 January.
1552: Nicholas Crowe, 3 October.

Burials
1542: Robert Crowe, 28 May.
1557: Georguis Crowe, 15 October.
1558: Cristoferus Crowe, 10 August; John Crowe, 9 November.

Ferror

Baptisms
1560: Johnes Ferror, 4 June.
1562: Nicholas Ferror, 25 January.
1579: Johes Ferror, 8 March.

1581: Edmundus Ferror, 3 September.
1588: Henrious Ferror, 14 October.
1592: Richardus Ferror, 20 September.
1593: Hamond Ferror, 16 January.
1696: Honora Ferror, 16 September.

Burials
1590: Richardus Ferror, 8 February.
1592: Richardus Ferror, 8 September.
1692: Johanes Ferror, 14 February.
1607: Edmundus Ferror, 6 April.
1620: Henry Ferror, 12 March.
1632: Saraleof Harnon Ferror, 26 June.
1637: Hamon Ferror, gent, 10 August.

Hammond

Baptisms
1580: Maria Hammond, 15 March; Robertus Hammond, 8 March.
1655: Mary, daughter of John Hammond and his wife Anne, 26 November.
1655: John son of same, 29 December.
1660: Robert son of same, 28 May.
1661: Thomas son of same, 10 August.
1663: Bodie son of same, 7 March.

Burials
1600: Nicholas Hammond, 15 April.
1606: Anna Hammond, 29 June.
1620: Johes Hammond, 14 November.
1630: Robert, son of John and Anne his wife, 3 July.
1669: Anne, wife of John, 3 July.
1681: John, son of John and Sara his wife.

Markant

Baptisms
1637: Judith daughter of Thomas and Mary Markant, 20 October.
1640: Thomas son of same, 12 May.
1642: Ferrour son of same, 29 September.
1648: Hamon son of same, 6 April.
1649: Maria, daughter of Thomas late deceased gent and Maria his wife, 7 February.
1667: Eliza daughter of Thomas and Eliz his wife bore 25 February, Baptised 12 March.
1673: Thomas son of Thomas Markant and Eliz his wife born 2 August, baptised 14 August.

Burials

1648: *Hamon Markent son of Thomas and Maria, 1 March.*
1649: *Thomas Markant, 18 December.*
1666: *Richard Markant, 2 March.*
1697: *Thomas Markant, 8 June.*

Nelson

Baptisms

1582: *Aria Nelson, 9 December.*
1629: *Edmundus Nelson, 29 November.*
1636: *Joanna daughter of Edmund and Joann his wife, 29 June.*
1637: *Anne daughter same, 28th May.*
1652: *Bridgett, daughter of Edmund and Alice his wife, born 20 February baptised 24 February.*
1654: *William Nelson son of same, 24 March.*
1656: *John son of same, 2 February.*
1661: *Edmund Nelson sone of Edmund and Mary, 15 September.*
1664: *Edmund son of same 3 July.*

Burials

1632: *Alice Nelson, 27 July.*
1636: *John Nelson, 30 June.*
1637: *Anne, daughter of Edmund Nelson and Joan, 28 August.*

Miscellaneous

Baptisms

1539: *John Hovell, 25 February.*
1542: *Georgduis Hovell, 28 July.*
1543: *Willmus Hovell, 5 August.*
1550: *Georgius Hovell, 2 June.*
1557: *Georgius Mynne, 27 January.*
1564: *Xpoferus Hovell, 20 March.*
1565: *Thomas Hovell, 15 April; Vinsent Becke, 15 April.*
1568: *Hoggon Jewell, 8 August.*
1585: *Francisen Cosen, 30 August.*
1592: *Franciscus Hovell filius thorne, 1 August.*
1593: *Hooggon Hovell filius throne, 25 November.*
1595: *Hooggon Hovell filius thorne, 28 December.*
1606: *Henricas Barrel baptised, 1 February.*
1615: *Maria Whiskard, 12 November.*
1626: *Maria Beckham, 14 January.*
1638: *Henrie son of Henrie Darvie and Margaret his wife, 2 December.*
1642: *John son of Henrie Darvie and Margaret his wife, 8 November.*
1645: *Thomas son of Henrie Darvie and Margaret his wife, 22 February.*
1646: *Robert son of Robert Dave and his wife Elizabeth, 19 May.*
1647: *James son of Henry Davy and his wife Margaret, 12 March.*
1648: *Mary daughter of Willyme Neave, 8 July.*
1649: *Thomas, son of Robert Brett gent and his wife Maria, 16 July.*
1650: *Edward, son of John Sherre and Margaret his wife, 23 June.*
1651: *Prudence, daughter of Henry Davey and his wife Margaret, 1 October.*
1652: *Sara, daughter of Hillary Forby and Maria his wife*

born 12 April, baptised 2 May.
1653: *Robert son of Robert Brett and Mary his wife bore 24 February, baptised 1 March.*
1657: *Hillary son of Hillary Forby and his wife Mary bore 4 May.*
1659: *Elizabeth Scarlett daughter of James and his wife Margaret born 22 June, baptised 21 September 1661.*
1679: *Robert son of John Hammond and Mary his wife baptised 19 January.*

Miscellaneous

Burials

1542: *Georgius Hovell, 14 August.*
1557: *Johnes Pumfrett, 12 December.*
1558: *Thomas Hooggon, 15 March.*
1559: *Margareta Hooggon, 19 May.*
1562: *Edwardus Minne, 10 April.*
1563: *Vinsent Hovell, 10 January.*
1564: *Xpoferus Hovell, 30 March.*
1566: *William Minne, 9 December.*
1589: *Maria Bozum, 15 March.*
1591: *Thomas Jewell, 16 January.*
1598: *Gitiliana Clerke, 27 October.*
1607: *Willmus husband of Hester Jewell, 7 May.*
1608: *Thomas Hovell, 25 March.*
1612: *Adamus Bozum, 22 September; Doritea Jewell, 26 January.*
1613: *Sislea Backvid, 20 February.*
1634: *Hester Jewell, 26 July.*
1637: *William Neave, 14 September.*
1646: *Robert son of Robert Davy gent and Elizabeth his wife, 31 January.*
1662: *Henry Davie, 4t August.*
1663: *James Scarlet, 10 May.*

Marriages

1558: *Adamus Bozous and Maria Pickering, 15 June.*
1559: *Robertus Barnes and Alicia Hooggon, 12 February.*
1567: *Thomas Jewell and Dorothea Hovell, 18 October.*
1591: *Thomas Hovell and Ava Barnes, 9th October*
1594: *Vincent Becke and Margareta Dunn, 16 June; Nichus Wright and Margareta Nelson, 20 September.*
1600: *Johnes Hammond and Martha Brett, 4 February.*
1606: *Dennis Barratt and Maria Ferror, 12 May.*
1614: *Edwardus Shene clicus and Elizabeth Ferror, 16 November; Hamondus Ferror and Elizabeth Sharrington, 16 November.*
1615: *Robertus Whiskard and Alicia Hay, 9 September.*
1633: *Robertus Whiskard vidius and Alicia Blade, 6 August.*
1636: *Thomas Markant and Maria Ferror, 24 November.*
1645: *James Wollnall, widower and Honor Ferror, single, 1 May.*
1646: *John Davy, widower and Anne Newman, widow, 1 August.*
1647: *Thomas Cockett, single and Ann Rumer, single, 28 November.*
1648: *John Whiskard, widower and Anne Purvis, single, 8 May.*
1649: *John Rippinghall, single and Anne Guibson, single, 8 April; William Bardwell, single and Frances Hawke, 21 May.*

Will of Robert Hovell of Wendlyng, 24 February 1567

Dorothye my wife, Noye my son, Thomas my son, Maud my daughter when married or if she do not marry, then to my daughter Bryget and Robert Allen and William Allyn, sons of said Briddget. Brydget and Clemence Ferrour, my mayds. Executors, Dorothye my wife and my brother Christopher Rouse.

Thomas Sherie a witness

Proved 9th July, 1567

Cur. EP. Norw.

On concluding the extracts from Wendling registers it is noted that changes in the character of hand writing appear in 1600, 1615, 1618, 1636, 1653, 1659, 1666 and 1673.

Extracts from Wendling Directories

From White's *Directory of Norfolk*, 1845

Wm. Boddy, Blacksmith.

Thomas Claxton, Vict. Red Hart.

Matha Jarvis, Miller and Shopkeeper.

John Moore, Wheelwright.

Rev. Richard Packe Waldegrave BA officially Curate.

Henry Philippo, Baker.

Mrs Elizabeth Skikelthorpe.

John Wright, Carpenter.

Farmers, 1845

Benjamin Baker, Thos Baley to J. Mason Abbey Farm, Wm. Curry, Edwd. Dunthorn, Henry Hubbard, Wm. Hubbard, Daniel Lovell, John Stringer, Jas. Thompson, John Wherry, Jerk.Wiffen.

From White's *Directory of Norfolk*, 1854

Wendling is a parish with scattered houses 78, 385 souls and 1,330 acres of land the property of John Margerson Esq. executors of the late J. Mason Esq. Mrs Skikelthorpe, Mw Burcham, Page Scott and Jon Hudons Engrs. Wendling House is a neat residence on the Lynn and Swaffham turnpike road, the seat and property of Mrs Eliz. Skikelthorp. Rev. Robt. Howlett is clergyman. The East Anglian Railway, opened September, 1848, has a neat station here.

East Anglian line trains to Dereham, Lynn and Ely four times a day (Sundays excepted) when there is but one Mr Mat Smith stationmaster.

Other occupations, 1854

Edward Askkew, Vict. and Carpenter, Red Hart; Wm. Boddy, Blacksmith; Robt. Claxton, Shopkeeper and School; Ed. Dunthorne, Farm Bailiff; Chas. Horsley, Corn Merchant and Miller; Mr Hubbard, Hy; Miss Kent, Wendling House; Win Lewin, Farm Bailiff; Jon Moore, Wheelwright; Henry Porter, Coal Dlr. and Vict. Railway Tavern; Mrs Skikelthorpe, Wendling House; Wright Jnr., Carpenter.

From White's *Directory of Norfolk*, 1864

The fuel allotment awarded in 1815 is 10 acres. The poors stock £400. 3% consals was derived from the sale of a house and land in 1816. The dividends have for some years been improperly carried to the poor rates. The widows 6A 1R 36p is let for £12 a year which is divided among poor widows belonging to the parish. The primitive methodist chapel was built in 1848.

Farmers, 1864

George Baker, George Baxter, John Bayfield, Humock Bone, William Bone, Noah Claxton, Walter Claxton (Castrate and Dealer), William Forby, George Greaves, James Haynes, William Hubbard, John Margerson.

Other occupations, 1864

Dinah Badcock, Schoolmistress; Lucuis Banham, Butcher; Wm Boddy., Smith; John Sayer, Shopkeeper; William Cook, Station Master; John Nichols Gibbs, Gardener, Nurseryman and Vict. Railway Tavern; Robert Greaves, Beerhouse; William Green, Carpenter; C. Horsley, Miller and Merchant; J. Moore, Wheelwright; Mr Hubbard, Hy; L. Sculthorpe; Mrs Eliz. Skikelthorp, Wendling House.

Farmers, 1954

Benjamin Baker, Lucius Banham, Bayfield junr, Wm. Bone, Jas. Duffield, Wm. Forby, Jas. Hains, Jas. Hains junr, Wm. Hubbard, Geo. Makin, Jno. Shipley.

Longham Registers and Census

White's Directory of Norfolk, 1854

Longham, a small parish and scattered village, 4½ miles north-west of Dereham, has 337 souls, 74 houses, and 1,284 acres of land, mostly belonging to the Earl of Leicester, the lord of the manor, impropriator and patron of the Church, dedicated to St Peter, and is a perpetual curacy, valued in 1831, at £30, and now enjoyed by the Rev. Robert. Howlett. At different periods, from 1756 to 1792, the curacy has been augmented with £1,000 Queen Anne's Bounty. There is a school supported by the Earl of Leicester.

Occupations

Thomas Allcock; George Watling, and Robert. Winter, shoe-makers; Mrs. Julia Cooper; Rev. Robert Howlett, incumbent; Jason Leeds, jun. dealer; George Murrell, vict. Ostrich; Fraises Reynolds, relieving officer; Philip Reynolds. Veterinary surgeon; Christmas Rust, baker; Eliza Watling, schoolmistress; Samuel White, wheelwright; Richard Winter, vict. and smith, White Horse; Thomas Brown; Jno. Francis; Jno. Hastings, Hall; James Leeds; Hasting Sayer, and Wm. Steel, farmers.

Kelly's Directory of Norfolk, 1883

Longham is a village and parish 2 miles north from Wendling station on the Great Eastern railway and 5 west-north-west from East Dereham, situated on the road from East Dereham to Lynn, in the Western division of the county, Launditch hundred, Mitford and Launditch union, East Dereham county court district, rural deanery of Brisley and archdeaconry and diocese of Norwich. The church of St Peter is a structure of flint and rubble in the Perpendicular style, has chancel, nave, a south porch, and square tower containing 1 bell; in 1878 it was thoroughly restored and re-seated and new pulpit added. The register dates from the year 1539. The living is a vicarage, with Wendling rectory annexed, joint yearly value £150, with residence, in the gift of the Lord Chancellor and held since 1869 by the Rev. Wm. Ray Eaton B.A. Corpus Christi College, Cambridge. Here is a small Wesleyan chapel, built in 1836. There are two cottages built as almshouses to accommodate two old married couples, or four single women. The Earl of Leicester is lord of the manor, chief landowner and lay impropriator. The soil is mixed: subsoil, clay and gravel. The chief crops are barley, wheat and roots. The area is 1,304 acres; rateable value £1,615; and the population in 1881 was 361. Parish Clerk, Charles Rudd.

Pillar box cleared at 5 p.m. No collection on Sundays. Letters received through East Dereham; Litcham is the nearest money order & telegraph office.

A Church of England school was erected by the Earl of Leicester in 1862 & is supported by voluntary contributions, to hold 100 children, average attendance 70; Miss Annie Ransome, mistress.

Occupations

Alcock, George & Jacob, shopkeepers; Alcock, Thomas, coal dealer; Balderow, Barnard, wheelwright; Barbe,r John, flour dealer &c; Brown, Peter, shoemaker; Brown, Thomas (Mrs), farmer; Burgess, William, shopkeeper; Chapman, Jones, Ostrich; Clamp, Thomas, White Horse & blacksmith; Hastings, John, farmer, The Hall; Horne, Joseph, relieving officer for the Litcham district; Hunter, William, farmer; Kemp, Mary (Mrs), shopkeeper; Kendle, William, farmer & landowner; King, Robert, painter &c; Leeds, George, farmer & cattle dealer; Leeds, James, cattle dealer & farmer; Syer, James, cattle dealer; Wiskar, James, thatcher.

1901 Census

Surname	Forename	Age	Position	Status	Occupation	Born
STANNER	Thomas	52	head	married	farm bailiff	Longham
STANNER	Jemima	50	wife	married		Longham
STANNER	Esther	23	daughter	unmarried		Longham
EVERETT	Alfred Arthur	42	head	married	yardman on farm	Fouldon
EVERETT	Maria	40	wife	married		Saham
EVERETT	Beatrice	18	daughter	unmarried		Fouldon
EVERETT	Amelia	17	daughter	unmarried		Fouldon
EVERETT	George	15	son	unmarried	cattle man on farm	Fouldon
EVERETT	Ruth	10	daughter	child		Fouldon
EVERETT	Edwin	8	son	child		Fouldon
EVERETT	Elsie	5	daughter	child		Longham
EVERETT	Cecil	2	son	child		Longham
EVERETT	Albert	3wks	son	child		Longham
HASTINGS	John	47	head	married	farmer	Gressenhall
HASTINGS	Helen	40	wife	married		Weeford, Staffs
HASTINGS	Edith	6	daughter	child		Longham
HASTINGS	John	5	son	child		Longham
HASTINGS	Ernest	2	son	child		Longham
DYE	Mary	36	servant	unmarried	nurse (domestic)	Wells
SCOTT	Maud	28	servant	unmarried	cook (domestic)	Longham
GRIMES	Mary	20	servant	unmarried	housemaid	Harpley
RANSOME	Louis Henry	49	head	married	clergyman (C of E)	North Elmham
RANSOME	Emily	48	wife	married		Newark, Ntt
WADE	Gertrude	21	servant	unmarried	cook (domestic)	Fakenham
MILES	Eliza Annie	17	servant	unmarried	housemaid	Wendling
DACK	Thomas	40	head	married	shepherd on farm	Stiffkey
DACK	Elizabeth	41	wife	married		Sculthorpe
DACK	Nathaniel	16	son	unmarried	ag. labourer	Cley Next Sea
DACK	Frederick	15	son	unmarried	shepherd	Hindringham
DACK	Ethel	12	daughter	unmarried		Hindringham
DACK	Margaret	10	daughter	child		Flitcham
DACK	Thomas	8	son	child		Flitcham
DACK	Walter	7	son	child		Flitcham
DACK	Edward	5	son	child		Flitcham
DACK	Harold	2	son	child		Gt Massingham
PURPLE	Jane	70	head	widow	parish relief	Gressenhall
PURPLE	Susannah	43	daughter	unmarried	works on farm	Longham
WINTER	Susan	78	head	widow	parish relief	Longham
RAYNER	Robert	67	brother	widower	parish relief	Longham
PURPLE	Bertie	7	grandson	child		Longham
PARKER	Elizabeth	45	head	unmarried	laundress	Gt Fransham
BAILEY	Emma Ann	5	visitor			Longham
BAILEY	Edward	28	head	married	ag. labourer	Longham
BAILEY	Florence	25	wife	married		Longham
BAILEY	Ernest	5	son	child		Longham
BAILEY	George	3	son	child		Longham
BAILEY	Horase (sic)	1	son	child		Longham
BAILEY	Reginald	3mths	son	child		Longham
ALCOCK	Thomas	72	uncle	married	own means	Longham
HALL	William	24	head	married	ag. labourer	Gt Ellingham
HALL	Ellen Louisa	25	wife	married		Thetford
HALL	Hilda Irene	1	daughter	child		Colton Forehoe
POLL	William	45	head	married	ag. labourer	East Harling
POLL	Sarah Ann	44	wife	married		Gt Ellingham
THROWER	Evelyn M	4	g.daughter	child		Thetford
FOX	Robert	42	brother	unmarried	parish relief	Gt Ellingham
BUNN	James	64	head	married	farmer	Beeston
BUNN	Eliza	54	wife	married		Middleton
BUNN	Annie	30	daughter	unmarried		Mileham
BUNN	William Henry	25	son	unmarried	farmer's son	East Dereham
BUNN	Frederick Charles	22	son	unmarried	farmer's son	East Dereham
BUNN	James Leeds	19	son	unmarried	farmer's son	Wymondham
BUNN	Arthur George	15	son	unmarried	farmer's son	Wymondham
BUNN	Clara	13	daughter	unmarried		Wymondham
LEEDS	Elizabeth	85	boarder	unmarried	own means	Mileham

PURPLE	Elizabeth	68	visitor	widow	parish relief	Longham
WEBSTER	Sophia	82	head	widow	own means	Hevingham
KILLENGREY	Jane	35	servant	unmarried	gen. servant (domestic)	Eastmoor
KENDLE	William F	31	head	married	farmer	East Dereham
KENDLE	Martha	39	wife	married		Crockerton, Wilts
WATTS	Robert	62	head	married	ag. labourer	Norwich
WATTS	Anna Maria	51	wife	married		Whissonsett
WATTS	William	22	son	unmarried		Whissonsett
WATTS	Lily	13	daughter	unmarried		Guist
WATTS	Frederick	11	son	child		Guist
PURPLE	John	47	head	married	ag. labourer	Longham
PURPLE	Sarah Jane	45	wife	married		Hillington
PURPLE	Albert Winter	19	son	unmarried	ag. labourer	Longham
PURPLE	William Edward	17	son	unmarried	ag. labourer	Longham
PURPLE	Jesse Robert	15	son	unmarried	ag. labourer	Longham
PURPLE	Noah	13	son	unmarried	ag. labourer	Longham
PURPLE	Dora Maud	11	daughter	child		Longham
PURPLE	Edith Ada	8	daughter	child		Longham
PURPLE	Rosa Mariam	2	daughter	child		Longham
POOLEY	Ada Basham	3	g.daughter	child		Longham
PURPLE	George	51	head	married	fowl dealer	Longham
THOMPSON	Mary Ann	49	boarder	widow	housekeeper	Wendling
THOMPSON	Walter	20	son	unmarried	ag. labourer	Mileham
THOMPSON	George	10	son	child		Longham
THOMPSON	Richard	8	son	child		Longham
THOMPSON	Herbert	4	son	child		Longham
PURPLE	Henry	53	head	married	parish relief	Longham
PURPLE	Catharine		wife	married		Longham
PURPLE	Ernest	12	son	child		Longham
PURPLE	Eley (sic)	9	son	child		Longham
PARKE	Frederick	34	head	married	butcher/slaughterer	Gayton
PARKE	Mary Jane	34	wife	married		Hornchurch, Essex
PARKE	William Frederick	6	son	child		Beeston
PARKE	Thomas Garod?	5	son	child		Beeston
PARKE	John	3	son	child		Beeston
PARKE	Henry	2	son	child		Beeston
PARKE	Edwin	1	son	child		Beeston
PARKE	Elizabeth	3wks	daughter	child		Longham
HOWARD	Mary Ann	27	boarder/nurse	unmarried	monthly nurse	Tittleshall
SYER	Edward	56	head	married	ag. labourer	Longham
SYER	Elizabeth	60	wife	married		Swanton Morley
FRANKLIN	Ephraim	61	head	widower	hurdle maker	Tittleshall
FRANKLIN	Elizabeth	17	daughter	unmarried		Mileham
KILLENGREY	Robert	32	head	married	innkeeper	Eastmoor
KILLENGREY	Caroline	32	wife	married		Longham
KILLENGREY	Dorothy	6	daughter	child		Longham
KILLENGREY	Caroline	5	daughter	child		Longham
KILLENGREY	Robert	4	son	child		Longham
KILLENGREY	Violet	2	daughter	child		Longham
KILLENGREY	Edith	6mths	daughter	child		Longham
THOMPSON	Mary Ann	62	mother-in-law	unmarried	retired housekeeper	Longham
POOLEY	John	27	head	married	road man (labourer)	Wendling
POOLEY	Rosanie Maria	24	wife	married		Gressenhall
POOLEY	John William G.	11mths	son	child		Longham
HUNTER	Ann	86	head	widow	parish relief	Longham
SYER	James A.C.	60	head	married	castrator of pigs	Beeston
SYER	Emily	55	wife	married		Horningtoft
SYER	Ethel	21	daughter	unmarried	assistant teacher	Longham
SYER	Amy	16	daughter	unmarried		Longham
SYER	Herbert L.W.	13	son	child		Longham
HENDLE	Harriett	70	head	widow	pig & fowl rearer	Little Bentley, Essex
THOMPSON	James	78	head	married	ag. labourer	Longham
THOMPSON	Harriett	79	wife	married		Beeston
THOMPSON	Charles	34	son	unmarried	ag. labourer	Longham
THOMPSON	James	16	g.son	unmarried	ag. labourer	Mileham
HORNE	James Joseph	63	head	married	grocer/sub-postmaster	Kenninghall
HORNE	Frances		wife	married		Colkirk
HEWITT	Lilian Winifred	13	servant	unmarried	gen. servant (domestic)	Longham

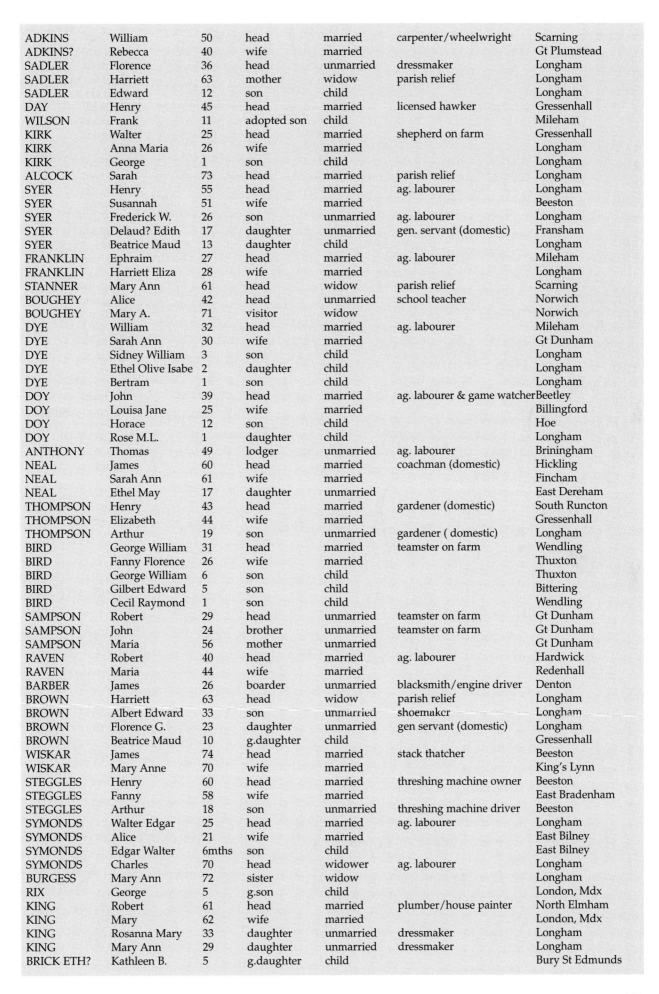

ADKINS	William	50	head	married	carpenter/wheelwright	Scarning
ADKINS?	Rebecca	40	wife	married		Gt Plumstead
SADLER	Florence	36	head	unmarried	dressmaker	Longham
SADLER	Harriett	63	mother	widow	parish relief	Longham
SADLER	Edward	12	son	child		Longham
DAY	Henry	45	head	married	licensed hawker	Gressenhall
WILSON	Frank	11	adopted son	child		Mileham
KIRK	Walter	25	head	married	shepherd on farm	Gressenhall
KIRK	Anna Maria	26	wife	married		Longham
KIRK	George	1	son	child		Longham
ALCOCK	Sarah	73	head	married	parish relief	Longham
SYER	Henry	55	head	married	ag. labourer	Longham
SYER	Susannah	51	wife	married		Beeston
SYER	Frederick W.	26	son	unmarried	ag. labourer	Longham
SYER	Delaud? Edith	17	daughter	unmarried	gen. servant (domestic)	Fransham
SYER	Beatrice Maud	13	daughter	child		Longham
FRANKLIN	Ephraim	27	head	married	ag. labourer	Mileham
FRANKLIN	Harriett Eliza	28	wife	married		Longham
STANNER	Mary Ann	61	head	widow	parish relief	Scarning
BOUGHEY	Alice	42	head	unmarried	school teacher	Norwich
BOUGHEY	Mary A.	71	visitor	widow		Norwich
DYE	William	32	head	married	ag. labourer	Mileham
DYE	Sarah Ann	30	wife	married		Gt Dunham
DYE	Sidney William	3	son	child		Longham
DYE	Ethel Olive Isabe	2	daughter	child		Longham
DYE	Bertram	1	son	child		Longham
DOY	John	39	head	married	ag. labourer & game watcher	Beetley
DOY	Louisa Jane	25	wife	married		Billingford
DOY	Horace	12	son	child		Hoe
DOY	Rose M.L.	1	daughter	child		Longham
ANTHONY	Thomas	49	lodger	unmarried	ag. labourer	Briningham
NEAL	James	60	head	married	coachman (domestic)	Hickling
NEAL	Sarah Ann	61	wife	married		Fincham
NEAL	Ethel May	17	daughter	unmarried		East Dereham
THOMPSON	Henry	43	head	married	gardener (domestic)	South Runcton
THOMPSON	Elizabeth	44	wife	married		Gressenhall
THOMPSON	Arthur	19	son	unmarried	gardener (domestic)	Longham
BIRD	George William	31	head	married	teamster on farm	Wendling
BIRD	Fanny Florence	26	wife	married		Thuxton
BIRD	George William	6	son	child		Thuxton
BIRD	Gilbert Edward	5	son	child		Bittering
BIRD	Cecil Raymond	1	son	child		Wendling
SAMPSON	Robert	29	head	unmarried	teamster on farm	Gt Dunham
SAMPSON	John	24	brother	unmarried	teamster on farm	Gt Dunham
SAMPSON	Maria	56	mother	unmarried		Gt Dunham
RAVEN	Robert	40	head	married	ag. labourer	Hardwick
RAVEN	Maria	44	wife	married		Redenhall
BARBER	James	26	boarder	unmarried	blacksmith/engine driver	Denton
BROWN	Harriett	63	head	widow	parish relief	Longham
BROWN	Albert Edward	33	son	unmarried	shoemaker	Longham
BROWN	Florence G.	23	daughter	unmarried	gen servant (domestic)	Longham
BROWN	Beatrice Maud	10	g.daughter	child		Gressenhall
WISKAR	James	74	head	married	stack thatcher	Beeston
WISKAR	Mary Anne	70	wife	married		King's Lynn
STEGGLES	Henry	60	head	married	threshing machine owner	Beeston
STEGGLES	Fanny	58	wife	married		East Bradenham
STEGGLES	Arthur	18	son	unmarried	threshing machine driver	Beeston
SYMONDS	Walter Edgar	25	head	married	ag. labourer	Longham
SYMONDS	Alice	21	wife	married		East Bilney
SYMONDS	Edgar Walter	6mths	son	child		East Bilney
SYMONDS	Charles	70	head	widower	ag. labourer	Longham
BURGESS	Mary Ann	72	sister	widow		Longham
RIX	George	5	g.son	child		London, Mdx
KING	Robert	61	head	married	plumber/house painter	North Elmham
KING	Mary	62	wife	married		London, Mdx
KING	Rosanna Mary	33	daughter	unmarried	dressmaker	Longham
KING	Mary Ann	29	daughter	unmarried	dressmaker	Longham
BRICK ETH?	Kathleen B.	5	g.daughter	child		Bury St Edmunds

MIDDLETON	?	62	head	unmarried	parish relief	Scarning
MIDDLETON	Lily Alice 1	3	g.daughter	unmarried	gen. servant (domestic)	Gressenhall
WATTS	Matthew	61	head	married	stockman on farm	Beeston
WATTS	Hannah	60	wife	married		Longham
WATTS	Elvina	31	daughter	unmarried	cook (domestic)	Longham
WATTS	Stephen Matthew	15	son	unmarried	stockman on farm	Longham
KILLINGREY	George	61	head	married	teamster on farm	Stoke Ferry
KILLINGREY	Elizabeth	58	wife	married		Eastmoor
KILLINGREY	Florence	14	g.daughter	unmarried		Longham
KILLINGREY	Elsie	5	g.daughter	child		Longham
THOMPSON	Rosa Anna	28	head	unmarried	laundress	Longham
PALMER	Bessie	5	nursechild	child		unknown
PALMER	Ethel	8mths	nursechild	child		unknown
KILLINGREY	James	38	head	married	ag. labourer	Eastmoor
KILLINGREY	Laura	39	wife	married		Longham
KILLINGREY	Eva	15	daughter	unmarried		Shipdham
KILLINGREY	Ethel	10	daughter	child		Longham
KILLINGREY	Daisy	8	daughter	child		Guist
KILLINGREY	Evelyn	4	daughter	child		Gressenhall
KILLINGREY	Ellen	2	daughter	child		Longham
RIX	(J?)oy (female)	6	visitor	child		London, Mdx
WALES	George	76	head	married	parish relief	Beeston
WALES	Charlotte	74	wife	married		Wendling
WALES	Frederick Nash	34	son	unmarried	cattleman on farm	Bittering
BUXTON	Alfred	45	head	married	farmer	Billingford
BUXTON	Caroline	48	wife	married		Saxlingham Holt
BUXTON	Lettice Jane	10	daughter	child		Fakenham
NICHOLS	Edward C.	39	head	married	innkeeper	Ashwellthorpe
NICHOLS	Maria	35	wife	married		Swaffham
NICHOLS	Daniel	69	father	widower	gardener (domestic)	Ashwellthorpe

Beeston and Bittering Registers and Census

1801 Census (Surnames) for Beeston with Bittering

Airs (1); Aldridge (1); Allison (1); Andrews (1); Ashey (1); Barker (2); Barnwell (5); Barnes (1); Baxter (1); Bear (2); Bowen (1); Bridges (1); Bunn (1); Burton (2); Claxton (2); Coker (2); Capps (2); Cooper (2); Case (2); Curson (2); Crome (2); Davey (2); Dearns (2); Dennis (3); Farrer (3); Filby (3); Flupott (3); Fox (3); Frost (3); Fuller (3); Gage (3); Gooderson (3); Goward (3); Hammond (3); Hart (3); Harvey (3); Head (3); Howes (3); Hunter (3); Johnson (3); King (3); Leeder (3); Linn (4); Makings (4); Marham (4); Melton (5); Moulton (4); Murrell (4); Orton (4); Powley (4); Payne (4); Rowe (4); Rudd (4); Ryall (5); Santy (4); Saunders (4); Sooley (4); Spicer (4); Sprags (4); Stanner (4); Stimpson (4); Tann (4,5); Tuck (5); Walker (5); Wheals (5); Whitesides (5); Winter (5); Wiscard (5); Wright (5).

Occupations
Beeston (agriculture): 95
In Bittering with Beeston: 6
Trade manufacture or Handicraft: 39
All Other Persons not [included] in the two above classes, Women & Children (Beeston): 358
Bittering: 13
Number of Inhabitants: 511

BEESTON-NEXT-MILEHAM

Francis's Directory of Norfolk, 1854

*B*EESTON, or Beeston-next-Mileham, is a large scattered village and parish, 7 miles W. of East Dereham united with Bittering Parva, for the support of the poor, the two parishes containing 696 souls, 187 houses, and 2,456a. of land, of which only 16 souls and 392a. are in Bittering Parva. The Rev. C.B. Barnwell is patron of the Church and lord of the manor of Beeston, in which the copyholds are subject to a fine of 2s. or a ploughshare, on every death or alienation. The Church, dedicated to St Mary, is a rectory, valued in the King's book at £13, enjoyed by the Rev. Junior. Nelson, M.A., who has a yearly rent of £550, in lieu of tithes. The Free School, founded by the Rev. C.B. Barnwell, in 1806, for twelve poor children, is endowed with £6 a year for the master, and £1 a year to provide bibles. The poor have 36s. left by Thos. Gooch; £2 by Wm. Allee; £2.8s. by Jno. Halcot; £6 by Thos. and Mary Huke; and 20s. paid by the rector for a plantation enclosed

from the waste. They have also 2½ acre of land, and a cottage let for £4 a year. The Fuel allotment, 20 acre, is let for £49.10s.

Occupations
Capps Wm. vict. Ploughshare; Coker Robert. farrier Curson, Samel. farm bailiff; Gooderston, Wm. shoemaker; Miles, Wm. baker; Nelson, Rev. Junior. M.A. Rectory; Perry, Junior. baker; Pescod, Eliz. M. Free school; Rayner, Junior. blacksmith; Sainty, Chpr. vict. Bell; Watling, Robert. smith, wheelwright, and grocer; Westby, Junior. schoolmaster; Wyett, Wm. vict. Holkham Arms.

Farmers
Brown, Geo.; Claxton, Arthur; Claxton, Noah; Francis, Wm.; Frankland, Junior.; Gathergood, Junior.; Godfrey, Rt. Wm.; Horton, Junior.; Hudson, Samuel.; Large, Wm.; Palmer, Junior;. Preston, Rayner; Rivett, Jas.; Roy, Mark; Rush, Junior.; Rush, Wm.; Sayer, Jas.; Tann, Junior.; Whitesides Wm.

Kelly's Directory of Norfolk, 1888

The living is a rectory, title rent charge £550 gross yearly value £600 including 19½ acres of Glebe with residents, in the gift of the trustees of the late Rev John Charles Barnwell, and held since 1865, by the Rev John Swaffield Corton of Kings College London. The Rectory House formally surrounded by a moat, which has been filled in on one side. This rectory was burnt down in the reign of James I and rebuilt on the same site. There is a Wesleyan chapel. Charities at this were: the Rectory dole of £1; the Almshouse £4 yearly; Hakes Charity £5 for the poor, £1 to the Rector for preaching on Good Friday; Holcott's Charity £2.8s for bread to be distributed every Sunday; Alec's Charity £1.12s. given away in bread; Gooche's Charity (year 1634) about £4.8s to be given to the poor in money; And the fuel allotment of 20 acres, rented at £45.

The trustees of the late Rev Barnwell are lord of the manor:
William Thomas Collison esq. of Bilney hall; Robert Harvey Mason esq. of Necton Hall; Miss Hoste, the trustee of the late C Wallis esq.; And Matthew Robert Stedman of Alethrope.

The village had acreage of 2,073, with a rateable value of £3,684. Population in 1881 was 513.

A School Board of five members was formed in 1875 for Beeston and Little Bittering. The school was built in 1879 at a cost of £850.

Beeston Wesleyan Methodist Chapel, 24 December 1853

Appointment of new trustees of a Wesleyan Methodist Chapel situated at Beeston-next-Mileham in the County of Norfolk with conveyance of a Trust Estate. Surviving Trustees: William Shingles of Kempston; William Balding of Narborough. New trustees: Mark Roy, Beeston Farmer; Jonathan Bunger, Gt Dunham Shopkeeper; John Parry; Gt Dunham Labourer; Charles Templeman Hewett; Swaffham Farmer; John Torby; Swaffham Shopkeeper; James Fuller; Swaffham Bricklayer; Samuel Crisp, Little Fransham Labourer.

Mortgage Agreement Between Trustees of Beeston Methodist Chapel and Mr Thomas Forster, 1864

The mortgage of the chapel and premises to secure £60 + interest. Indenture between: Jacob Guerton, Litcham; Robert Clamp, Mileham, Blacksmith; William Green, Wendling, Carpenter; John Mowing. Wendling, Carpenter; James Preston. Beeston, Boot maker; Thomas Frost. Beeston, Labourer; Crispin Todd Gray, Beeston, Farm Bailiff; John Baker, Beeston Grocer; William Walpole, Beeston, Labourer...

1891 Census (Surnames) for Beeston and Bittering

Barnes, Barrett, Bateson, Baxter, Bell, Bird, Bishop, Blackweell, Blowers, Bolton, Burgess, Burkett, Buscall, Carman, Cason, Claxton, Colman, Cooper, Cranmer, Culley, Cullyer, Dickerson, Dodman, Dowling, Dunnett, Dye, Eke, Frost, Gales, Gooderson, Gowing, Green, Gunton, Hall, Harris, Head, Hewett, Hill, Holman, Jackson, Jarrett, Johnson, Jordan, Kendrick, Knock, Land, Mann, Manns, Mason, Melton, Milk, Moore, Mower, Naylor, Orton, Parke, Parnell, Pond, Pooley, Potter, Preston, Pye, Pyle, Rackham, Ravin, Rayner, Reeve, Rivett, Rox, Robinson, Rudd, Rush, Sadler, Seamon, Sellars, Sennett, Shinfield, Smith, Stanner, Starling, Steggles, Stimpson, Symonds, Tilney, Turner, Wales, Walls, Ward, Watling, Watson, Wheals, Whites, Winter, Wiskar, Woodhouse, Wyett.

BITTERING MAGNA

White's Directory of Norfolk, 1845

BITTERING MAGNA was formerly a parish, lying between Gressenhall and Beetley, to which parishes it was annexed many years ago, after the dilapidation of its CHURCH, of which no traces now remain. Like Little Bittering, it maintains its roads separately. Near Gressenhall village, are a number of scattered houses called Bittering Street.

BITTERING PARVA

White's Directory of Norfolk, 1854

BITTERING PARVA, or Little Bittering, 5½ miles W. by N. of East Dereham, is a parish which keeps its poor conjointly with Beeston, and has 16 souls, and 392 acres of land, all in one farm, occupied by Mr. John Hastings, of Longham. The Church is dedicated to St. Peter, and the living is a rectory, valued in the King's book at £2.13s. 6½d., and in 1831 at £100. It has been augmented with £800 Queen Anne's Bounty. Hy. Dover, Esq., is patron and owner of the soil, and the Rev. Chas. Goodrich is the incumbent.

Subscribers

Christopher J. Allen, Fransham, Norfolk

The Andrews Family and The Neale Family, Norfolk

Mrs P.R. Anema

Kenny Austin, Dereham, Norfolk

Karen Baxter (née Footit), Beeston

Hazel M. Benfield, Longham, Norfolk

Katia R. Benfield-Griffiths, Beeston, Norfolk

Pauline Bennett, The Old Rectory, Gressenhall

Michael and Jenny Bloomfield, Wendling, Norfolk

Amanda J. Brunton (née Brooks) and Lee Brunton, Beeston, Norfolk

Sheila M. Brunton (née Skipper), Dereham, Norfolk

Mrs M. Buck, Gressenhall, Norfolk

Tara L. Burton, Beeston, Norfolk

M.C. Butler-Stoney, Burwood Hall, Mileham

Mrs J. Campen, Gt Fransham

The Canham Family

Peter and Pam Carr, Hoddesdon, Hertfordshire

James, Sandra and Thomas Clayton, Wendling

Mr Gavin Codman, Beeston, Norfolk

Karen Codman, Beetley, Norfolk

David E. Coleman, Beeston, Norfolk

Andy and Carol Cooke, Wendling

J.I. Cooper (née Spaull), Thetford, Norfolk

Richard M. Cross, Beeston, Norfolk

Vivienne D. Cross, Longham, Norfolk

David Denham-Smith, Beeston, Norfolk

Monica and Terry Durrant, Longham

Jack Gordon Dye, Scarning

Margaret R. Dye (née Pooley), Longham, Norfolk

Norman Eagle, Scarning, Norfolk

Daphne and Keith Evans

Danny Fenn, Litcham, Norfolk (formerly of Wendling)

Phylis Footit (née Holmes) deceased, Beeston

Mr and Mrs K. Fowler, Manor House, Bittering

Anthony P. French, Wendling, Norfolk

Mrs Elizabeth Galer (née Walthew), Beeston, Norfolk

Mr G. Garwood, Beeston

Mr J. Gilbert, Wendling

D. Green (née Spaull), Leigh, Lancashire

David L.F. Greenacre, Wisbech, Cambridgeshire

Alan and Alison Greenwood, Litcham, Norfolk

Geraldine Gunton (née Howe), Wendling/now Fransham

Joy Hammond

Hortis Dale Hanna, Tennessee, USA

Brian Hawes and Linda Baker, Beeston

J.B.M. Holbeach, Spring Farm, Gressenhall

Steve Horton, Beeston Cum Bittering, Norfolk

The Houston Family, The Old Steading, Wendling

Julie Howard, Beeston

Arther Denis Howard (deceased)

Verity Howden

Sir Ralph and Lady Margaret Howell, Wendling

Paul Ireland, Dereham, Norfolk

Mr and Mrs R.T. Jackman

Mr and Mrs Johnston-Gotts, Beeston, Norfolk

Mr and Mrs G. Keppler

V.P. and W.R. Keron (Robert and Ruth), Hall Farm, Wendling

Sarah Knights, Longham, Norfolk

Mr G.I. Lawes, Gt Dunham, Norfolk

Mr G.M. Lawes, Fransham, Norfolk

Brian Laws, Beeston

Jean Laws, Beeston

Jean M. Laws, Beeston, Norfolk

Maurice and Heather (née Skipper) Laws, Beeston, Norfolk

Maurice Roy Laws, Beeston

Imogen Leeder, Beeston, Norfolk

Mrs R.H. Leggett

The Mackneys

T.R. and R.E. Matsell (Peter and James), Cameron House, Wendling, Norfolk

Ewen McLeod, Longham Hall

Neil and Sheila McLeod, Longham

Nicholas McLeod, Longham Hall

Peggy Meen, Wendling, Norfolk

Mr W.J. Meen, Wendling

Michael and Carol, Longham, Norfolk

Patricia M. Mindham, Longham

Sheila and Dorothy Moore, Wendling School 1945–1951

Audrey Newsome (née Parker)

Andrew Nightingale, Longham, Norfolk

Mr G. and Mrs M. Olley, Wendling, Norfolk

William R. Palmer, Longham, Norfolk

Ploughshare Public House, Beeston, King's Lynn

Mr Barry C. Pooley, Longham

Mrs J. Prior, Mileham

Peter Roberson and Co., Holly Farm, Longham, Norfolk

Gordon K. Robinson, Tittleshall, Norfolk

Edwin G. Roegele, Beeston, Norfolk

Paul Roegele, Gressenhall, Norfolk

Peter Roegele, Dereham, Norfolk

Jean K. Rowland, Beeston, Norfolk

Mrs M. Sadler, E. Dereham, Norfolk

Wendy Secker (née Short), Beeston

Kathleen Rosemary Shinn (née Wright), 1915–1996

David W. and Lena E. Smith, Wendling, Norfolk

Neil and Kathy Smith, Wendling, Norfolk

M.J. Taylor, The Mount, Litcham

Kenneth C. Thorne, Longham, Norfolk

Mr Alec Wales

John F.W. Walling, Newton Abbot, Devon

John and Beverly Walsh, Wendling

Tim C. Walthew

D. Webster, Wendling, Norfolk

Doreen O. Webster, Longham, Norfolk

Eddie Whales, Beeston, Norfolk

Margaret Whitehead (née Footit) deceased, Beeston

D.J. Winterbone, Beeston

Michael E. Wright, Wendling, Norfolk

Mildred M. Wyett, Beeston, Norfolk

Community Histories

The Book of Addiscombe • Canning and Clyde Road
Residents Association and Friends

The Book of Addiscombe, Vol. II • Canning and Clyde Road
Residents Association and Friends

The Book of Ashburton • Stuart Hands and Pete Webb

The Book of Axminster with Kilmington • Les Berry
and Gerald Gosling

The Book of Bakewell • Trevor Brighton

The Book of Bampton • Caroline Seward

The Book of Barnstaple • Avril Stone

The Book of Barnstaple, Vol. II • Avril Stone

The Book of The Bedwyns • Bedwyn History Society

The Book of Bergh Apton • Geoffrey I. Kelly

The Book of Bickington • Stuart Hands

The Book of Bideford • Peter Christie and Alison Grant

Blandford Forum: A Millennium Portrait • Blandford Forum
Town Council

The Book of Boscastle • Rod and Anne Knight

The Book of Bourton-on-the-Hill, Batsford and Sezincote •
Allen Firth

The Book of Bramford • Bramford Local History Group

The Book of Breage & Germoe • Stephen Polglase

The Book of Bridestowe • D. Richard Cann

The Book of Bridport • Rodney Legg

The Book of Brixham • Frank Pearce

The Book of Buckfastleigh • Sandra Coleman

The Book of Buckland Monachorum & Yelverton •
Pauline Hamilton-Leggett

The Book of Budleigh Salterton • D. Richard Cann

The Book of Carharrack • Carharrack Old
Cornwall Society

The Book of Carshalton • Stella Wilks and Gordon
Rookledge

The Parish Book of Cerne Abbas • Vivian and
Patricia Vale

The Book of Chagford • Iain Rice

The Book of Chapel-en-le-Frith • Mike Smith

The Book of Chittlehamholt with
Warkleigh & Satterleigh • Richard Lethbridge

The Book of Chittlehampton • Various

The Book of Codford • Romy Wyeth

The Book of Colney Heath • Bryan Lilley

The Book of Constantine • Moore and Trethowan

The Book of Cornwood and Lutton • Compiled by
the People of the Parish

The Book of Crediton • John Heal

The Book of Creech St Michael • June Small

The Book of Crowcombe, Bicknoller and Sampford Brett •
Maurice and Joyce Chidgey

The Book of Crudwell • Tony Pain

The Book of Cullompton • Compiled by the People
of the Parish

The Book of Dawlish • Frank Pearce

The Book of Dulverton, Brushford,
Bury & Exebridge • Dulverton and District Civic Society

The Book of Dunster • Hilary Binding

The Book of Easton • Easton Village History Project

The Book of Edale • Gordon Miller

The Ellacombe Book • Sydney R. Langmead

The Book of Exmouth • W.H. Pascoe

The Book of Grampound with Creed • Bane and Oliver

The Book of Gosport • Lesley Burton and
Brian Musselwhite

The Book of Haughley • Howard Stephens

The Book of Hayle • Harry Pascoe

The Book of Hayling Island & Langstone • Peter Rogers

The Book of Helston • Jenkin with Carter

The Book of Hemyock • Clist and Dracott

The Book of Herne Hill • Patricia Jenkyns

The Book of Hethersett • Hethersett Society
Research Group

The Book of High Bickington • Avril Stone

The Book of Honiton • Gerald Gosling

The Book of Ilsington • Dick Wills

The Book of Kingskerswell • Carsewella Local
History Group

The Book of Lamerton • Ann Cole and Friends

Lanner, A Cornish Mining Parish • Sharron
Schwartz and Roger Parker

The Book of Leigh & Bransford • Malcolm Scott

The Second Book of Leigh & Bransford • Malcolm Scott

The Book of Litcham with Lexham & Mileham • Litcham
Historical and Amenity Society

The Book of Llangain • Haydyn Williams

The Book of Loddiswell • Loddiswell Parish History Group

The New Book of Lostwithiel • Barbara Fraser

The Book of Lulworth • Rodney Legg

The Book of Lustleigh • Joe Crowdy

The Book of Lydford • Compiled by Barbara Weeks

The Book of Lyme Regis • Rodney Legg

The Book of Manaton • Compiled by the People
of the Parish

For details of any of the above titles or if you are interested in writing your own history, please contact: Commissioning Editor, Community Histories, Halsgrove House, Lower Moor Way, Tiverton, Devon EX16 6SS, England; email: katyc@halsgrove.com